# THE ANTONINES

# THE ANTONINES

## The Roman Empire in Transition

*Michael Grant*

London and New York

First published 1994
by Routledge
11 New Fetter Lane London EC4P 4EE

Simultaneously published in the USA and Canada
by Routledge
29 West 35th Street, New York NY 10001

© 1994 Michael Grant Publications Ltd

Phototypeset in Baskerville by Intype, London
Printed and bound in Great Britain by Biddles Ltd, Guildford and King's Lynn

*British Library Cataloguing in Publication Data*
A catalogue record for this book is available from the British Library.

*Library of Congress Cataloging in Publication Data*
Grant, Michael
The Antonines : The Roman Empire in Transition / Michael Grant.
p. cm.
Includes bibliographical references and index.
1. Rome–History–Antonines, 96–192. 2. Rome–Civilization.
3. Roman emperors. I. Title.
DG292.G73 1994
937'.07–dc20        94–597

ISBN 0–415–10754–7

# CONTENTS

# ILLUSTRATIONS

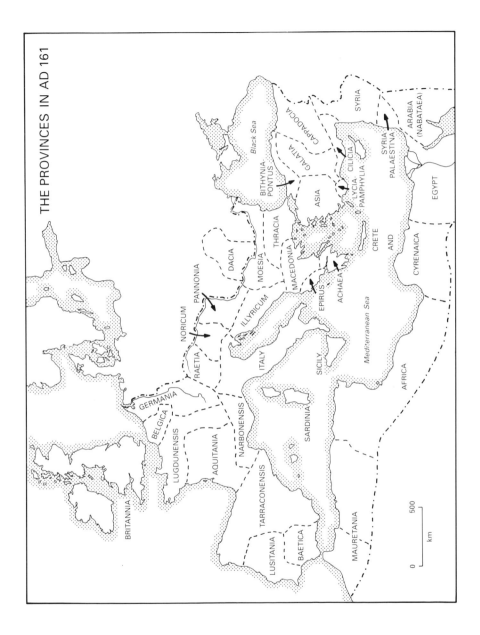

THE PROVINCES IN AD 161

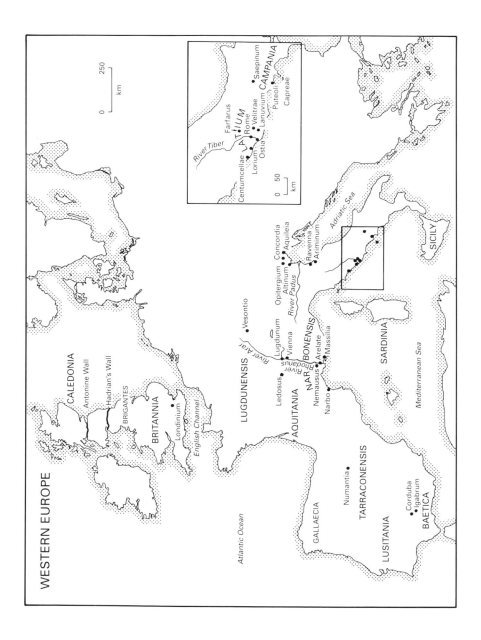

WESTERN EUROPE

250

km

0

CALEDONIA

Antonine Wall

Hadrian's Wall

BRIGANTES

BRITANNIA

Londinium

English Channel

Atlantic Ocean

GALLAECIA

Numantia

TARRACONENSIS

LUSITANIA

Corduba
Igabrum

BAETICA

AQUITANIA

LUGDUNENSIS

Ledosus

River Arar

Lugdunum

Vienna

Vesontio

NARBONENSIS

Nemausus
Arelate

Narbo

Massilia

River Rhodanus

SARDINIA

Mediterranean Sea

Opitergium
Altinum

River Padus

Concordia

Aquileia

Ravenna

Ariminum

Adriatic Sea

SICILY

River Tiber

Farfarus

Centumcellae

Lorium

Ostia

LATIUM

Rome

Velitrae

Lanuvium

CAMPANIA

Saepinum

Puteoli

Capreae

0     50

km

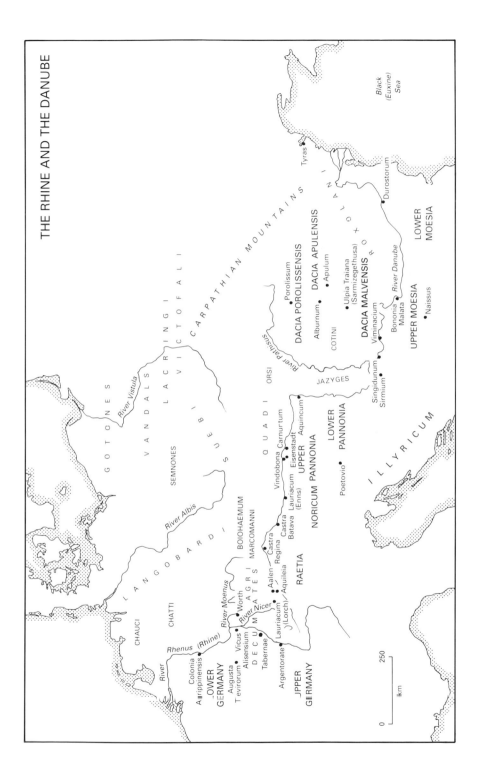

THE RHINE AND THE DANUBE

Black
(Euxine)
Sea

Tyras

Durostorum

LOWER
MOESIA

Porolissum

DACIA POROLISSENSIS          DACIA APULENSIS

Alburnum          Apulum

Ulpia Traiana
(Sarmizegethusa)

COTINI          DACIA MALVENSIS

Bononia          River Danube
Viminacium          Malata

Naissus          UPPER MOESIA

River Pathissus

ORSI          JAZYGES

Singidunum
Sirmium

CARPATHIAN MOUNTAINS

River Vistula

GOTONES

VANDALS          LACRINGI          VICTOFALI

SEMNONES

S U E B I

QUADI

Aquincum

Carnuntum
Vindobona          Eisenstadt

UPPER          LOWER
PANNONIA          PANNONIA

Lauriacum
(Enns)

Poetovio

ILLYRICUM

River Albis

LANGOBARDI

BOIOHAEMUM

MARCOMANNI

Castra
Regina          Batava

Castra

River Moenus          A G R I

Worth          D E C U M A T E S

Aalen          River Nicer

Lauriacum
(Lorch)          Aquileia

RAETIA          NORICUM

CHAUCI

CHATTI

River
Rhenus (Rhine)          Vicus

Tabernae          Augusta
Treverorum          Alisensium

Argentorate

Colonia
Agrippinensis

LOWER
GERMANY          UPPER
GERMANY

0          250
km

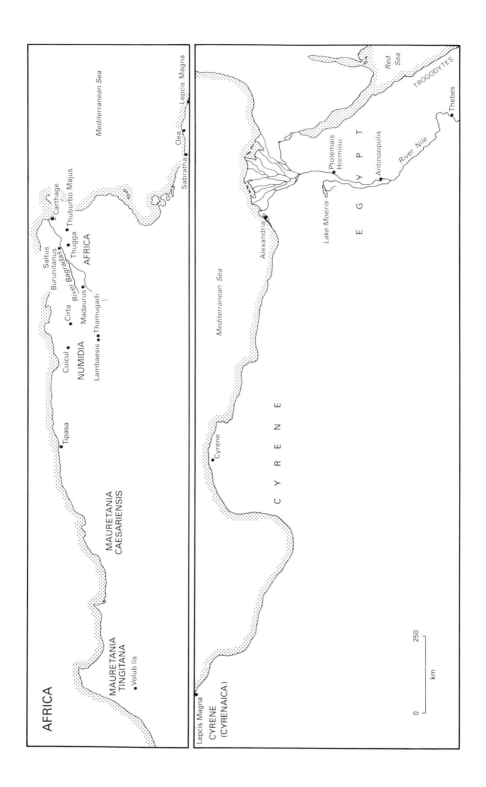

AFRICA

MAURETANIA
TINGITANA

• Volub lis

MAURETANIA
CAESARIENSIS

• Tipasa

NUMIDIA

Cuicul •

Cirta •

River Bagradas

Lambaesis • • Thamugadi

Madaurus •

Thugga •

AFRICA

Saltus
Burunitanus

• Carthage

Thuburbo Majus

Mediterranean Sea

Sabratha •

Oea •

• Lepcis Magna

Lepcis Magna

CYRENE
(CYRENAICA)

C Y R E N E

• Cyrene

Mediterranean Sea

Alexandria •

E G Y P T

Lake Moeris

Ptolemais •
Hormiou

Antinoopolis •

River Nile

• Thebes

Red
Sea

TROGODYTES

0    250

km

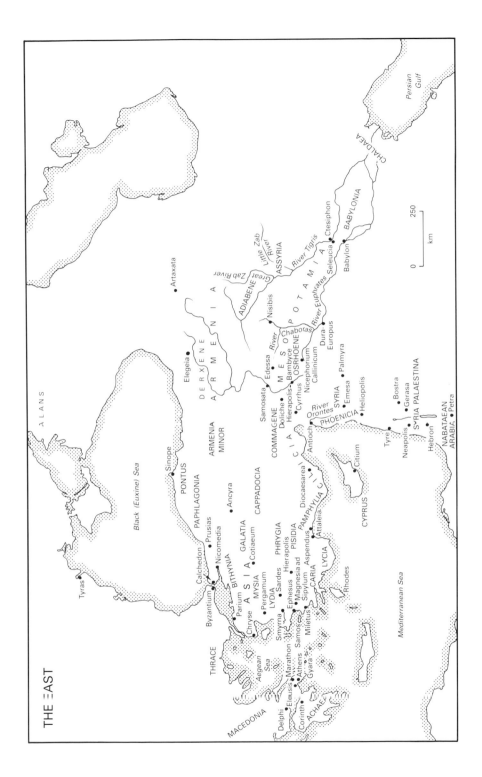

THE EAST

*Persian Gulf*

CHALDAEA

250

km

0

BABYLONIA

*River Tigris*

Ctesiphon

Seleucia

Babylon

*Little Zab River*

ASSYRIA

ADIABENE

*Great Zab River*

Nisibis

M E S O P O T A M I A

*River Euphrates*

*River Chaboras*

Edessa

OSRHOENE

Dura Europus

Artaxata

D E R X E N E

A R M E N I A

Elegeia

Samosata

COMMAGENE

Doliche

Bambyce

Hierapolis

Callinicum

Nicephorium

Palmyra

*River Orontes*

SYRIA

Emesa

Heliopolis

Cyrrhus

Antioch

PHOENICIA

Tyre

Neapolis

Bostra

Gerasa

SYRIA PALAESTINA

Hebron

NABATAEAN

ARABIA

Petra

*A L A N S*

*Black (Euxine) Sea*

Sinope

PONTUS

PAPHLAGONIA

ARMENIA MINOR

Ancyra

CAPPADOCIA

A S I A

C I L I C I A

Diocaesarea

Citium

CYPRUS

Tyras

Calchedon

Nicomedia

Prusias

BITHYNIA

GALATIA

Cotiaeum

Byzantium

Parium

MYSIA

Pergamum

PHRYGIA

Sardes

LYDIA

Hierapolis

PISIDIA

Aspendus

PAMPHYLIA

Attaleia

LYCIA

Magnesia ad Sipylum

Ephesus

Smyrna

Samos

Miletus

CARIA

Rhodes

*Mediterranean Sea*

THRACE

MACEDONIA

*Aegean Sea*

Chryse

Delphi

Eleusis

Marathon

Athens

Corinth

Gyara

ACHAEA

# INTRODUCTION

The Roman Empire was a startling achievement, partly because of its size. It was enormous, extending from the Atlantic to the Euphrates and from the Rhine and Danube to the Sahara. It is therefore of relevance and interest to those people of today who are thinking of rising above and beyond small national frontiers to multi-national unities, such as Europe and the other endeavours of a similar kind. For it has been done before: the Romans did it, and on a scale which has never been equalled since their day and will never be equalled again. The question of how well this gigantic empire worked is a matter of concern to those who are attempting, at least in part, to repeat the pattern today, at least as far as Europe is concerned (Chapter 8).

In the development of that empire the Antonines played a crucial part. By the Antonines I mean three successive emperors of the second century AD, Antoninus Pius (138–61), Marcus Aurelius (161–80); until 169 his colleague was Lucius Verus), and Commodus (180–192). It was they who controlled this huge machine during more than half a century of its most testing period. They were not, of course, the first Roman emperors. Augustus (30BC–AD 14) had converted the Republic into an empire ruled by one man, known as the Principate, and he had been followed by four more emperors descended from or related to him, known as the rulers of the Julio-Claudian house (AD 14–69). Then, after a period of civil war, followed the Flavian dynasty founded by Vespasian (69–79) and continued by his two sons, Titus and Domitian (79–96). Next came a series of rulers often known as the 'adoptive' emperors because, having no sons around, they promoted the most meritorious successors they could find: the ageing Nerva, the popular, imperialistic Trajan, and the brilliant, controversial, widely travelled Hadrian (96–138).

The eighteenth-century historian Edward Gibbon observed that the epoch of the Antonines, the second century AD, was the happiest period the world had ever known. This statement needs reexamination (Chapter 8). It has been fashionable, in recent years, to contradict Gibbon's assertion, on the grounds that it was written from the point of view of

1

the upper class: the other social classes of the Roman empire enjoyed a far from happy existence. On the other hand it can well be argued that in subsequent centuries – today for example – the lot of the unprivileged has not been any more satisfactory. Certainly in Western Europe and the United States there exist distinctly unprivileged and depressed groups, but they are not as numerous, proportionately, as those that existed in the Roman empire. Yet in the world as a whole an enormously large proportion of the population lives below subsistence level – certainly a proportion large enough to give credence to Gibbon's assertion.

On the other hand it must also be conceded that Gibbon was referring *only* to the Roman empire, and not to the vast areas of the world that lay outside it – about which he did not know or care. So his statement that the Antonine world was unequalled for happiness must be considered in that light. Nevertheless, his assertion must be given due weight. The Antonine period did achieve something for its people, and something substantial. It was founded on the famous Roman Peace, which had never before been so complete and far-reaching, and never would be again: an achievement which is well worth looking at afresh, in this troubled late twentieth century in which hopes for universal peace have seemed within our reach (after the collapse of the Soviet empire) and then been dashed.

No one, as far as I know – at least in recent years or decades – has attempted to describe the reign of Antoninus Pius. It has been regarded as a model reign of peace and good administration, and he has been regarded as a model ruler: the man who worked so hard and so conscientiously that he trained himself only to go sparingly to the bathroom. But there are certain points that need to be studied once more. Why, for example, did he leave his heritage jointly to two men, one of whom was obviously unfit for it? And, most serious of all, is it true that this long period of peace and tranquillity concealed within itself the seeds of future decay – the origins of the decline and fall of the Roman empire? Here is a matter of significance which we ought to investigate.

As to Marcus Aurelius, saintly man though in many ways he seems to have been, he had his personal problems: his reputedly unworthy colleague Lucius Verus and his allegedly immoral wife Faustina the younger. And it is interesting to note how he dealt with those problems. But the most striking of all of the difficulties that he encountered was the fact that this man of markedly intellectual and introspective tastes had to spend, or felt that he had to spend, such a very large part of his reign in military camps on the Danube, commanding Roman armies. This did not stop him from writing his *Meditations,* and it is to this astonishing work that I would particularly direct attention. The *Meditations* perhaps seem less remarkable than they should because they so often appeared in Victorian editions, bound in soft leather; and they have been far too rarely republished or looked at since then. This ought to be rectified.

The work needs to be examined with great care, because it is one of the most acute and sophisticated pieces of ancient thinking that exists. It is also, incidentally, the best book every written by a major ruler.

Marcus Aurelius has often been blamed for abandoning the theory that the empire ought to go to the best man, by 'adoption', seeing that he instead nominated his own son Commodus as his successor: and Commodus proved a disaster. That Commodus turned out to be so disastrous, and effectively put an end to the blessings of the Antonine monarchy, can scarcely be contradicted. But that does not excuse the fact that far too little attention has been devoted to his biography and his reign. Here I would single out only two matters that seem to need careful reconsideration. The first is Germany. Three attempts were set in motion, in ancient times, to place Germany within the boundaries of the Roman empire, which would then have a shorter Elbe-Danube frontier than the long, right-angled Rhine-Danube frontier which actually existed. The first attempt was made, by Augustus, from the west: it collapsed catastrophically in AD 9, when Varus was ambushed by Arminius in the Teutoburg Forest. The second attempt was made by Germanicus, very soon afterwards, but is hardly worth mentioning because it was called off by his uncle Tiberius. The third attempt was launched by Marcus Aurelius, who intended to occupy Germany from the south, by way of the Czech Republic and Slovakia. When Aurelius died, the plan was immediately abandoned by his son Commodus, who – acting perhaps on the suggestion of a Greek adviser – returned to Rome instead. For this he was fiercely criticized by ancient imperial writers, and the criticisms have persisted to this day. But was he right or wrong? It would certainly have been satisfactory if Germany had been brought within the Roman empire, and it is possible to conjecture that such a step might have not only prevented or postponed its fifth-century Fall but also saved us from the two World Wars of the present century. But could Rome have afforded the hugely increased military expenditure and, for that matter, could the number of men in the army have been raised to an adequate strength? These are points which, as far as I know, have not been sufficiently considered, and I propose to do just that before pronouncing a verdict on Commodus.

The second element in Commodus's policies which seems to me to need equally urgent reconsideration is his attitude to Roman religion. It is as a numismatist that I am particularly struck by the changes that occurred. The religious slogans on his coinage are markedly different from those of previous reigns; and, in particular, they show a novel tendency towards monotheistic aims. True, Commodus was a new sort of autocrat, and that too is echoed by his coins and medallions. But this autocracy is enshrined within a distinctly monotheistic approach to the traditional Roman religion. In the late second century AD things were changing. It is part of the purpose of this book to show how they

3

were changing, and why. The answers, I think, point the way towards the shift to Christianity which was becoming apparent and which would find full imperial expression less than a century and a half after Commodus's death.

All of these emperors were, in their diverse fashions, remarkable men, and each of them has been so inadequately dealt with by ancient and modern historians that a new treatment is needed. This certainly applies to the first and last of the three emperors, both interesting personages; Marcus Aurelius, although more fortunate in his biographers, also demands further attention, because of his exceptionally complex character and career.

The importance of the Antonines is manifold, but it mainly lies in the fact that they represent an age of transition, one of the major turning-points in the history of the world. At the beginning of the period the great empire was at its height: at the end it had experienced the first signs of the disaster that were to lead to its collapse. These developments brought about enormous social changes, which heralded a new era. There were remarkable writers in Greek and Latin (far too neglected in our academic curricula); and there was a host of other writers, whose existence bears witness to a high level of culture and a breadth of educational diffusion.

Moreover, to take up a point mentioned earlier, whereas at the outset of the epoch the old paganism was still at its height, at the end an altogether new sort of paganism was coming into being; and the age of Christianity (represented, as time went on, by an increasing number of Apologists and critics) had been clearly foreshadowed.

Simultaneously, the old classical art and architecture were giving way to something new.

In another book I have described the time which was now coming into existence as the age of *The Climax of Rome* (1968). It was the Antonines who presided over the transitional phase which brought about all of these developments. They all played leading parts in this massive historical drama that was unfolding, and that would change the Roman empire from its ancient mould into what, with our love of labels, we describe as the Middle Ages.

In this book I shall quote a good deal from the ancient Greek and Latin writers. That will, I think, be generally accepted as justifiable, since whatever their faults they are our principal source of information. I shall also be quoting quite a lot from modern authors. That, perhaps, will be more widely questioned. But I believe it is right because, for all their incompletenesses that have been mentioned, they have had a lot to say about the period. To ignore this and to assert that I am entirely striking out on my own would, I suggest, be immodest. I shall be original where

I can, but my debts to others remain incalculable and it would be wrong not to admit them.

Underlined words refer to the notes at the back of the book.

I am particularly grateful to Richard Stoneman and Victoria Peters of Routledge for seeing this book through the press. I also want to express my appreciation to Sarah C. Butler, Maria Ellis, Thomas Howard-Sneyd, Sarah-Jane Woolley, Ros Ramage and Jayne Lewin for their assistance. And I am happy to thank my wife, as always, for all of the help that she has given.

Michael Grant<br>
1994

# Part I

# THE EMPERORS

# 1

# ANTONINUS PIUS

Hadrian (117–38), whose relations with his wife Vibia Sabina (d. 128) were not very cordial, had no son to become his heir, just as Nerva and Trajan before him had also lacked sons. In 136 he adopted as his son and presumptive successor an elegant, luxuriously living and not apparently very impressive senator in his mid-thirties, Lucius Ceionius Commodus, thenceforward known as Lucius Aelius Caesar; and he was appointed governor of the key frontier province of Upper and Lower Pannonia. In the same year, Hadrian brought about the execution of his elderly brother-in-law, Lucius Julius Ursus Servianus, and the latter's grandson who, Hadrian suspected, was being prepared as a rival candidate to Aelius. In January 138, however, Aelius died. Hadrian was so upset and dejected that he did not bother to have him deified.

About a month later he adopted Antoninus Pius (Titus Aurelius Fulvus Boionius [?] Antoninus). He convened at his house the most prominent and most respected of the senators and, lying upon his couch, he spoke to them as follows:

> I, my friends, have not been permitted by nature to have a son, but you have made it possible by legal enactment. Now there is this difference between the two methods – that a begotten son turns out to be whatever sort of person Heaven pleases, whereas one that is adopted a man takes to himself as the result of deliberate selection.
>
> Thus by the process of nature a maimed and witless child is often given to a parent, but by process of selection one of sound body and sound mind is certain to be chosen. For this reason I formerly selected Lucius [Aelius Caesar] before all others – a person such as I could never have expected a child of mine to become.
>
> But since Heaven has bereft us of him, I have found as emperor for you in his place; the man whom I now give you, one who is noble, mild, tractable and prudent, neither young enough to do anything reckless nor so old as to neglect anything, one who has

9

been brought up according to the laws and one who has exercised authority in accordance with our traditions, so that he is not ignorant of any matters pertaining to the imperial office, but can handle them all effectively.

I refer to Aurelius Antoninus here. Although I know him to be the least inclined of men to become involved in affairs and to be far from desiring any such power, still I think that he will not deliberately disregard either me or you, but will accept the office even against his will.[1]

Antoninus, after prolonged consideration, accepted the proposal. He had been born in 86 at Lanuvium (Lanuvio) in Latium, had served as consul (120) and proconsul of Asia, and was a member of the emperor's council. His family, described as eminent but not particularly old,[2] came from Nemausus (Nîmes) in Gallia Narbonensis (southern Gaul), but moved to Rome where his grandfather and father – both bearing the names Titus Aurelius Fulvus – each became consul. Antoninus's mother was Arria Fadilla, whose father Arrius Antoninus, who was also from southern Gaul, had likewise twice obtained consulships. It was from him that Antoninus Pius took the name Antoninus, following a habit common among upper-class Romans of favouring names from the female line.

He was linked to most of the new governing class of Rome – the nobility who had risen to this rank under the Flavians, Vespasian and his two sons. He had lived on the revenue from his country estates, which included fine inherited villas at Centumcellae (Civitavecchia), built by Trajan, and Lorium (near La Bottaccia, two miles from Rome, on the Via Aurelia); and he augmented his income by lending money at 4 per cent interest.

When Hadrian adopted Antoninus, the latter took the name Imperator Titus Aelius Caesar Antoninus. His assumption of the name 'Aelius', which immediately appeared on coinage issued with his head,[3] was no doubt a tribute to Hadrian's earlier appointee, who had borne this name. It will be noted that Antoninus, although he was invested with the titles 'Imperator' and 'Caesar', was not called 'Augustus', so that this was not truly a dual monarchy in which he was a full colleague. Nevertheless, during the few months of Hadrian's life that remained he was virtually regent. Some modern writers are surprised by this development, others are not, pointing out that he had already been Hadrian's closest adviser.

It is pretty clear, however, that the promotion caused a certain amount of jealousy among others, who felt that the move was unexpected and that they themselves were equally qualified. This included the prefect of the city, Lucius Catilius Severus Julianus Claudius Reginus, backed, no doubt, by a group which had supported Servianus's grandson(?) now dead. There were also, probably, some doubts about whether the armies would support Hadrian's new appointee, since the coins that were now issued in Antoninus's name gave hopeful prominence to CONCORDIA EXERCITVVM and to figures of 'Securitas', testifying to a certain fear.[4]

Then, on 10 July of the same year, Hadrian died, and Antoninus, without opposition, succeeded him on the imperial throne, becoming 'Augustus' and being hailed as such on the coinage. His reign began, however, with a considerable amount of embarrassment: when Antoninus requested the deification of his predecessor and the ratification of his official actions, the senate proved recalcitrant on both issues, remembering that it had cordially disliked Hadrian for diminishing its authority and executing a number of its members. Antoninus, who stressed his role as follower of Hadrian, complained that if the senate annulled Hadrian's acts it would also be undermining his own position, since one of those acts had been his own adoption. Thus, although there were still men who objected to his elevation, he finally secured the deification of Hadrian, as was obliquely referred to by coins of early 139 which displayed *Aeternitas* standing beside an altar.[5] No army hostility manifested itself, so that another coin was able to portray the Loyalty of the Troops (FIDES MILITVM), which was depicted by a female figure holding a standard.[6] And the senate too, despite rumours of plots, eventually complied; indeed it was perhaps partly because of the attitude of the army that it did so.

But it was also because Antoninus gave the senate a *quid pro quo*. This was the abolition of circuit judges (*juridici*) in the Italian peninsula. There were four of these and, although they were senators (usually former praetors), the senate did not like them because their existence diminished its control of Italy.

When the senate dropped its objection to Hadrian's deification, Hadrian's body was duly buried in the mausoleum that he had erected for the purpose (now the Castel Sant'Angelo), which was dedicated to him, as an inscription shows.[7] Work was also started on a temple in his honour at Rome, the Hadrianeum – which was dedicated at a later date – and temples commemorating his divinity were erected at Cyzicus (Balkiz) and elsewhere. Nevertheless, Antoninus continued to feel that he had to be somewhat careful about all of this, and there is reason to suppose that Hadrian became only a type of second-class imperial god, whose deification did not obtain a great deal of public celebration, being limited, on the whole, to an inner circle.

Antoninus Pius, on becoming emperor, assumed the tribunician power. Augustus had introduced the power in order to show how democratic he was, posing as a tribune who stood up for the people's rights. He had also used the power as a technical means for proposing motions in the senate. There is no evidence that Antoninus did this. Indeed, there was nothing distinctive about his assumption of the *tribunicia potestas*, since every earlier emperor had assumed the same power. Nor was there anything unusual about his acceptance of the title 'Father of his Country' in 139, after initially refusing it.

What was exceptional, however, was the bestowal upon Antoninus of the appellation 'Pius', by which he is so generally known. The precise reasons behind the allocation of this name to him have been much discussed, by ancient and modern authorities alike. The *Historia Augusta* offers five of these reasons:

> He was given the name of 'Pius' by the senate either (1) because, when his father-in-law was old and weak, he lent him a supporting hand in his attendance at the senate (which act, indeed, is not sufficient as a token of great dutifulness, since a man were rather undutiful who did not perform this service than dutiful if he did), or (2) because he spared those men whom Hadrian in his ill-health had condemned to death, or (3) because after Hadrian's death he had unbounded and extraordinary honours decreed for him in spite of opposition from all, or (4) because, when Hadrian wished to make away with himself, by great care and watchfulness he prevented him from so doing, or (5) because he was in fact very kindly by nature and did no harsh deed in his own time.[8]

Reason (5) is repeated by other ancient authors, but is not particularly plausible; nor are (1), (2) or (4), although, in respect to the last, his dutifulness to the memory of Hadrian has been held to have played a part. But (3), which is also recorded by Dio Cassius, may well have been relevant. And so, in all likelihood, was Antoninus's general meticulousness in matters of religion,[9] of which more will be said later, and his graciousness of character and correct performance of all of his duties, in every branch of life, relating both to gods and to humankind.

This was the start of a period when emperors felt obliged to show how dutiful they were. However, it should not be forgotten that 'Pius' may well have been a proper name in Antoninus's family, which he felt entitled to revive for himself. People could interpret the appellation in various ways, and there was no good justification for preventing them from doing so; multiple meanings were familiar enough to the Romans, as the poet Horace, for example, was well aware. In any case Antoninus, in addition to calling himself 'Pius', immediately showed that he was not averse to placing *Pietas* on his coins and medallions,[10] on which, moreover, she was soon explicitly named.[11] And his role as family man and dutiful paterfamilias – paterfamilias, one might add, to the whole nation – was stressed by the appearance of the goddess with small children, as well as by her close link with the deified empress Faustina the elder – on whose coinage, abundant in life and after death, a temple is labelled PIETAS AVG.[12]

Antoninus overcame his initial friction with the senate and in deference to it accepted (like other emperors before him) a second consulship, in

139, followed by a third and fourth in 140 and 145. And so, in 140–43, his coins were already paying tribute to the Genius of the Senate (GENIO SENATVS).[13] Antoninus, as we have seen, had ostensibly restored its full powers, by abolishing the four circuit judges in Italy. The new aristocracy could forget that he was no better than they were; they were well off, and what they wanted most was to relax and enjoy their wealth and position. Antoninus was content to allow them to do so.

Nevertheless, he knew perfectly well that the senate was weak compared to himself: the myth that the Principate could be seen as a Restored Republic was threadbare. Besides, in practice, while paying outward respect to the senate, Antoninus reserved all of his consultations about important business for his much smaller imperial council (*consilium principis*). Local initiatives mostly came to nothing because, with the aid of an ever-growing bureaucracy, he was quite an inflexible centralizer, his humanity being of a distinctly paternalistic character. Deference to him became more marked and explicit, and he did not prevent the appellation of 'god and master' (*deus et dominus*); the deification after her death in 141 of his wife Faustina the elder (despite the questioning of her character by tradition) was celebrated both by temples and by coinage on a wholly unprecedented scale – in honour, no doubt, not only of herself but also of her husband's imperial house. At Sardes (Sart), for example, a joint cult of Faustina and Artemis was established.

A series of coins labelled LIBERAL(*itas*)[14] recalls that Antoninus Pius, no doubt eager to contradict accusations of stinginess, was generous in his distributions of cash. The *Chronographer of AD 354* (composer of an illustrated calendar) recalls that he doled out 800 *denarii* (32 *aurei*) per head. Probably the first distribution was on quite a modest scale, reducing Hadrian's usual dole of 150 *denarii* to the original figure of 75, but later this was raised to 100. The total of 800 finally reached was unprecedented and has been criticized as unduly indulgent, but it only serves to show what lengths the emperor was prepared to go in order to counter the charges of meanness that have been mentioned, and to keep his people happy and so prevent them from thinking of sedition.

For the same reason, he encouraged the making and restoration of roads as an aid to commerce, and was keen that the Romans should be properly fed, by means of good harvests in Italy and regular supplies of imported grain. Thus it was that coins of 140–4 are dedicated to Ops, the goddess of the abundance of such products (OPI AVG.).[15] And when LAETITIA (Joy) was celebrated in 149–50 – later she was defined as LAETITIA PVBLICA[16] – the inscription was accompanied by a figure of the grain-goddess Ceres (Demeter), attended, on occasion, by her daughter Proserpina (Persephone).[17] Nor were the provinces forgotten; when the customary crown-gold (*aurum coronarium*) was offered to Antoninus from all quarters on the occasion of his adoption, he remitted not only the whole of Italy's share but also half of what was provided by the provinces. They must also have benefited when, in 147–8, on the occasion when the tenth anniversary of his accession was celebrated, he remitted arrears of debt to the treasury.

It was mentioned earlier that he relied for advice on his imperial council. This included military experts, on whom he depended as a result of his lack of personal experience in this field. And, naturally, he was in close consultation with his praetorian prefects (not yet senators), of whom five are attested during his reign: the first, Marcus Gavius Maximus, held office for twenty years. Outside Italy, he listened to the advice of his agents (procurators), creating nine new posts of this character (and abolishing seven).

Meanwhile, however, attention was given to making the <u>laws</u> as good, fair and comprehensive as possible. Hadrian had already incorporated legal assessors in the imperial council, or had given a more formal character to those who were already there; no less than four successive praetorian prefects of Antoninus were eminent lawyers, and the rulings of legal experts (*responsa iurisprudentium*) were now recognized as a source of law. So were the enactments of the emperor himself, which obtained full validity without question; and the adoption of imperial decrees was greeted with applause by the senate – as it had been since the days of Trajan.[18]

Laws at this time were more humane than they had been, and displayed a somewhat new spirit of liberalism, partly because of the influence of Greek philosophical doctrines such as Stoicism. As for Antoninus, despite his own conservative instincts, his laws, which were numerous and covered a wide field, reflected this trend. He increased the exemptions and privileges of university teachers, and his public works showed a consciousness of social welfare. Moreover, he initiated humane regulations (up to a point) in relation to slaves, justifying these measures on the grounds that the unrest of slaves could become injurious to society. True, this liberalism did not go very far; the distinction between the legal treatment accorded to the upper and lower classes, the *honestiores* and *humiliores*, was maintained, if not widened, and a tendency to regulate everything became more and more noticeable.

Nevertheless, in many respects Antoninus's laws not only removed anomalies but also softened harshnesses, and displayed the human conscience and moral progress at work, as befitted the caring nature of his regime. Nor was there any hesitation in proclaiming this policy on the coinage, which portrayed *Aequitas* – with her scales – and went on to include IVSTITIA among the imperial virtues, in 150–1, and then, a year later, to commemorate the leniency of Antoninus (INDVLGENTIA AVG.).[19] It was partly because of his benevolent lawgiving, as well as his devotion to religion (see p. 16), that Antoninus was hailed as the reincarnation of the second king of antique Rome, Numa Pompilius.

Hadrian had been the great traveller; Antoninus, although he was careful to combine Hadrian's philhellenism with his 'national' tastes, deliberately followed exactly the opposite policy, staying continuously, it would seem probable, inside Italy.

> He did not engage on any expeditions – except that he set out to his own landed properties and in Campania – saying that the retinue of a *princeps*, even a very economical one, was burdensome to the provincials. Yet he had immense authority among all nations, since he purposely resided in the city so that he could receive messengers from all sides the more rapidly, seeing that he was at the centre.[20]

It was by design, therefore, that TIBERIS appeared among his 'Birthday of Rome' propaganda pieces (see below), and that sovereign ITALIA was portrayed on an *aureus*, quite distinct from his commemoration of provinces;[21] and Italy benefited markedly from his acts of generosity and charitable endowments. Money was spent on its harbours, bridges, baths and amphitheatres, and a plan was promoted to assist Italian orphan girls. The project which was, in fact, a continuation and expansion of earlier alimentary schemes, was dedicated to the memory of his late wife Faustina the elder and was celebrated on the coinage as the PVELLAE FAVSTINIANAE.[22] In order to contradict rumours of over-carefulness, other coins honour the emperor's generosity (MVNIFICENTIA AVG.),[23] with special reference to his provision of wild animals for the Games, represented by an elephant (148–9).

All of this was intended to honour the central country of the empire: in which Antoninus was well placed to receive messages from all quarters with speed,[24] since the imperial system of roads and posts was now at its best.

It must be added, however, that Antoninus's persistence in staying at Rome corresponded with his personal tastes. This is particularly evident in the field of religion (in contrast to astrology, against which he legislated). Many of his coin-types are selected to illustrate the heroic, mythical past of Rome and Italy. Ancient Roman legends are displayed on a series of coins and medallions which was issued over eight years in preparation for the ninth centenary of Rome,[25] which, when it arrived in 147/8, was celebrated by a further massive output of medallions. Moreover, Antoninus's coinage reflects his keen attention to the anniversaries of temple foundations at Rome.

The whole atmosphere of Antoninus's regime was well adapted to retrospective Roman religion, and this was largely at the initiative of the emperor himself, who not only, as we saw, was hailed as the new Numa Pompilius but also replaced Hadrian's 'Romulus the Founder' (ROMVLO

CONDITORI) on his coins by ROMVLO AVGVSTO,[26] thus identifying himself with the founder king, as he also identifies himself with the Augustan Palatine Apollo (APOLLINI AVGVSTO).[27] It is no surprise to find an inscription honouring Antoninus for 'his outstanding care and religious observance in relation to public rituals' (*ob insignem erga caerimonias publicas curam ac religionem*). Thus, a relief in the Vatican identifies the deified Antoninus and his wife Faustina the elder with Jupiter and Juno.

And yet it is the cult of Jupiter himself which also shows that, despite Antoninus's preference for Rome and Italy, this was a time when the provinces and all that they stood for were powerfully gaining ground. Antoninus, therefore, whatever his personal views, commemorated each of the regions of the empire on his coinage[28] and on friezes of the Temple of Hadrian, who had been so keen on visiting them all. Moreover, the Jupiter whose temple on the Aventine Hill was dedicated soon after 138 was Jupiter Dolichenus, Jupiter of Doliche (Duluk) in Commagene (northern Syria), that is to say Baal. And that is only one of innumerable shrines of orientalized Roman deities which were erected at this time, all over the empire and in Rome itself, as assimilation proceeded apace. Indeed, Antoninus and his wife Faustina the elder felt a strong personal devotion to the Great Mother (Cybele), who, although long since Romanized, was of Asian origin. Now, on a medallion of Antoninus, the goddess made her first official appearance in connection with an emperor.[29] Furthermore, as befitted her popularity among women, her cult assumed particular importance in the apotheosis of his wife.

The empire was seen as a unity, and the keynote of Antoninus's propaganda was the Peace that prevailed throughout its vast extent. It seemed virtually the equivalent of the Earth, *Tellus (Terra Mater)*, who appears on his medallions,[30] and there are references on his coins to the PAX AVG(*usti*) over which he presided, and to the TRANQVILLITAS AVG(*usti*) which came with that Pax.[31] Even HONOS bears the branch of peace (140–4) – although it is a military type; and Antoninus was depicted as the war-god who brought peace, Mars Pacifer.

Certainly the army was still formidable and all-important. Indeed its role was always expanding; a coin-type repeats Hadrian's DISCIPLINA AVG(*usti*).[32] Legionary pay continued to rise, but only four key provinces were garrisoned by as many as three legions: an insufficient defence, as the next reign would show. But Antoninus felt in a strong enough position to curtail the privileges of the fleet and auxiliaries, whose children, born in service, ceased to receive Roman citizenship as they had before. Thenceforward, instead, they could only become enfranchised by joining the legions. Thus, the new restriction was intended to encourage legionary recruiting. (Conscious of the possibly illiberal appearance of this measure, Antoninus's coins stressed that he was, in fact, an expander of the citizen body [S.P.Q.R. AMPLIATORI CIVIVM]).[33]

However, peace was not as universal as propaganda liked to show. True, the revolt of 'Celsus', mentioned by the *Historia Augusta*,[34] may well be fictitious, and nothing came of a plot which a certain Titus Atilius Rufus Titianus was supposed to be fomenting – indeed, Antoninus directed that his accomplices should not be tracked down. However, on the frontiers troubles did occur.

> Through his legates Antoninus waged a number of wars. He conquered the Britons through his legate Quintus Lollius Urbicus, and compelled the Mauri to sue for peace; and he crushed the Germans and Dacians and many peoples, including the Jews, who were rebelling, through governors and legates. In Achaia (Greece) also, and in Egypt, he put down rebellions. He frequently curbed the Alani when they began disturbances.[35]

Moreover, some of the trouble had occurred quite quickly. As the coinage of 138–9 suggests, Antoninus's accession was accompanied by the danger of wars in different zones. One of them, mentioned, as we have seen, by the *Historia Augusta*, was north Africa. Large portions of the area were suffering from brigand marauders, such as were also to be found elsewhere (Chapter 8); and it would appear that at this period independent nomadic tribes began an unprovoked attack across the African frontier.[36]

Thus, the elaborate defence system in north Africa, probably dating back to Hadrian, had to be maintained or strengthened. In Numidia, a road was built across the hills behind Lambaesis (Tazzoult), to open up the Saltus Arausius (Aurès Mountains), a district where brigands congregated. In Mauretania, excavations at Tipasa have revealed fortifications: as Colonia Aelia Augusta, the place served as a basis against rebellious Mauri (*c.* 144–50). Reinforcements were brought in, and in *c.* 150 the dissidents had to take refuge in the extreme west and elsewhere, and were forced to sue for peace. There were also disturbances among the peoples living along the Red Sea coast, presumably Trogodytes.[37] At Alexandria, too, there was a serious riot, in which the prefect of Egypt was killed.

In Britain, in *c.* 140–1, there was a rising of the Brigantes, who lived in north Britain just south of Hadrian's Wall. As we saw from the *Historia Augusta*, Quintus Lollius Urbicus, moving troops from other British camps, put down the revolt, an event which was commemorated by coins with the inscription BRITANNIA,[38] displaying her seated figure in a pose which was repeated centuries later on the British currency. Quintus Lollius Urbicus was also credited with the expansion of imperial territory in this region, marked by the construction, by the soldiers of three legions, of a new rampart, the Wall of Antoninus, extending for thirty-seven miles from the River Clota (Clyde) to the Bodotria (Firth of Forth). The Wall

17

was of turf, standing on a cobbled foundation fourteen feet wide, behind a deep ditch. The garrison was stationed in eighteen small forts, only about two miles apart, instead of the larger and more widely separated forts of Hadrian's Wall. In conjunction with that Wall, its Antonine successor formed a double line of defence, although the garrison, despite its considerable size (comprising 30,750 auxiliaries, as well as legionaries), was too small to man the whole length of the new wall.

The reasons that lay behind the creation of this new fortification have been much debated. One suggestion is that Hadrian's Wall was too far away to be in touch with the principal centres of opposition to Rome in Caledonia (Scotland), where the tribes of the Scottish lowlands had caused disturbances and needed to be brought under more direct Roman military rule. An alternative theory is that the creation of the Antonine Wall, and the enlargement of the Roman province of Britain that it involved, may not have been motivated by the local situation at all but was due to the accession of a new emperor, who needed to make his mark. Antoninus Pius, it is recalled, was not Hadrian's first choice as his successor, and there were other men who did not regard his claims to the throne as superior to their own. In these circumstances the new emperor, who had never commanded an army before, would be well advised to back his peaceful accession by a military success – a short and victorious foreign war – which would give him the prestige that he lacked.

However, it may reasonably be concluded that the Antonine Wall was intended as a symbol of Roman sovereignty, calculated to overawe the tribes – which were also subjected to extensive trading influences. The Roman army could well have moved forward to the conquest of the whole of the rest of the island. But it did not do so. Evidently Antoninus Pius considered that this limited expansion was enough to achieve the aims that he had in mind.

Nevertheless, a renewal of the trouble caused earlier by the tribe of the Brigantes in c. 154 brought about the withdrawal, towards the south, of certain military units from the Antonine Wall, which resulted in the devastation and demolition of some of its forts by raiding tribesmen. It may well have been at this juncture that Blatobulgium (Birrens) fort in Dumfriesshire was destroyed (and had to be rebuilt). The many earthwork defences of the period show how unsettled conditions were.

These developments seem to have prompted Antoninus to evict some or most of the population from between the two walls. Yet the measures in this twilight area proved ineffective. Although Antoninus reoccupied his Wall in c. 158 [?], not long after he was dead it no longer seemed tenable, since it possessed no defence in depth and no large camps to the rear. After further destruction the Wall was abandoned altogether, under Aurelius or Commodus.

As for the evicted Britons, they were transplanted to Germany and settled on either side of the River Nicer (Neckar), a tributary extending eastwards from the Rhenus (Rhine), where they were formed into units of 'Brittones' and required to take part in the local defences. This frontier, like the frontier in Britain, was pushed forward soon after 155. That is to say, it was extended some eighteen miles beyond the Rhine. The purpose of the expansion was to eliminate the rather impractical reentrant between the Upper Rhine (Germania Superior) and Upper Danube (Raetia), and thus to shorten the frontier considerably – even if the natural lie of the land tended to be ignored.

Where the old frontier line had left the River Moenus (Main) at Wörth to pass to the River Nicer (Neckar) at Vicus Alisinensium (Wimpfen), its new counterpart was constructed some way to the east, extending southwards from Miltenberg-Ost (Bürgstadt) to beyond Welzheim (on the Raetian border). The new line probably incorporated earlier outposts which had exercised some supervision across what had hitherto been the frontier, for example at Vicus Aurelius or Aurelii (Öhringen; Burgkastell). The fortifications of the new border-line were equipped – at least eventually – not only with palisades (like the earlier line further back) but also with stone towers (there were no timber towers on this outer *limes*).

The expansion thus attempted and achieved in Germany was quite an important development. But it does not appear to have involved any noticeable campaign, and there is no evidence that Antoninus Pius accepted any triumphal salutation because of what had been done. Indeed, it has been suggested that, although auxiliary troops were moved up to the new frontier, the reason for the advance was not military at all, but was based on economic advantages. The region now enclosed within the empire, lying on the edge of a sandstone area containing thick pine afforestation, was good agricultural land. (As regards the old, 'inner' *limes*, new fortlets were now planted between its forts, not on any rigid pattern but as local conditions required).

An equivalent adjustment necessarily followed to the south, at the adjoining, western end of the Raetian *limes*, where a unit advanced from its earlier camp at Aquileia (Heidenheim) to a newly constructed fort at Aalen, perhaps in *c*. 152–5. Once again the whole frontier of the province of Raetia was pushed forward, to join the Danube shortly before Alcimoennis (Kelheim). This was the last forward move of the Raetian *limes* (which survived intact for a further century).

The area between the old and new frontier was demilitarized and given over to civilian administration. The Brittones were kept on the old inner line, where they were entrusted with the building of forts. while new German settlers may have been planted in the newly occupied zone. The new outer line was not sufficiently strong to constitute a really effective military barrier, as breakthroughs in its southern portion were to show

19

in the following reigns. But it is probable that this extension of the frontier made it possible to relax martial law in the area, and to increase the number of townships to the rear of the new line; and Augusta Raurica (Augst) was largely rebuilt. Roads were also restored in many parts of Gaul.

Further east, beyond the Danube, Antoninus was proud because he sanctioned the appointment of a new king of the tribe of the Quadi (REX QVADIS DATVS, 140–4),[39] of whom we shall hear a lot more in the reign of Marcus Aurelius. This was a sign that Antoninus was not altogether neglecting the area (although unrest did not cease).

Further east again, there were troubles and military operations in the Trans-Danubian country of Dacia, which had been annexed by Trajan. After a revolt, in c. 158–9, its northern region, Dacia Superior, was divided into two (Apulensis and Porolissensis, a name that had become known in the previous reign). The larger of the camps at exposed Porolissum (near Moigrad) was rebuilt in stone and strongly walled. The southern portion of the land, Dacia Inferior, became known as Malvensis. There was a senatorial governor of Apulensis at its capital, Apulum (Alba Julia), whereas Porolissensis and Malvensis were governed by procurators of knightly (equestrian) rank. The Black Sea area of Scythia Minor (part of Lower Moesia, now Dobruja) reached the height of its prosperity and Romanization under Antoninus Pius. Many milestones of this time bear witness to the quantity of well-repaired roads.

As for the eastern portion of the empire, a rebellion in Greece had to be put down – as we saw from the *Historia Augusta* – and in Egypt the demand for compulsory contributions (*leitourgiai*) and/or the imposition of forced labour, to an extent regarded as excessive, caused the flight of people from their homes and culminated in an armed uprising (153). This had to be suppressed by military force (Chapter 3), and was followed by further flights to escape compulsory contributions and labour.

There may also have been violent incidents in Judaea. There Antoninus modified his predecessor's ban on circumcision but he did not completely reverse it, although he attempted to establish a *modus vivendi*. That is to say, he permitted Jews to circumcise their sons but prohibited them from enrolling converts. Moreover, the ban forbidding Jews to enter Jerusalem was maintained, and indeed enforced, by the construction of a ring of military outposts round the city. All of this caused discontent, which probably resulted in the occasional forcible outbreak.

In Asia, an edict of the reign of Antoninus Pius forbade the stacking of heavy pieces of marble or the sawing up of blocks of the same material on the dockside at Ephesus (Selçuk), so as to prevent the quay from becoming choked. At Sardes (Sart), as was mentioned earlier, cult statues of Antoninus Pius and Faustina the elder were set up.[40]

On the Asian frontier of the empire, Antoninus Pius was not averse to the cults of Zeus (Jupiter) Dolichenus and other eastern deities (see p. 16). But he may have admonished King Abgar VIII of Edessa (Urfa), in Osrhoene, for aggressive behaviour towards the Parthians.[41] He also, quite early, recorded that he had given a king to the Armenians – and he warned the Parthian monarch, who ruled beyond the Roman frontier, to leave Armenia untouched. Nevertheless, there seem to have been two Parthian crises during the reign, although nothing much happened.

It does appear, however, that Antoninus intended, had he lived, to proceed against the Parthians on a substantial scale, believing that their king, Vologaeses III, was preparing for war against him; and in his last years he sent Lucius Neratius Proculus to Syria 'for the Parthian War' (*ob bellum Parthicum*).[42] But, again, nothing happened until the next reign, when there was a major Parthian explosion. Antoninus had allowed the Parthians to choose their own time, and it is probable that he ought to have acted more decisively against them. Indeed, he himself, on his death-bed, seems to have felt the same, since we are told that 'while he was delirious with fever, he spoke of nothing save the state and certain kings with whom he was angry'.[43] These may well have been the monarchs across the Euphrates, from whom he rightly expected an attack which he had failed to forestall.

It is possible to see the frontier tensions and disturbances of Antoninus's reign in two conflicting lights. They can be regarded as contradictions of his continual assurances that there was universal peace. Alternatively, they and their subsequent resolution by himself and his officers can be interpreted as the unavoidable conditions for establishing and enforcing that peace – events which took place far from the principal centres of the empire and their inhabitants, and which enabled force to be kept right away from them so that they could live out their peaceful lives. This second interpretation is the fairer of the two; although it must be added that Antoninus, while establishing peaceful conditions for his own time, had not created, in west or east, a peace that would last, as events after his death almost immediately showed.

It has been suggested that prices may have fallen during his reign, but the evidence is inconclusive, and if this had happened one might have expected the continual increases in army pay to have been arrested, instead of continuing. Despite frontier troubles and a general policy which by no means deserved the reproach of stinginess (considering, for example, the generosity of his *congiaria*), Antoninus succeeded in saving vast sums, and on his death left as much as 675 million *denarii* to the Treasury.

He died tranquilly in 161; this was the first really serene death that any Roman emperor had experienced. He earned the immense praise of his successor Marcus Aurelius,[44] who set up a column in the Campus Martius (no longer to be seen there, although some of its friezes have survived;

Chapter 7) to celebrate the consecration which Antoninus duly received. The *Roman Regionary* links the Column with the Temple that was erected for his divinity.[45] The later emperor Gordian I (238) wrote an epic in his honour, and Julian the Apostate (361–3) praised his public life.[46] Down to the fourth century the day of his accession was celebrated.

Nevertheless, Marcus Aurelius, while praising Antoninus Pius so warmly, was aware that after his death Antoninus belonged to the past, and that, like everyone else, he could make no claim to perpetual recognition.[47] To a large extent Aurelius was right, because today, although there are fine portraits of Antoninus, little is really known about him as a man. On the whole, Aurelius's eulogistic picture seems well deserved. It is confirmed by the *Historia Augusta*.[48] Alone among almost all *principes* Antoninus lived entirely free from the blood of either citizen of foe, as far as lay within his own power, and he was a man who, as we have seen, was compared with Numa Pompilius, whose good fortune, pacific dutifulness, and religious scrupulousness he always maintained.

We can dimly discern a man who was 'a blend of Italian landowner and petty bourgeois, unambitious, unelastic and uncreative',[49] a man who enjoyed the pleasures of a rural proprietor and had a taste for self-consciously rustic pursuits; a man who, despite his services to imperial universality and his tributes to Hadrianic philhellenism, was not particularly keen on Greek culture (or particularly interested in beauty); a man who could display touches of humour and could show patience with criticism and even the capacity for gentle sarcasm; a man who reputedly (as the emperor Julian suggested) was not 'a wise lover', since he tolerated the excessive frankness and levity of his wife; a man who, above all, was enormously dutiful in regard to his tasks as the director of a huge empire.

He was said to have tolerated open criticism, and that may have been partly the significance of his early coin-type LIBERTAS PVBLICA.[50] He kept a statue of Fortune, his obedient follower (the FORTVNA OBSEQVENS of coins), in his bedroom.[51] It is conceivable, however, though by no means certain, that the prominence of Health or Well-Being (SALVS AVG.) on his coinage and medallions[52] indicates some recurrent anxieties about his physical condition, which included a tendency towards acute headaches, despite general good health. But it must be admitted that, just as we do not know a great deal about the man himself, the history of his reign remains little short of 'almost a complete blank',[53] denuded of chronological framework.

One can deduce from Marcus Aurelius's tribute that Antoninus himself was a bit too conservative.

> Antoninus pursued his own calm and steady way, disdaining anything that savoured of the flashy or new-fangled. . . . All his actions were guided by a respect for constitutional precedent (though he

would never go out of his way to court public recognition of this). He disliked restlessness and change, and had a rooted preference for the same places and the same pursuits.[54]

Under this man as ruler, the empire, with all of its merits and faults, was running smoothly. It could be described as a good time (TEMPORVM FELICITAS).[55] In fact, things were running so smoothly that they hardly seemed to move at all. Everything had become rather <u>static</u>. The Roman world seemed in a state of equipoise, propped up by its rich accumulation of wealth and experience, and apparently destined to continue indefinitely according to this established pattern. (As it turned out, of course, this was not to be the case.) It is not, therefore, entirely wrong to detect a certain *immobilisme*, which was not wholly inhumane – even if the lowest classes did not benefit much – but was based on traditional ways of thinking.

# 2

# MARCUS AURELIUS AND LUCIUS VERUS

A relief from Ephesus (Selçuk) – now in the Kunsthistorisches Museum at Vienna – has been interpreted as depicting the imperial family in 138, between the adoption of Antoninus Pius and the death of Hadrian.[1] It shows both Marcus Aurelius and Lucius Verus. Although it has been variously interpreted, it does not, in fact, throw a great deal of light on the intended future relationship of the two men. No doubt the Ephesian authorities preferred to remain equivocal, biding their time in order to see what happened.

Subsequently, Antoninus Pius, when he came to the throne in 138, lost his own two sons, Marcus Aurelius Fulvus Antoninus and Marcus Galerius Aurelius Antoninus, to premature deaths and thereafter adopted, as his sons, the seventeen-year-old Marcus Annius Verus (the later emperor Marcus Aurelius) and Lucius Ceionius Commodus (Lucius Verus).

Marcus was the nephew of the new ruler's wife Faustina the elder, and so could well be regarded, by those in favour of hereditary succession, as his natural heir. In consequence the youth assumed the names Marcus Aurelius Caesar (Aurelius being one of Antoninus's names), and broke off his engagement to Ceionia Fabia (daughter, as we shall see, of Aelius Caesar) so as to become betrothed instead (first unofficially, then officially) to Antoninus's own daughter, Annia Galeria Faustina – Faustina the younger. He married her in 145, when she was perhaps about fourteen, and the occasion was accorded great and continued attention, the relation of the new bride to Antoninus himself being stressed.[2]

For the twenty-three years of Antoninus's reign after 146/7 Marcus lived at Antoninus's side. Like Antoninus, he scarcely moved outside the palace; indeed, he was not absent from it for more than two nights. He was Antoninus's closest helper and greatest friend, and virtually co-emperor. He held the consulship in 140 and 145 as Antoninus's colleague, and in 146 was invested with the tribunician power, clearly indicating his position as heir to the throne, and was granted a proconsular post of superior authority (*imperium*) outside Rome. Moreover, from the year 140 (when he became consul for the first time) onwards, coinage had been issued in his name, as son of the emperor (PII *Filius*).[3] Early types included PIETAS AVG (*usti*) and HILARITAS – commemorating the joyful prospect of his heirship and marriage – and IVVENTAS, who was Hebe, the spirit of the youth of Rome and Italy which Marcus Aurelius represented.[4] It fitted in well with Antoninus's religious policy that the last-named type, like its contemporary, military but peaceful counterpart HONOS, coincided with an ancient Roman anniversary of the virtue's temple.[5]

Coins were also issued for Marcus Aurelius's wife, Faustina the younger, who was made Augusta (when her husband had not yet become Augustus), and was described as AVGVSTI PII FIL(*ia*).[6] These issues celebrate her piety and alleged chastity (PVDICITIA), the harmony of the imperial family (CONCORDIA), and the blessedness of the age (SAECVLI FELICIT*as*), already mentioned, which was indicated and symbolized by an allusion to her sons, so that Venus is personified as GENETRIX and Juno as LVCINA, the goddess of childbirth.[7]

A statue in the Capitoline Museum shows, with great sensitiveness, what the young Marcus Aurelius looked like. Meanwhile his elaborate education continued. His surviving correspondence with Fronto (Chapter 6) gives a remarkable impression of the atmosphere surrounding this process. At first the training concentrated on oratory, perhaps on the instigation of the practical Antoninus who saw that it would be useful. But then, when Marcus was in his twenties, he was persuaded (by Quintus Junius Rusticus) to turn to philosophy, much to the disappointment of Fronto.

Marcus Aurelius (161–80) was born in 121, and his original name, Marcus Annius Verus, was that of his forebears.[8] His paternal great-grandfather, from Ucubi (Espejo) in southern Spain (Baetica), had founded the family fortunes by rising to the rank of senator and praetor. The emperor's grandfather, Marcus Annius Verus, the first patrician of the family, held three consulships, in 97, 121 and 126, and his father of the same name, who died when his son was still a boy, became the husband of Domitia Lucilla, whose rich family owned a tile factory (inherited by Marcus Aurelius) outside Rome; a terracotta seal bearing her name has been discovered. In his earlier years Marcus bore the additional names of Catilius Severus in honour of his step-grandfather on his mother's side, Lucius Catilius Severus Julianus Claudius Reginus, consul in 110 and 120 (and subsequently in trouble). Also on his mother's side Marcus was descended from the famous orator Cnaeus Domitius Afer, who had died in 59 [?]. Marcus had numerous, wealthy and influential relatives belonging to the 'new establishment', and was the darling of high society.

When he was still very young he had attracted the attention of the emperor Hadrian, who made him a priest of the antique ritual association known as the Salian Order (at the time Marcus was only eight years old), and nicknamed him – after his name Verus – 'Verissimus'.[9] This was a compliment based on his uncommon moral qualities, but a slightly double-edged one, suggesting that Hadrian found the solemn child something of a prig; he was *a prima infantia gravis*, although he played ball well and managed to enjoy taking part in the wine harvest. The nickname became widely known, and found its way into writings and on to coins (of Tyras [Belgorod Dniestrovsky]) and inscriptions (notably from Ostia), as well as on to inscribed silverware. Hadrian entrusted his education to the best teachers of the day, including the famous Fronto to whom Marcus Aurelius became so close.

Hadrian seems to have been keen, perhaps excessively keen, to regulate the imperial succession. But whether he really envisaged Marcus Aurelius as an eventual emperor has been the subject of debate. The text of Dio Cassius that has come down to us asserted that he did, but Dio's original version perhaps indicated that the ruler who did so was Antoninus, not Hadrian: though this has been disputed.

On the one hand it has been suggested that Hadrian did *not* aim at the eventual succession of Marcus Aurelius, since he wanted a Ceionius on the throne, and therefore envisaged the much younger Lucius Verus (who was a Ceionius, and was the son of Hadrian's destined and beloved heir Aelius Caesar, who had died) as Antoninus's son-in-law and eventual successor. But it seems more probable that Hadrian, who arranged for Marcus to become engaged to Aelius Caesar's daughter Ceionia Fabia, *did* see him as an eventual successor, because of his personal qualities and family and social connections, but that Eutropius was right to say that he did not feel that this could take effect immediately, since Marcus was only seventeen in 138.[10] Thus, he adopted someone else instead, Antoninus Pius, entrusting Marcus Aurelius to his care. (It has also been suggested that he deliberately chose a successor who would not live long, so that Marcus could follow: but this seems uncertain, and anyway did not happen.) But Antoninus, at the same time, very probably did suppose, out of dutifulness to Hadrian, that Lucius Verus would become Marcus's colleague, and eventually perhaps sole emperor.

However, Antoninus's attitude to Lucius Verus (as he was later called) is hard to reconstruct. It is true that he never gave him the title of Caesar – which Aurelius had possessed since 139 – or any important job, even when he was thirty; and there is no coinage in Verus's honour under Antoninus. On the other hand, he did adopt him jointly with Marcus, and therefore kept him in the family. And he seems to have liked him. To quote the *Historia Augusta*, 'Pius loved the frankness of Verus's nature and his unspoiled way of living [?], *simplicitatem ingenii puritatemque vivendi*: or was the original text *hilaritatem*, referring to his geniality and high spirits?[11] And the same work continues, 'Antoninus encouraged Marcus to imitate him like a brother' (*hortatusque est ut imitaretur ut fratrem*). This

26

may seem surprising in view of the wave of denigrations of Verus's character, just as surprise has also been caused by Justin's description of him as a 'philosopher and lover of culture',[12] and has inspired some to conclude that the account is wrong, and that the reverse was the case. But such a rejection is not justifiable. Evidently Antoninus saw something in Verus, which he felt would make a useful complement to the solemnity of Marcus.

At all events, when Antoninus died Marcus Aurelius made Verus his colleague with a thoroughness that had never been seen before; it was now that he was given the name 'Verus', to make him a family connection. Lucius (Aurelius) Verus, as he now became, was proclaimed Augustus and granted the tribunician power; indeed, he held equal powers to Marcus in every respect, except that Marcus alone was chief priest (*pontifex maximus*). True, as the *Historia Augusta* asserted, the senate had presented the sovereignty to Marcus alone,[13] but when Ammianus Marcellinus records that the new partnership caused no impairment of Marcus's own imperial majesty,[14] he is missing the point that the two men *did rule jointly*, creating a novel precedent which was to be very often followed in the subsequent life of the empire. Several earlier rulers, it has been suggested, had intended something like a joint succession; but on nothing like so thoroughgoing a scale.

Marcus Aurelius's motives in taking this decisive step may have been three. First, he was carrying out the wishes of his predecessors, as he had supposedly promised to do. Second, he himself was fond of Verus, as his *Meditations* testify. He called him 'a brother whose natural qualities were a standing challenge to my own self-discipline at the same time as his deferential attention warmed my heart'.[15] Others also praised Verus. Third, Marcus Aurelius is very likely to have felt, as many including Valerian, Diocletian and Valentinian I felt after him, that two men were indeed needed to shoulder the enormous responsibilities of the imperial role and to deal with its massive press of business.

So he praised Lucius Verus to the senate, and meticulously showered honours upon him. He gave him his own third child, <u>Lucilla</u> (Annia Aurelia Galeria Lucilla), as his future wife. She was only eleven at the time of their betrothal in *c.* 159, and they married, at Ephesus (Selçuk), five years later; she was given the title Augusta. Nor did Aurelius believe the rumour that Lucius Verus (with his sister Ceionia Fabia, the former fiancée of Aurelius) was plotting against him; and the story that Aurelius was responsible for Verus's death, as we shall see, is absurd. To scotch these rumours of dissension, the latter's coins lay great stress on 'the Harmony between the emperors' (CONCORDIA AVGVSTORVM).[16]

Verus looked striking, as we can tell from his busts. He had a mass of curly hair, which was golden – an attribute of the gods.

He was physically handsome, with a genial face. His beard was allowed to grow almost in barbarian profusion – perhaps to assert his masculinity, and independence of Marcus Aurelius. He was a tall man, and his forehead projected somewhat above his eyebrows, so that he commanded respect. He is, of course, said to have taken so much care of his blond hair that he used to sprinkle gold dust on his head so that his hair might become brighter and blonder. In speech almost halting, he was very keen on gambling, and his way of life was always extravagant.... He was a voluptuary and excessive in his pleasures, and very suited, within proper limits, to all sports, games and jesting.[17]

The bad things that were said about Lucius Verus were partly concocted, no doubt, in order to provide a rhetorical contrast with the saintly Marcus Aurelius, and here the biographer Marius Maximus has been blamed.[18] But Verus does seem to have had 'an almost childish estimation of his own merits',[19] and, even if he was a not wholly inadequate administrator and general, he does not seem to have been quite energetic or conscientious enough for the position of emperor. Though pointing the conventional contrast with Marcus, the *Historia Augusta* does seem to have got it right when it says that 'Verus neither bristled with vices nor abounded with virtues' (*non inhorruisse vitiis, non abundasse virtutibus*), and refers to the 'laxity of his principles and the excessive licence of his life' (*lascivia morum et vitae licentioris nimietas*). The same work goes on, with unusual perceptiveness (probably borrowed), to remark that 'in character he was utterly ingenuous, and unable to conceal a thing' (*erat enim morum simplicium et qui adumbrare nihil posset*).[20]

This meant that he was easily led astray. There were plenty of intelligent men about at this time, imitating the virtuous Marcus Aurelius, and Verus did keep a number of eloquent and learned people in his employment – he was something of a philosopher himself.

Lucius Verus attended classes with [numerous scholars]. All these he loved most particularly and was in turn cherished by them, although not talented in literature. He did, to be sure, in boyhood love to compose verses, and, later on, speeches. In fact he is said to have been a better orator than a poet, or rather, to speak more truthfully, to be worse as a poet than as a rhetorician.

Nor are there lacking those who say that he was assisted by the talent of his friends and that those very things credited to him, such as they are, were written by others. And in fact he is said to have always had with him many eloquent and learned men. He had as his tutor Nicomedes – who was also his foster-father, and later (though a freedman) became a procurator and a knight.[21]

28

However, Lucius Verus was also said to have been excessively keen on a famous beauty at Antioch (Antakya) named Panthea (this enthusiasm caused Aurelius to send out his daughter Annia Lucilla, to whom Verus was engaged, to marry him promptly); and it was believed that he was too much influenced by unscrupulous freedmen, among whom Coedes, Eclectus (not the same as Commodus's later chamberlain), Geminus, Apolaustus (named after a famous actor), Agaclitus and Pergamus were mentioned. The criticism of these advisers may, of course, be partly due to the senatorial bias of so many historians, but it is also likely that they formed an unsatisfactory clique, which helped to develop the worse sides of Verus's character.

And yet, at the same time, Verus maintained a dutiful and affectionate reverence for his wiser colleague (far from plotting against him). It was even said to have been Verus who prompted Marcus Aurelius to give Caesarships to the latter's own sons, and Verus remained unoffended by Aurelius's appointment of most of the members of Verus's staff when he moved to the east, as will now be described.

Although there were troubles in Britain and Gaul, attention was almost at once focused upon the eastern question. The background to this situation needs to be appreciated, as a counterpart to what was about to happen on the other, northern frontier of the empire. The eastern neighbour, and invariably the potential or actual rival and enemy of Rome, was the Parthian kingdom, massive and varied and ruled by kings whose successions were even more turbulent than those of the emperors of Rome, although we actually have little information about the Parthians, owing to the lack of contemporary records.

We do know that the frontier between the two states was the River Euphrates, even if as a barrier it now proved useless, without some adjustment. Beyond the river, between it and the Tigris (in what is now Iraq), lay Mesopotamia in the northern region, and Babylonia (Lower Mesopotamia) to the south towards the Persian Gulf – the country in which lay the usual Parthian capital, and centre of dynastic struggles, Ctesiphon (Taysafun), opposite the very important, originally Greek, city and commercial entrepôt Seleucia-on-the-Tigris (Tell Umar).

The Parthians, like the Romans, believed in controlling sensitive frontier areas through client-states (quasi-independent satrapies), and in this category were Osrhoene, just to the north-west of Mesopotamia but still on the eastern, Parthian side of the Euphrates, Adiabene (as well as its southern neighbour Assyria) on the eastern bank of the Tigris – fertilized by the Great and Little Zab rivers – and, above all, the land of Armenia (Major), a buffer-state in the mountains north of the Upper Tigris, fought over by Rome and Parthia, and shuttling between clientage under the one and the other.

The Parthians' huge army consisted of permanent frontier garrisons plus 'feudal' levies summoned for military operations. The wars of the second century AD showed that these forces were no match for the Romans in protracted wars, but they could still steal surprise successes. Because of <u>pressure from central Asian tribes</u>, the Parthian centre of gravity had shifted westwards into Mesopotamia; and it was Mesopotamia which the Romans regarded as the key to their hoped-for reduction of Parthia and Armenia – both of which seemed to them, or to many of them, essential to the preservation of their own provinces. Trajan had invaded Mesopotamia, but probably almost all of it had already been evacuated before his death in 117, or at least shortly afterwards.

Later, in 162 at the beginning of the reign of Aurelius, the major eastern war which Antoninus had foreseen but shelved broke out. It was deliberately provoked by the powerful <u>King Vologaeses III of Parthia</u> (148–92), who placed his own son, Pacorus, on the throne of Armenia. As part of the same operation a Parthian general, Chosroes, used his cavalry to defeat the Roman governor of Cappadocia (Marcus Sedatius Severianus, who had rashly penetrated into Armenia) at Elegeia (Ilica?) in Derxene on the Armenian border, whereupon Severianus, who was responsible for this expensive and unnecessary interlude, committed suicide. The governor of Syria, where Parthia had many friends and the Roman legions were in poor shape owing to inactivity, suffered an equally serious setback.

It was the task of Marcus Aurelius and Lucius Verus to remedy this situation. The departure of both emperors for the east was probably thought inadvisable, since they had only so recently come to the throne. It was therefore decided that only one, Lucius Verus, should take command of the forces, since he was younger, more vigorous, and seemingly less unmilitary.[22] Or, rather, he was not much more military than his colleague, but he had able generals under him to do the job.

It took Verus, unfortunately, at least nine months to reach as far as Antioch. People attributed the delay to his pleasure-loving temperament. Hostile biographers and historians made the most of this.

> While a legate was being slain, while legions were being slaughtered, while Syria meditated revolt, and the East was being devastated, Verus was hunting in Apulia (Puglia), travelling about through Athens and Corinth accompanied by orchestras and singers, and dallying through all the cities of Asia that bordered on the sea, and those cities of Pamphylia and Cilicia that were particularly notorious for their pleasure resorts.
>
> And when he came to Antioch, there he gave himself wholly to riotous living.[23]

This may well be exaggerated; as we saw, there was a tendency to contrast the bad Verus with the virtuous Aurelius. And Verus may not have been in the best of health. Nevertheless, for one reason or another it did take him a long time to reach Syria, and when he arrived he showed no great eagerness to travel to the front, to which he only went once or twice, 'treating Syria as his own kingdom'.[24]

Meanwhile, however, his generals who undertook the fighting, their forces strengthened by reinforcements from Europe, were very active. In the first phase, the Armenian War, Marcus Statius Priscus invaded Armenia (163) and captured and destroyed its capital Artaxata (Etchmiadzin), founding an entirely new city (Kaine Polis) in its place, and crowning a Roman protégé, Sohaemus of Emesa (Homs), king of Armenia in 164. The victorious title 'Armeniacus' had been conferred on Lucius Verus in 163, while Marcus Aurelius, so as not to diminish the glory of his colleague, delayed his own acceptance of the title until the following year, as the coins reveal. It has been suggested that after these victories achieved by his generals Lucius Verus could have negotiated peace with Vologaeses III, but this, like so many other aspects of these campaigns, remains uncertain.

A second, more particularly Parthian, War now followed. In 165 Gaius Avidius Cassius, after taking over the governorship of Syria and subjecting its legions to an exacting re-training programme, undertook the first phase of the war by collaborating with Publius Martius Verus in easterly moves, penetrating by the difficult southern route far into Mesopotamia. The cities of Nicephorium Callinicum (Raqqa) on the Euphrates, Edessa (Urfa) further north (east of the river bend in Osrhoene, near the source of the Euphrates tributary of the Balissus [Belich], and Nisibis (Nüsaybin) far to the east in northern Mesopotamia, near to where the plains rise into the mountains, all surrendered to the Romans. Sohaemus was restored to the kingship of Armenia, which he had lost four years earlier (the task being performed by Thucydides, an agent of Martius Verus). Lucius Verus was hailed as Parthicus Maximus, a title which was probably designed to set him above Trajan (and compensated for his lack of the title *pontifex maximus*). Once again Marcus Aurelius, so as not to lessen Verus's honours by sharing them with him, postponed his own acceptance of the same title until the following year.[25]

After Avidius Cassius had won a bloody victory at the Greek or Graeco-Roman (but largely Parthianized) city of Dura-Europus (Salahiye) on the Euphrates (164 or 165), operations were brought to a conclusion (after he had been reinforced by another column) in late 165, or the following year, by the capture and destruction of the two great cities of Babylonia, on either side of the Tigris, the Greek emporium and cultural metropolis of Seleucia (Tell Umar) and the Parthian centre, Ctesiphon (Taysafun). (His burning of Seleucia, which was probably prompted by motives of security, meant the end of Hellenism in Babylonia.) No steps were taken to annex Babylonia or Mesopotamia, however, although the latter, at least seemingly, became a Roman dependency and sphere of influence, like Osrhoene. Roman garrisons were planted along the River Chaboras (Khabur), an eastern tributary of the Euphrates.

Next, in 166, Avidius Cassius penetrated across the southern reaches of the Tigris into the mountainous country of Media, a final show of might which marked the easternmost penetration of Roman arms, and earned both emperors the title of 'Medicus' after they had staged a triumph at Rome. The designation occasionally appears on inscriptions, but was soon dropped from the coins because it seemed so empty of significance, since the campaign did not lead to any lasting occupation. Indeed, despite dazzling successes in the field, no spectacular permanent results were produced by these operations as a whole – about which Verus no doubt consulted Aurelius, and for which Aurelius, in a brief moment of disloyalty to Lucius Verus, is said to have taken the credit,[26] perhaps with justification, though we cannot tell. Even Armenia did not remain a Roman client for very long (Sohaemus lasted until *c.* 185 or *c.* 192). And the failure to subjugate Parthia has sometimes been judged disappointing, though Aurelius and Verus had never intended to annex it or to give it a king.

What the emperors did achieve was to strengthen the Euphrates line and, while otherwise restoring the status quo, to go beyond this frontier and straighten it by occupying northern Mesopotamia, thus cutting off the river bend in its middle reach – and facilitating trade outside the empire (notably in slaves). They also caused the Parthians to remain inactive for a number of years. But Septimius Severus (193–211) rightly decided that the whole business had to be accomplished all over again, and not long after his time Parthia, permanently weakened by these two sets of wars, was transformed into the even more formidable Sassanian Persia.

It was a dreadful and lamentable fact that the Roman troops under the command of Lucius Verus in the east brought the plague back to Italy and the west – apparently from Seleucia on the Tigris, in Babylonia. Its character has been disputed[27] – was it smallpox, or exanthematous typhus, or bubonic plague? – and also the degree of its severity. Attempts have been made to minimize this, but they are unconvincing in face of strong evidence to the contrary. Corpses were piled on carts, and whole districts and legions were depopulated. The Roman revenue from taxes and imperial estates was much diminished, and some have suggested, although others will not have it, that the plague contributed more than any other factor to the decline of the empire.

The extraordinary, unprecedented crisis that characterized the reign of Marcus was brought about by the serious troubles that menaced the northern frontier, only just after the eastern frontier was pacified. The troubles were, it is true, of a different character, because the northern frontier area harboured no political power comparable to that of the Parthians in the east. Yet the northern tribes, although we learn little about them from Roman sources, were extremely perilous for the Romans, all the same. Not only had they learnt the Roman art of war by contact with the garrisons but they were also, at this time, gradually moving from semi-nomadism into a condition of permanent settlement. This augured badly for the Roman defences, although agriculture, long since practised,[28] was still largely left to women and prisoners of war.

There was, initially, trouble across the Rhine, where the Chatti (taking advantage of the change of emperor) caused devastation in the Wetterau and apparently destroyed Argentorate (Strasbourg), before suffering defeat in 162 at the hands of Gaius Aufidius Victorinus, governor of Germania Superior (Upper Germany). But, most serious of all, the tribes that lay just beyond the Danube were themselves under severe pressure from other Germans who lived further to the north and north-east. Notable among these were the Gotones (Goths), who were currently in the Vistula region – or were just beginning to move westwards from that area – and who would later prove such a curse to the Romans. These and other northern tribes pushed their more southerly compatriots along and across the Danube, in a process of escalation that had spread out through the Carpathians, forming a big population shift and collusive movement of the peoples such as the Romans had never experienced before and found exceptionally daunting.

The people that particularly needed watching were the Marcomanni, most of whom lived in the plateau region of Boiohaemum (Bohemia: which is now the Czech Republic); that is to say, where the Romans could see them across the river from Castra Regina (Regensburg), or further east from the second Lauriacum (Enns) and Castra Batava (Passau). Although generally quiescent, they had turned against the Romans in 89 (when Domitian was emperor) and were now preparing to do so again. To the east of them dwelt the Quadi, north of the bend of the middle Danube or, further west, north of Carnuntum (Petronell) and Vindobona (Vienna); opposite the Roman provinces of Noricum and Upper and Lower Pannonia, in what are now Austria and western Slovakia. The Cotini worked Moravian iron for them, and the Quadi had often been friendly to the Romans in the first century AD, and had traded with them. However, they could not be relied upon. It was better not to forget that Julius Caesar had described them as by far the greatest and most bellicose of the large group of German peoples known as the Suebi.[29] This might no longer be true, and the Quadi, like the Marcomanni, were often regarded as performing the cliental function of acting as Roman protégés, but the Quadi, in common with their neighbours, had not forgotten their warlike reputation.

Moreover, a peculiarity of the Roman frontier was the deep reentrant between the Danube, where it turned south, and its tributary the Pathisus (Tisza, Theiss), which was inhabited by a non-Germanic people, the Jazyges, who together with the Roxolani (further to the east) formed the somewhat vaguely defined Sarmatian nation. The Jazyges, to whom the Cotini and the Orsi (north-east of Aquincum [Budapest]) paid tribute, became famous for their heavy cavalry of 'iron-clad knights', which was not, perhaps, an entirely early creation, but was notable in the time of Marcus Aurelius.

A few richly furnished barrow graves, known as the 'Nagyhegy group', which are scattered throughout Jazygian territory, are of interest. They evidently belonged to the ruling class and differ from other graves in their burial ritual and grave goods. Weapons are common and a horse was often buried with its master. Many of the objects are of eastern origin: Indian beads and small thin Parthian gold and bronze plates sewn on to garments. A notable example was discovered at Szil in Hungary, possibly the grave of a Sarmatian prince who fell in battle during a raid in the second century AD.

It seems likely that the situation was pretty disturbed in the land of the Jazyges, partly, perhaps, because they were overrun by their more easterly Sarmatian cousins, the Roxolani. It is uncertain, however, whether these incursions took place before 166, or a decade and a half later. If the former, then the consequent establishment of a new and more aggressive leadership may have been partly responsible for the dangerous situation which Marcus Aurelius had to face. But all of this remains conjectural.[30]

The Jazyges, who seem to have crossed the Carpathians and settled in the Hungarian plain soon after AD 20, had originally been made a buffer vassal state by the Romans to keep away their Dacian enemies. Trajan, when he conquered Dacia (101-5), had been helped by the Jazyges (although they had been hostile to Domitian), and he had subsequently left their low, flat, swampy land of dunes alone, probably because it seemed to him hard to defend and not worth taking. But its exclusion greatly extended the frontier, and the Jazyges were not reliable, since under Hadrian they attacked Roman Dacia (117-19).

Indeed, in general terms the Danube frontier was not satisfactory. Long ago, Augustus had planned to conquer Bohemia and to annex south Germany, and in 9 BC Nero Drusus had reached the Albis (Elbe). After a major revolt in Illyricum (AD 6-9), and the ambushing of Varus by Arminius (AD 9), these expansionist plans, which envisaged the Carpathians instead of the Danube as the empire's northern border, had been abandoned, and Germanicus's subsequent claim that he had conquered the lands between the Rhine and the Elbe amounted to nothing. Possibly such plans could not, realistically, amount to anything (see the Introduction), because the Romans would not have been able to find enough soldiers to garrison these vast territories; indeed, it is highly questionable whether even the Carpathians would have been an effective northern frontier, since beyond them were the menacing Gotones (Goths), who could not safely be left outside the empire, even if there were not sufficient Roman manpower to bring them inside its borders.

So trouble, one day, was expected. Meanwhile, as has been said, there were cliental and commercial relationships to stave it off, and Rome had, on occasion, intervened in the dynastic troubles of the Quadi. However, the garrisons in the frontier zone were not sufficient for the purpose. For instance, along the Raetian *limes* and Upper Danube there were inadequate camps, mobile rear troop reserves were lacking, and the units that were in existence were weakened by the plague. Yet trouble, it may be repeated, was bound to come one day, and in the earliest years of Marcus Aurelius too little was done to avert it, because of the war in the east.

The trouble came, in no uncertain fashion, in 166 or 167 (not later, as has been sometimes supposed). It appears that the first invaders were six thousand people belonging to what had formerly been remoter tribes, the Langobardi and Obii (Osi), who had migrated a little earlier from the lower Albis (Elbe), taking with them from their old homeland sections of other peoples, the Lacringi and Victofali. What was sinister was that these tribesmen reached the Danube frontier through the lands of the Quadi, with whom – possibly not for the first time – they had evidently reached an agreement. Then, a few months later, the Quadi and Marcomanni themselves crossed the Danube, severely damaging Aquincum (Budapest), and broke through into the flat lands on the Roman side. It was the first of many attempts by the Marcomanni to expand beyond Bohemia, and was done for reasons of land hunger, that is to say, for settlement rather than mere plundering. 'The enemy peoples were on the move in a serious way.'[31]

Dacia and Upper Moesia were immediately at risk, massacres took place, villas were burnt, and gold mines at Alburnum (Roşia Montană) were lost; at Verespatak tablets were found which had been buried hastily because of the invasion. But the main targets were the whole of Upper and Lower Pannonia and Noricum and Raetia, where appalling damage was done. Carnuntum (Petronell) was one of a number of fortresses which were burnt to the ground, vast numbers of the population were taken prisoner, and something like 20,000 soldiers were killed. A general and praetorian prefect, Titus Furius Victorinus, was 'lost' – possibly he died of the plague, but more probably he too was slain by the invading Germans, somewhere in Pannonia (?168); other Roman generals, too, were killed in battle. Worst of all, the invaders penetrated right through into north Italy (probably in 167). Opitergium (Oderzo) was destroyed,[32] and Aquileia, with the aid of its strong natural defences, saved itself only by the most determined and efficient resistance to a formidable siege.

Not long afterwards another tribe, the Costoboci, from the eastern slopes of the Carpathians in northern Transylvania, took advantage of Roman disorganization to penetrate the empire, apparently by land through Lower Moesia, as far as Greece, where they sacked Eleusis (Lefsina). Pausanias described them by the emotive term of 'bandits', used for all manner of seditious people (Chapter 8).[33]

It was the worst crisis to which the empire had ever been subjected, a 'war of many nations in which all the tribes from the [Danube] *limes* to Gaul conspired together' in a collusive drive,[34] that is to say, of quite a new character and new dimensions; it was the first occasion on which the Romans had been forced to confront a mass migration of tribesmen determined to settle on their territory. Eutropius was indeed right to see this Marcomannic War as the most terrible of all wars, comparable even to the Punic Wars of the past.[35]

Marcus Aurelius was faced with this emergency on top of the eastern wars and the plague. The situation was compounded by the lack of a capital reserve or sinking fund and by Aurelius's own generosity in remitting debts to the treasury; in addition, floods had destroyed great quantities of grain at home and seem to have been at least partly responsinle for a famine. He did everything that he could. He even sold imperial property in the Forum of Trajan at Rome, partly to raise much-needed money, but partly to show that even the emperor valued his own personal possessions less than the welfare of the empire (he claimed to possess nothing himself). But he also demanded ruinously large contributions from the richer people in the provinces.

He had recourse to exceptional measures to recruit the necessary troops, a step that was all the more necessary because the Roman army was losing many deserters to the Marcomanni and Quadi. He mobilized even slaves as *voluntarii*, as well as 'brigands' from Dalmatia and Dardania (Upper Moesia; Moesia Superior). The Legio VII Claudia received at least twice its normal intake of recruits, and legionaries were poured into inadequately defended Raetia and Noricum. There had not been such active recruiting since the time of Hannibal. Moreover, to counteract heavy rises in price, military pay continued to increase, and Aurelius (who, as we have seen, remitted debts to the treasury) felt it necessary to be rather extravagant with his largesses. He also continued the inflation of the currency by lowering the silver content, so as to cut down costs, as well as decreasing the amount of gold in the *aureus* to 75 per cent and debasing the *orichalcum* in brass coinage to 65 per cent zinc.[36]

The crisis was considered so severe that Aurelius told the senate that both emperors, he and Lucius Verus, were needed to go north. When there had been war in the east, Aurelius had allowed Verus to go alone, on the grounds that one emperor had to stay behind and that he himself was better equipped for peace than for war. But now the northern situation was so serious that no such considerations were held to apply. Verus had hastened home from the east in 166, owing to the threats on the German frontier, and after time had been taken to make the armies ready to engage the attackers both emperors set out together for the north, in spring 169, pausing for a considerable time at Aquileia.

Meanwhile, there had been heavy fighting in the Danube-Pathisus reentrant, resulting, it was said, in a major victory on the frozen Danube. Not only were the Jazyges defeated – and Dacia reorganized – but the king of the Marcomanni, Ballomarius, seeing what a wasp's nest had been stirred up, had gone with ten other envoys – one for each tribe involved – to seek peace from Marcus Iallius Bassus Fabius Valerianus, the governor of Pannonia Inferior (Lower Pannonia).[37] Verus thought that this was satisfactory, and that the time had now come for the emperors to turn back.[38] (The loss of the praetorian prefect Titus Furius Victorinus and the large number of other Roman casualties [see p. 35] had distressed him.) Aurelius, however, persisted in crossing the Alps, penetrating as far as Pannonia – in the company, at first, of Verus. Aurelius did this because he mistrusted the intentions of the Marcomanni: rightly as it turned out, since Ballomarius broke the truce and attacked once again. Nevertheless, once this renewed threat had been dealt with, a halt was called – partly, perhaps, because the plague had reappeared in the army.

On their way to the north Lucius Verus died.

Not far from Altinum (Altino), Lucius was struck down in the carriage with the sudden illness which they call apoplexy. After being set down from the carriage and bled, he was taken to Altinum, and after living on speechless for three days he died there.

There was gossip that he had committed incest with his mother-in-law Faustina: he is said to have died through her treachery, after poison had been sprinkled on oysters, the reason being that he had betrayed to the daughter the relations he had had with the mother ... There is [also] a well-known tale that Marcus Aurelius handed Verus part of a sow's womb smeared with poison after he had cut it with a knife poisoned on one side.

But it is sacrilege for this to be thought about Marcus, even if both Verus's thoughts and his deeds might have deserved it. We shall not leave it in the balance, but reject the whole story as disproved and refuted.[39]

Indeed, there is every reason to suppose that Lucius Verus died a natural death, from apoplexy; and rumours to the contrary can be ignored. As the *Historia Augusta* surmised, it is not likely that Aurelius poisoned him, or that Faustina the younger (or Verus's wife Lucilla) did so either.

Aurelius's feelings about his death, however, cannot be reconstructed. There were those who felt that he must have heaved a sigh of relief that such a comparatively inadequate colleague was out of the way: 'perhaps the burden of Lucius Verus dead and divine was lighter than the burden of Lucius alive and human'. On the other hand he had needed an imperial collaborator, and he seems to have appreciated good points in Verus that others failed to detect.

It is no less easy to understand what Marcus Aurelius thought he had so far achieved by his German operations. Probably all that he felt was that he had turned back the would-be invaders, and reduced them to an appropriate cliental status, signified by the construction of many Roman posts and roads. He wanted to justify the wars as defensive, *bella iusta*,[40] and the idea of more comprehensive annexation may not yet have occurred to him (though this is disputed). Nevertheless, the notion of crusading against barbarians was popular among the Romans and it was celebrated by medallions showing Jupiter throwing a thunderbolt at the German foe.[41]

# 3

# MARCUS AURELIUS

In spite of the philosophical liberalism displayed in his *Meditations* (Chapter 6), Marcus Aurelius did quite a lot to shore up the position of the upper classes.

This tendency is illustrated by the incident relating to Saepinum (Altilia),[1] a place situated at an altitude of two thousand feet in the country of the Samnites. In about 168 the local functionaries of this place came into hostile confrontation with the emperor's herdsmen. The people of Saepinum had found that their harvests were damaged by the nibbling of these herdsmen's cattle as they were moved, in the annual process of transhumance, to the mountain pastures; and the Saepinians reckoned that if they could not secure protection against these encroachments they would never again make a success of their cultivation. The age-long historical struggle between sedentary populations and nomads was symbolized by this incident.

So Saepinum reacted with vigour, and complained to the emperor. And the attitude which the imperial administration was going to adopt would prove decisive for a long time ahead. The emperor passed the decision to his praetorian prefects, Marcus Bassaeus Rufus and Marcus Macrinius Avitus Catonius Vindex, and their ruling gave the Saepinians no satisfaction whatever. One wonders whether Marcus Aurelius, if he took cognizance of the matter at all, was just letting matters take their course, or if he was quite deliberately subordinating the interests of the people of Saepinum to those of the large landowners – of whom he was one of the largest himself: since the failure of the ordinary Saepinians would mean that the local landowners became more powerful. In any case, the consequence of the decision was the same: the victory of the wealthy element. And with it came the decline of agriculture, and the recession of the imperial economy.

In Achaia (Greece), too, steps were taken to bolster up the richer section of the population by Marcus Aurelius's expulsion of freedman (ex-slaves) from the Council of Athens; and he also took steps to restrict the membership of the Areopagus.

By the same token, at home, he adopted measures which increased the privileges and prestige of senators. When there was a war crisis, he made the extraordinary request that the necessary funds should be voted by the senate (see note, p. 179). And he helped individual senators by reducing their compulsory investment in Italian land from the Trajanic figure of one-third to one-quarter. On a medallion he celebrated the 'Genius of the Senate'.[2] If he shared Fronto's view that the upper classes were mostly inhuman,[3] then he did not show it. True, he preferred to consult an inner circle (*consilium*) of personal associates (*comites*) – who had existed before but now became more important – rather than the senate itself. But the members of this *consilium*, some of whom but not all possessed military expertise, were mostly senators.

However, he was well aware of, and shared, the Stoic view that the ruler was there to serve his subjects as a whole: 'Let all actions', he advised himself, 'aim solely at the common good.'[4] So the emperor ought to be careful 'not to affect the monarch too much, or to be too deeply dyed with the purple', which, after all, is only 'sheep's wool stained with a little gore from a shell-fish'.[5] He had views of his own about the 'virtues' which Romans had habitually personified. He had something to say about liberty, about happiness – and about unity, since he was aware of possible disturbances in the army when he celebrated *Concordia* and *Fides Exercituum*. But he emphasized *Justice*. It may well be that IVSTITIA AVG. has some special reference to disputes with barbarians over the frontier, but it also possesses a very general significance, as Marcus Aurelius believed strongly that injustice is an unforgivable sin.[6]

This belief emerged from his concentration on his duties in the lawcourts. Roman emperors were heavily engaged in the practical tasks of legislators, and this process reached its climax under Aurelius, of whom no less than two hundred imperial rescripts have survived. Certain of their features admit generalization. First, they are somewhat conservative, as the *Historia Augusta* pointed out. *Ius magis vetus restituit quam novum fecit*:[7] he was more keen to restore the old law than to create anything new. In this respect he was a continuator of Antoninus Pius.

Aurelius also maintained his predecessor's policy of helping orphans (*pueri et puellae Lucilliani et Veriani*: see note, p. 175) and may even have set up a central alimentary office. But it will not surprise those who have read what has already been said that there are additional signs that he supported the upper classes. The *honestiores* receive much more attention than the *humiliores*, who, incidentally, do not get a mention in the *Meditations*. Furthermore, Aurelius tried to enhance the citizen body. He was perhaps the last emperor to make an effort to strengthen the dividing wall between citizens and non-citizens (though he thanked the Peripatetic Claudius Serenus for teaching him democracy). That is how he interpreted his duty, which he sought at all times to carry out, and despite his support for the upper classes his laws did help the helpless as well – widows, and minors, and slaves.

How far was all of this due to the Stoicism which, as we know from the *Meditations* (Chapter 6), was his personal creed? Aurelius upheld, as we have seen, the Stoic view that the ruler should serve his subjects as a whole. Yet it is, surely, an exaggeration to say that Stoicism dominated his laws. But it would probably be legitimate to conclude that Stoicism exercised an indefinable, but never entirely absent, general influence on his humanitarian legislation.

True, it must be remembered that the emperor himself did not usually play a strong personal role in framing these laws. Indeed, this was a time when distinguished legal experts flourished. Tradition assigns Quintus Cervidius Scaevola (who taught Septimius Severus) the role of Aurelius's principal legal counsellor. And this was also the age of Gaius, on whose publications our modern knowledge of the law of Rome is largely based (Chapter 6). Gaius recognized the full legal validity of imperial enactments, and also listed the pronouncements of recognized lawyers (*responsa iurisprudentium*) as a source of law. The reign of Aurelius was a time when works of interpretation flourished, serving a government which they helped to make authoritarian, interfering ever more in people's private lives; and that interference was the result of the first systematic treatments of administrative law that we now find.

As for the emperor himself, he conveniently identified *Romanitas* and *humanitas* (which was beginning to mean 'humanity') as two indissoluble, indeed identical, synonyms for universality:[8] both are meant by *Tellus*, *Terra Mater*, the personification of the earth, called upon to personify and produce a prosperous agricultural new year.

Aurelius played a prominent part not only as a legislator but also as a judge. One of the principal differences between a Roman emperor and a British prime minister or American president is the amount of time that the former had to spend as a judge, and under Aurelius this task reached epic proportions. He raised the number of court days in the year to two hundred and thirty.[9] Ulpius Marcellus describes how he gave verdicts. In performing these judicial tasks, he was meticulously longwinded.[10] But he also laid great stress on *indulgence*. This became particularly apparent after the attempted revolt of Avidius Cassius in the east, when Aurelius took pains not to punish his accomplices but to spare them.

Outside his own court, too, he showed determination to improve the administration of justice. This was the principal motive behind his revival of the four travelling judges (*juridici*) in Italy – usually senators of praetorian rank – who had been suspended by Antoninus Pius (himself once a *juridicus*). Aurelius reckoned that their renewed existence, even if not welcome to all of the governing class, would make justice cheaper and more expeditious, and that was the sort of improvement that he had in mind.

Whatever may have been the exact meaning of the *Pietas* of Antoninus Pius, the same quality as constantly invoked and proclaimed on behalf of Aurelius refers to his traditionalistic devotion and care for religion, and his fatherly care for his subjects, which displayed both clemency and constancy to principle. As for religion, it was at this time, one might say, that paganism was reaching its climax, and it was embodied in Aurelius who in 172–3 proclaimed RELIG(*io*) AVG(*usti*) on his coinage.[11] But it is a somewhat changing and noteworthy *religio*, because the inscription on the coins is often accompanied by the picture of a temple of Mercury (Hermes) *in the Egyptian style*, so that the Mercury was the Egyptian Thoth.

Moreover, this was an age in which belief in miracles was not disdained. There was the Lightning Miracle and the Rain Miracle, both probably in 172; and both are recorded by graphic pictures on the Column of Aurelius (Chapter 7). The Lightning Miracle destroyed enemy siege engines, and the Rain Miracle intervened to save Roman troops from the Germans.

> When the Romans were in peril in the course of the battle, the divine power saved them in a most unexpected manner. The Quadi[?] had surrounded them at a spot favourable for their purpose and the Romans were fighting valiantly with their shields locked together. Then the barbarians ceased fighting, expecting to capture them easily as the result of the heat and their thirst. So they posted guards all about and hemmed them in to prevent their getting water anywhere; for the barbarians were far superior in numbers.
>
> The Romans, accordingly, were in a terrible plight from fatigue, wounds, the heat of the sun, and thirst, and so could neither fight nor retreat, but were standing in the line and at their several posts, scorched by the heat, when suddenly many clouds gathered and a mighty rain, not without divine interposition, burst upon them.
>
> Indeed, there is a story to the effect that Harnouphis, an Egyptian magician, who was a companion of Marcus Aurelius, had invoked by means of enchantments various deities and in particular Mercury, the god of the air, and by this means attracted the rain. . . . Dio goes on to say that when the rain poured down, at first all turned their faces upwards and received the water in their mouths. Then some held out their shields and some their helmets to catch it, and they not only took deep draughts themselves but also gave their horses to drink . . .
>
> A violent hail-storm and numerous thunderbolts fell upon the ranks of the foe . . . but the fire did not touch the Romans.[12]

Thus the miracle was ascribed to Mercury (Hermes Aërios, the god of the air; the Lightning Miracle was attributed to Jupiter), although the

Mercury was an Egyptian version of the God, because the Egyptian Harnouphis was supposed to have invoked his aid.

Aurelius's willingness to worship foreign gods is illustrated by his reaction to this alleged event, and celebrated by coinages depicting an oriental temple, with the inscription (as we have seen) RELIG(*io*) AVG(*usti*).

[On the Column] the downpour is personified as a frightening and semi-human figure, with gloomy face and long beard, whose hair melts into descending streams of water. . . . If the personification had a name, it can only have been the name of one of the gods whose aid was acknowledged on the coinage – presumably Hermes Aërios, although the grim and alarming figure is very unlike the normal youthful winged-footed Hermes or Mercury. The god described by Dio Cassius as 'Hermes Aërios' is apparently a native Egyptian deity, Thoth, whose aid was invoked by Harnouphis.

In other respects, too, Marcus Aurelius took a lively interest in the religion of Egypt, including the cults of Isis and Serapis.[13] Cults of other near-eastern countries, such as those of the Magna Mater and Jupiter (Baal) of Doliche (Duluk) and Heliopolis (Baalbek; Chapter 7), were also revered. But there was sharp rivalry to take the credit for the Rain Miracle between adherents of different sects and religions, including the 'Chaldaean' Julianus and the Christians. This, of course, was not generally accepted, though Aurelius was not averse to the superstition of the miracle.

Moreover, as his *Meditations* make clear,[14] he believed, like many others, that we are given advice in dreams. However, being philosophically inclined, he was 'sceptical of wizards and wonder-workers'. One wonders how he reacted (apart from rejecting his theory of the Rain Miracle) to Julianus who evolved theurgy (a higher or religious sort of magic), and to the arch-charlatan Alexander of Abonuteichus (Ionopolis, Inebolu) in Paphlagonia, who was denounced by Lucian but who impressed the eminent Marcus Sedatius Severianus (whose father-in-law was a senator who told Aurelius to throw two lions into the Danube).

As we have seen, the cults which took the credit for the Rain Miracle included the Christians, who claimed, notably through the voice of Claudius Apollinaris, bishop of Hierapolis (Pamukkale), that it was their god who had saved Aurelius's army (p. 124).[15] Christianity was now a religion to be reckoned with. Contemporary pagans were prepared to admire the cohesion and mutual assistance of the Christians, and even sceptics were impressed by their social services. Moreover, Christianity had worked itself up from the uneducated classes, and had reached the age of intellectual maturity, enlisting some of the leading minds of the age. The result was that some of the first and most important Christian 'Apologists' belong to this period (Chapter 6).

It is scarcely surprising, however, that these Christians did not find favour with the Roman authorities. Their growing numbers and tightly-knit social coherence seemed to distance Christianity from the imperial system, and the inward-turning secrecy of their society made it all too easy for horrible accusations of incestuous and cannibalistic banquets, and so forth, to be whispered against them: they were considered 'mad', and blamed for national and natural disasters.

Emperors had occasionally encouraged their persecution, when the Christians omitted formal gestures that proclaimed their loyalty, and in order to distract attention from unpopular hardships; this was notable under Nero, as Tacitus so vividly recorded.[16] Indeed, persecution went on automatically, if sporadically, whoever the emperor might be; the Christian distinction between 'good' emperors, who did not persecute, and 'bad', who did, is a myth. Yet at the same time the rulers did not usually want the Christians to be too roughly treated, out of a sense of justice, or so as not to stress fractures in the empire's social system. Thus, more recently, Antoninus Pius, although he presumably did not care for the beliefs of the Christians – and his officials were said to have persecuted them – on some occasions extended his protection to adherents of their faith, especially in the east, by suppressing incipient anti-Christian campaigns by over-zealous officials in Achaia (Greece) and Macedonia.

As for Marcus Aurelius, he only once refers to the Christians in his *Meditations* – when he is discussing suicide.

> Happy is the soul which, at whatever moment the call comes for release from the body, is equally ready to face extinction, dispersion or survival. Such preparedness, however, must be the outcome of its own decision; a decision not prompted by mere contumacy, as with the Christians, but formed with deliberation and gravity and if it is to be convincing to others, with an absence of all heroics.[17]

Efforts to delete this passage from the text, as a later fictitious addition, have failed. It is difficult not to regard them as unsuccessful endeavours to show that such a good man as Aurelius could not be anti-Christian; endeavours furthered by the alteration of one of his portraits, as a priest, into a figure of Christ.

But anti-Christian he was, and what he objected to was the taste of these increasingly numerous dissidents for spectacular martyrdoms, which seemed to him playing to the gallery, and doing so for a cause which conflicted with universal Roman unity. The fact that he had Stoic leanings did not help; the Stoics and the Christians emphatically did not see eye to eye. And Marcus Aurelius, with his keen belief in the individual's duty to the state, cannot have welcomed the Christian lack of concern for worldly life. His friend Fronto denounced the Christians, with ill-informed political clichés. But Aurelius did not much care for them either, although he probably knew little about them and they did not figure largely in his mental processes.

At all events, the Christians did not fare well during the reign of Aurelius. Not all of the information that has come down to us about their 'persecution' can be accepted, but it does appear that Justin was condemned in Rome in *c.* 165 (or 167) by the city prefect Quintus Junius Rusticus, and executed, with six of his disciples; that the aged Polycarp was seized and burnt to death at Smyrna, perhaps in *c.* 177, though other dates have been suggested; and that Carpus and Papylus and Agathonice suffered a similar fate at Pergamum (Bergama) after torture by the proconsul of Asia. The most decisive event took place at Lugdunum (Lyon) in Gaul, probably in *c.* 177, although the date has been questioned, when forty-eight Christians from Lugdunum itself and from Vienna (Vienne) were put to death.[18]

After they had already been subjected to local victimization, these Christians were brought before the 'governor' (presumably the *legatus* of Gallia Lugdunensis), who tried to make them either recant from their religion or else admit that they had taken part in the evil activities, such as incest and cannibalism, that were alleged to fulfil an essential role in the rituals of Christianity.

During the imprisonments and tortures that accompanied this process, some died, including Pothinus, the not very young bishop of Lugdunum. Those who survived, after further floggings and scorchings, were killed by wild beasts in the 'amphitheatre' – which was presumably the arena attached to the imperial cult centre at the suburb of Condate. Outstanding among these martyrs was the slave Blandina, who, in spite of the sufferings that she underwent, refused to give way or recant. The bodies of the dead Christians were publicly displayed, and then burnt, and their ashes thrown into the River Rhodanus (Rhône).

The Christians had shown personal bravery in dying, rather than abandoning their faith. Yet the general significance of their martyrdoms must not be overstated. For example, it must not be regarded as justifying the view that there was a substantial or powerful Christian community in Gaul at the time. The relatively few who existed were turned upon by a population which was distressed by the troubles that beset themselves and the empire, and wanted someone to blame. Furthermore, there were substantial groups of holiday-makers in town, attracted by the annual summer meeting of the delegates of the Gallic tribes at Condate, for which preparations were under way. It was July, and very hot, so that hysterical excitement could easily arise – and it was directed against the Christians: first by the crowd, and then by the civic authorities, and finally by the governor. The instinct of the Roman administration was to try to control the situation by giving way, rather than by saying 'no', or by attempting to divert the current high feelings in some other direction.

In 160 the pagan cult of the Great Mother (Cybele) had been made official at Gaul, which did not help when the persecution there began. Moreover, there had already been an angry public outcry against the Christians, whose oriental immigrants conducted extensive business activities in and around the Rhodanus (Rhône) valley. Rumours circulated about their way of life, as we saw, and now they were made the scapegoats for military, economic and natural disasters.

The provincial governor, faced with an enraged mob, wrote to Aurelius requesting his instructions. Those anxious to exculpate him from what followed have pointed out that he was on the Danube, and may never have received the letter. But it seems more natural to suppose that he did so – whether or not he shared the view that the Christians were partly responsible for the misfortunes of his reign – and replied that the law must take its course. He cannot be exempted from responsibility for the massacre that followed. Another took place at Carthage in 180, when six Christians, some of them natives of the area, were tried by the proconsul, and beheaded. The event is described in the Latin *Acts of the Execution of the Martyrs of Scillium* in Numidia.

Martyr Acts were also attributed to Irenaeus – who inveighed too against the dualist Gnostics, denounced as heretical (Chapter 6) – and Orosius, the Christian historian, saw the plagues as punishment visited upon pagan Rome for these persecutions. At all events, not only did such deaths provide a turning-point by strengthening the central church against off-centre sects, thus warding off disintegration, but also every martyrdom was a stimulating encouragement to Christianity – prompting a revival of the old enthusiasm of the primitive Christians, which was exactly the opposite of what Marcus Aurelius and his administration hoped.

Marcus Aurelius displayed the usual imperial vigilance on the frontiers. On the African continent, for example, he not only stimulated the provinces of Mauretania Tingitana and Africa – by providing a new strong wall for Volubilis (168/9; near Moulay Idriss) and appointing an official to buy up oil in Tripolitana – but also did a good deal to extend Roman influence *beyond* the frontier line. Antoninus Pius had already taken steps in this direction, and Marcus Aurelius did more. An inscription, which can be dated to AD 174,[19] was found at Agneb (Agueneb), at the northern extremity of Djebel Amour. This was some two hundred and fifty miles beyond the African *limes*; and yet the inscription was set up by a mixed force of imperial Roman cavalry. A search has been made for a fort on the spot, but one has not yet been discovered. We do know, however, that the soldiers were there long enough for a decurion (non-commissioned officer) to learn that he had been promoted. This posting of a force so far beyond the Roman frontier recalls the similar centres of military occupation which Marcus Aurelius hoped to impose on the Marcomanni and Sarmatians (Jazyges) across the Danube.

However, in that northern area, things were not going well for the Romans, who, far from successfully extending their area of control beyond the established line of the Danube, were having to cope with serious incursions and invasions into the provinces and even, as we saw, into Italy itself.

Marcus Aurelius tried to lull the fears of his people about these northern invasions by proclaiming Victory on his coins of 168,[20] but the effort of recovery had scarcely begun. For the time being, Aquileia had saved the day, and a new command in north Italy (the *praetentura Italiae et Alpium*) was established, under Quintus Antistius Adventus.[21] By *c.* 170 Marcus Aurelius was ready to hit back (it is uncertain where he spent the winter of 169–70). War was undertaken on a vast front along the <u>Rhine</u> and <u>Danube</u>.

It is possible that a first offensive across the Danube in 170 was not successful, but it seems that late in 171 his attack achieved results. The tide had begun to turn. Roman control over Raetia and <u>Noricum</u> was reestablished, partly through the efforts of the emperor's son-in-law Tiberius Claudius Pompeianus. At or near Carnuntum (Petronell), Marcus Aurelius's latest headquarters, from where the attack had been launched, the emperor met enemy envoys, including some from the Quadi. Castra Regina (Regensburg) became a legionary camp, housing the new Legio III Italica. Hard-hit Upper and Lower <u>Pannonia</u> were also dealt with,[22] and a *municipium Aelium* was founded at Durostorum (Silistra) in <u>Lower Moesia (Moesia Inferior)</u>, which sent reinforcements to Dacia. Then, in 172, a resounding victory was won over the Marcomanni, as they were trapped when they were trying to cross the Danube. The success was celebrated by the issue, in 172, of a coin depicting a bridge, and of other coins commemorating the 'conquest of Germany' (GERMANIA SVBACTA); while Marcus Aurelius allowed himself to be hailed as 'Germanicus'.[23]

The triumph was largely achieved, so it was said, with the help of two divine interventions, which may have taken place in 172 and which are vigorously depicted on reliefs upon the Column of Marcus Aurelius (Chapter 7). On the first occasion, the emperor summoned a thunderbolt from heaven by his prayers, and destroyed one of the enemy's military engines. The other story is the famous Rain Miracle (see p. 42), in which a sudden downfall of rain slaked the thirst of the parched Roman soldiers, thus saving the army from the Quadi (or Cotini).

However, it is very doubtful whether Marcus Aurelius himself was present at the alleged Rain Miracle. Neither the Column nor the account of Dio Cassius, summarized by his Epitomator, indicate that he was there at the time. Indeed, the fifth-century Christian historian Orosius records that only a small Roman force was concerned;[24] if he is right, then the main army was not involved. It is reasonable, therefore, to accept the statement of Eusebius that the Roman commander on this occasion was not the emperor himself but Publius Helvius Pertinax,[25] the future emperor. It is hard to see why Eusebius should have excluded Marcus Aurelius if the facts had not been against his inclusion.

The Christians, suffering martyrdoms at the time, built up the occasion as much as they could, attributing the 'miracle' to their God. This Marcus Aurelius rejected. Yet, whatever his private views about these kinds of alleged events, he did publicly accept that there had been a divine intervention in his favour. He repudiated not only the Christian claim to take credit for it but also that of the 'Chaldaean' theurgist Julianus, and portrayed on his coins a temple of the god Mercury (Hermes Aërios; invoked by the Egyptian magician Harnouphis, his companion, by means of enchantments), which Aurelius had constructed in gratitude. The coins, as we saw, were inscribed RELIG(io) AVG(usti). It must be added that the religion of Aurelius, which enabled him to accept (at least outwardly) divine interventions to save his troops, did not prevent him from exiling an inflammatory prophet and issuing a rescript ordering relegation to an island for anyone 'who alarmed fickle minds with dread of the supernatural'.[26]

Then a medallion of 173 celebrated his return to Rome, but it never happened. This was probably because of trouble from the Sarmatian Jazyges, who lived in the reentrant between the Danube and the Pathisus (Tisza, Theiss). It seems likely that they had been in touch with, and were set in motion by, the Quadi and Marcomanni, whose submission to the Romans was only apparent. The Jazyges attacked from the west (and excavations have revealed the destruction of a bakery at Albertfalva, near Aquincum [Budapest]). Thus, the second, Sarmatian phase of the northern wars began, the *Bellum Sarmaticum* (*c.* 174–75?). One of Marcus Aurelius's headquarters was Sirmium (Sremska Mitrovica), and the first book of his *Meditations* was written 'among the Quadi, on the River Granna' (Hrón, Gran), a northern tributary of the Danube.[27] This was near the border between the Jazyges and the Quadi, and Marcus Aurelius's aim was to drive a wedge between the two peoples, who could each then be conquered separately.

In this we must suppose that he was momentarily successful. There was an epic battle against the Jazyges on the frozen Danube. The Jazygian king, Zanticus, came to Marcus Aurelius as a suppliant. Tens or hundreds of thousands of Roman prisoners were restored, and many Roman soldiers were presumably posted in northern territories. Moreover, trading rights were granted both to the Jazyges and to the Marcomanni (and Quadi). But this was done with a certain amount of caution – some would even say harshness – and without granting full commercial freedom.

Although the tribesmen were not allowed within five miles of the Danube, *loca* were fixed by Marcus Aurelius across the river: that is to say, places where tribal meetings and markets were authorized on fixed days, under regular supervision, though not more than once a month. The Jazyges could probably be persuaded to agree to this sort of arrangement, since they were nervous of Roman concessions to the Quadi. This was a period when commercial undertakings of such a kind were of importance to Rome, which was increasing its trade beyond the frontiers of the empire (Chapter 8), as the development of Colonia Agrippinensis (Köln), for example, confirms. Legionary moves were made, and Marcus Aurelius also brought many northern prisoners of war to settle within the empire,[28] first of all in Italy, near Ravenna, and then (after troublesome incidents) in the provinces, especially Gaul and Britain and Scythia Minor (the Dobruja).

This massive series of arranged immigrations into the empire was not an altogether new policy, but was embarked upon by Marcus Aurelius with a new systematic thoroughness (although he refused entry to some). The German and Jazygian settlers were free, but legally tied to the land, and assigned to landowners or imperial domains. In addition to weakening hostile tribal pressure across the Danube, this policy provided much-needed agricultural labour and thus helped the provincials, who had suffered seriously from the plague. Furthermore, the new settlers found themselves hired by the Romans to join the army and to fight against their fellow-barbarians.[29] Thus, the 100,000 prisoners whom the Jazyges gave up included, it was said, 8,000 cavalry, of whom 5,500 were sent to Britain (*c.* 175), where they served on at least four sites in units 500 strong. Nevertheless, a high price would have to be paid by the Romans in the end, when these huge implantations of 'barbarians' were to transform, very thoroughly, the ethnical character of the Roman world and to prove one of the factors which eventually brought down the western empire.

At present, Marcus Aurelius was clearly determined to render the Marcomanni, Quadi and Jazyges impotent, by reducing them to client status, but whether he already intended to annex their territories as new Roman provinces must remain uncertain, because he had no chance to push his policy to its conclusions. This was because a rebellion broke out in the east, in 175. Its leader was Gaius Avidius Cassius, to whom Marcus Aurelius had given immense powers in the area. Avidius Cassius's father was Gaius Avidius Heliodorus of Cyrrhus (Kurus; prefect of Egypt 137–42).[30] Originally brought into Syria after the outbreak of the Parthian War, the younger Avidius (Cassius) had impressively revived the discipline of the Roman troops, much weakened by too close contact with Antioch and similar centres of dissipation, and had played a prominent part in the eastern wars, in the course of which he had, it appears, distinguished himself as a model military man, but had also burnt the great Greek city of Seleucia-on-the-Tigris (Tell Umar) to the ground (165). Not long afterwards (?166) he had been promoted to exercise control over all of Rome's eastern provinces,[31] superior to the powers of all provincial governors, whereupon he undertook a major reorganization of almost the entire eastern frontier, over a period which extended for nearly a decade.

One of the tasks that he had to perform was to put down quite a dangerous rebellion in Egypt, started by the *boukoloi* (herdsmen) of the Nile delta, in the marshes behind Alexandria (or perhaps the term may be the name of the district where they lived).[32] The material conditions of these men and their families were intolerably bad. They lived wretched lives in boats, feeding on fish dried by the sun. Now they rose in revolt, and persuaded the people round about to join them; a priest called Isidorus took the lead. A Roman centurion and soldier were dispatched to put them down. The rebels, however, disguised in women's clothes, managed to seize the two men and killed them both. It is hard to discover what exactly happened during the uprising, because a strong element of myth has entered into the story, but we are told that the rebels swore an oath on the intestines of the dead men, which they then proceeded to eat. Isidorus enjoyed an initial success against the Roman army, and became a national hero. He gained sufficient strength to pose a threat to cities, and even Alexandria feared that it might fall to the rebels.

The Roman government felt obliged to take serious steps; it requested Avidius Cassius to intervene. Initially he did not venture to take open action against the dissidents, 'because of their despair and their numbers', but he managed, in the end, to disarm them, by resorting to some trick or other.

Next, however, followed the rebellion of Avidius Cassius himself – one of the most serious events of Marcus Aurelius's reign. The circumstances surrounding Avidius Cassius's revolt against Aurelius in 175 contain certain mysterious elements. The *Life of Avidius Cassius* in the *Historia Augusta* is almost valueless, but his rising is described by the Epitomator of Dio in these terms:

> Cassius in rebelling made a terrible mistake, due to his having been deceived by <u>Faustina the younger</u>. The latter, who was the daughter of Antoninus Pius, seeing that her husband had fallen ill and expecting that he would die at any moment, was afraid that the throne would fall to some outsider, inasmuch as their son Commodus was both too young and also rather simple-minded; so that she might thus find herself reduced to a private station. Therefore she secretly induced Cassius to make his preparations so that, if anything should happen to Aurelius, he might obtain both her and the imperial power.

   Now while he was considering this project, a message came that
Aurelius was dead (in such circumstances reports always represent
matters as worse than they really are), and immediately, without
waiting to confirm the rumour, he laid claim to the throne, on the
ground that he had already been elected by the soldiers who were
then in Pannonia. And in spite of the fact that he learned the whole
truth before long, nevertheless, having once made a beginning, he
did not change his course, but speedily won over the whole region
south of the Taurus (Toros), and was making preparations to gain
the throne by war.[33]

What really happened, in all probability, is that Avidius Cassius learnt,
wrongly, that Marcus Aurelius – whose health had always been poor –
was dying or dead; and so he intended to take his place. This appeared
reasonable (though it might have enraged others), since, as the Epitomator of Dio observed, Aurelius's son Commodus, quite apart from his
failings, seemed too young to be able to take on the job. In Egypt (Rome's
main granary) a papyrus honoured Avidius Cassius as emperor, and most
of the eastern provinces followed suit. But only a short time afterwards
it became known that Aurelius was *not* dying or dead, and so two petty
officers put Avidius Cassius to death. The revolt was over, though it had
ominously pointed the way to similar difficulties in the future, often on
the peripheries of the empire. The ancient writers tell us of the generosity
with which Marcus Aurelius dealt with the defeated plot. But the situation
was not quite as straightforward as suggested by this dominant motif of
clemency which has distorted the tradition about the emperor's reactions
that has come down to us.
   In the east, the suppression of the rebel leader must have been followed
by further measures. These apparently included the killing of his son,
Avidius Cassius Maecianus, a lawyer at Alexandria, and of a senior official,
whose name cannot be recovered. After these tough initial reactions,
however, it does appear that Marcus Aurelius treated Avidius Cassius's
other supporters with restraint.
   As he pursued his eastern journey, accompanied by a strong force of
troops, he evidently took the view that he personally ought to sort out
the critical situation that had arisen. 'Barbarians', from beyond the frontier, had offered their help to the emperor. The ancient writers explain
that this assistance was refused, because it was not proper that such
people should have cognizance of fighting between Romans, but an
inscription suggests that, on the contrary, the offer was accepted, and
that contingents were received from 'client-states'.[34]
   Marcus Aurelius refused to look at the severed head of Avidius Cassius;
but he arranged for its burial. When he reached the provinces that
had revolted, he pursued his investigations with energy – tempered by

51

moderation. As for the possibly seditious correspondence that fell into his hands, he had it all burnt without reading it (Publius Martius Verus, the governor of Cappodocia who remained loyal to Aurelius, had done the same when Avidius Cassius was still alive). But the emperor did decide to banish certain persons, notably one of Cassius's sons, Avidius Cassius Heliodorus, who had not been executed like his brother. Other members of Cassius's family were left untouched, though some of them may have come to grief under Commodus. The prefect of Egypt, who had joined Avidius Cassius, was sent into exile, like Heliodorus.

In the army, certain serving personnel were condemned to death. Moreover, in partial contradiction of the emphasis on the emperor's clemency by the literary authorities, legal sources report that the confiscations provided for by the law of treason were put into force. Nevertheless, Marcus Aurelius was well aware that, if left to the judicial procedures of the senate, matters might well get out of hand, and so, while duly respecting the senate's rights, he ensured that enquiries into the behaviour of Avidius Cassius's accomplices should not be carried too far. He had never, he said, taken the initiative in causing the death of any senator, and he did not want the senate, while he was emperor, to condemn any of its own members. This put a stop to any witch hunt relating to those who had joined Avidius Cassius.

On the other hand, there is every reason to suppose that he rewarded for their loyalty those legions that had refused to side with Cassius. Conversely, he showed no tenderness towards the cities of Antioch and Alexandria, which had rallied to Cassius's cause and had, apparently, not concealed their disappointment when it had not prevailed. Marcus Aurelius also made it a rule that in future no one should govern the province from which he had originated.

The emperor had set out for Syria and Egypt via Byzantium, Ancyra (Ankara) and Tarsus – fearing for the safety of Publius Martius Verus, the governor of Cappadocia, one of the only two eastern governors who had remained loyal (the other was Decimus Clodius Albinus, proconsul of Bithynia, who later contested the throne with Septimius Severus). Subsequently, on his way back home to celebrate a Triumph against the Parthians (176), Aurelius passed along the coasts of Syria and Asia Minor, stopping off at Smyrna (Izmir) and Athens.

Avidius Cassius had not spoken against Aurelius – even declaring him *divus* when it asserted that he was dead – and Aurelius, for his part, as we have seen, refused to read the correspondence which would have incriminated his accomplices. What remains uncertain, however, is whether Dio was right in believing that Marcus Aurelius's wife, Faustina the younger, was one of them. Certainly, she had reason to fear what might happen to her and their son Commodus if Aurelius died; and it is conceivable that she allowed Avidius Cassius to believe that if her husband died she might marry Avidius. As it turned out, however, the whole thing went disastrously wrong, because the belief that Aurelius was dying or dead which prompted Avidius to revolt proved mistaken. In consequence Faustina was said to have gone on record as demanding the punishment of Avidius himself and his accomplices,[35] and that may well be true.

Many people in high society spoke of the infidelity and immorality of Faustina, and it is impossible for us at this late date to say if the reports are true or not. Certainly Marcus Aurelius's views about sex must have been, for his wife, more than a little depressing: 'copulation is friction of the members and an ejaculatory discharge'.[36] And it could also be suggested that there is 'no smoke without fire'.

In any case, Aurelius has often been criticized for his toleration of Faustina's alleged previous sexual irregularities. Most of the stories about these might very well be fictitious. The suggestion that she had an affair with a gladiator or sailor, for example, was no doubt prompted by the subsequent bad behaviour of her son Commodus, who could not possibly, it was felt, be the son of the high-minded Marcus Aurelius. It is, of course, not beyond the bounds of possibility that Faustina became unfaithful to him, now and then. But it must be remembered that she bore him many children – the two youngest were born in 159 and 160, and there were several more who died in infancy. All of these had kept her pretty busy.

Yet, when Marcus Aurelius was away from her for at least three years – from autumn 169 until autumn 172, if not longer – she may well have been tempted to stray a little. There were rumours, at this time, of her liaisons with ballet dancers (*pantomimi*). Earlier, too, in the east, temptation may have come her way (in 165–6). Men of a higher social class were mentioned, one of whom was said to have flirted with her when Marcus Aurelius was actually at home.

Finally, there was this story of her treasonable correspondence with Avidius Cassius. On balance, it does not look as if she were guilty. But she did have to think of her son Commodus, and of what would happen to him if Marcus Aurelius died before Commodus became an adult. If the matter is viewed from that perspective, it does not seem altogether unlikely that she felt that she would prefer to have Avidius Cassius as the eventual protector of herself and her son, rather than, say, her son-in-law Tiberius Claudius Pompeianus, whom, like his wife and her daughter Lucilla, she may not have greatly loved.

As for Marcus Aurelius's reaction, despite his ambiguous views on sex (which did not prevent them, as noted earlier, from having a considerable number of children), he not only asserted that he owed Faustina the empire,[37] since she was the daughter of Antoninus Pius (and, as we have seen, she had become Augusta before Aurelius became Augustus), but also proclaimed that he believed in her and loved her, as passages in the

*Meditations* make abundantly clear (though they would enrage women today). 'So submissive', he called her, 'so loving, and so artless'. And 'this is the plain fact;' he said, 'I would rather live with her in Gyara (Gyaros, Yigura) than in the palace without her.'[38] The coinage issued in her honour described her as 'Mother of the Camp' (MATER CASTRORVM),[39] and invoked, and thus compared her with, a wide range of goddesses (with a special emphasis on Venus), providing a vivid illustration of how an empress could be presented.

But then, shortly after Avidius Cassius's rebellion, and on her way back with Marcus Aurelius from the affected zone, Faustina died (perhaps of gout) at Halala (later Faustinopolis; Paşmakci or east of Ulukişla) in Cilicia. She was promptly <u>deified</u> and extensively worshipped, and a fresh burst of coinage celebrated her divinization. Other coins hopefully celebrated the Concord of the armies.[40]

The real taste of Marcus Aurelius was for studying and thinking, as his *Meditations* show (Chapter 6). Indeed, he was even said to have given public lectures on philosophical themes, although this may not be true. But he did appoint professors for the four great philosophical schools at Athens – a city for which he showed much concern. He himself dramatically abandoned rhetoric for philosophy (much to the annoyance of his tutor and friend, Fronto) when he virtually became co-emperor in 146/ 7: an abandonment for which he may have prepared himself much earlier, at the age of twelve.[41]

A philosopher is what he would have liked to be. What a miserable fate, then, it was for him, with this aim in mind, to have to spend such a huge part of his reign fighting against alien enemies from one headquarters or another among the misty, melancholy swamps and reedy islands of the Danube! This probably accounts for his transition from an early gaiety (which was reflected in his keenness on sports and in his letters to Fronto describing how much he had enjoyed hunting and taking a joyful – if slightly patronising? – part in the wine harvest)[42] to the grimness and depression of the *Meditations*, written in his later years.

Nevertheless, philosophy, founded on Reason, remained for him a sort of religion,[43] and he felt that it ought to be immensely useful to an emperor. Yet (and this was his tragedy), he realized that a philosopher was just what he could never be, because of all of the calls upon his time.

What is your trade? Goodness. But how are you to make a success of it unless you have a philosopher's insight into the nature of the universe, and into the particular constitution of man? . . .

Manifestly, no condition of life could be so well adapted for the practice of philosophy as this in which chance finds you today! . . .

I must thank heaven . . . that with all my addiction to philosophy I was yet preserved from either falling a prey to some sophist or spending all of my time at a desk poring over text-books and rules of logic or grinding at natural science. . . .

It will tend to avert complacency if you remember that any claim to have lived as a philosopher all your life, or even since reaching manhood, is now out of the question; indeed, it is as evident to many others as it is to yourself that even today philosophy is still far beyond you. Consequently your mind remains in a state of confusion, and it grows no easier to earn the title of philosopher.

Also, your station in life militates constantly against it. . . . You cannot hope to be a scholar.[44]

He could not hope to be a scholar because of his intense determination to do his imperial <u>duty</u>, which pulled in quite a different direction: 'by nature he was a saint and a sage: by profession a ruler and a warrior'. Yet he did continue to maintain that the best of all rulers would be Plato's philosopher-king[45] – though whether this is a correct conclusion is doubtful, when we think of all the things that a ruler has to do.

However, throughout the entire course of history no one has approached this ideal more closely than Marcus Aurelius. Yet, even in his case, it meant being a Roman more than a philosopher. 'As Marcus I have Rome, and as a human being I have the Universe.'[46] But he was first and foremost a dutiful Roman.

Hour by hour resolve firmly, like a Roman and a man, to do what comes to hand with correct and natural dignity, and with humanity, independence and justice. . . . The good within you should preside over a being who is virile and mature, a statesman, a Roman, and a ruler. . . .

At two points hold yourself always in readiness: first to do exclusively what Reason, our king and lawgiver, shall suggest for the common weal; and, second, to reconsider a decision if anyone present should correct you and convince you of an error of judgement. . . . Be like the headland against which the waves break and break; it stands firm, until presently the watery tumult around it subsides once more to rest. . . .

I do that which it is my duty to do. Nothing else distracts me. . . . Do without flinching what man's nature demands. Say what seems to you most just – though with courtesy, modesty, and sincerity. . . . Work hard, but not as if you are being made a victim, and not with any desire for sympathy or admiration.

Desire one thing alone: that your actions or inactions alike should be worthy of a reasoning citizen. . . .

The aim we should propose to ourselves must be the benefit of our fellows and the community. . . . Let every action aim solely at the common good.[47]

Aurelius had to drive himself continually in order to do his duty. It was all the harder for him because he disliked getting up in the morning. He implies as much himself.

> At day's first light have in readiness, against disinclination to leave your bed, the thought that 'I am rising for the work of man'. . . . Is this the purpose of my creation, to lie here under the blankets and keep myself warm? 'Ah, but it is a great deal more pleasant!' Was it for pleasure, then, that you were born, and not for work, not for effort?[48]

Moreover, his <u>health</u> was generally poor.

> Apollonius [a Stoic philosopher from Calchedon (Kadiköy)] . . . schooled me to meet spasms of acute pain . . . and the tedium of a chronic ailment with the same unaltered composure. . . . I must thank heaven . . . for remedies prescribed for me in dreams – especially in cases of blood-spitting and vertigo, as happened at Caieta [Gaeta] and Chrysa [see note, p. 182].[49]

And the Epitome to Dio fills in the picture.

> He was so frail in body that at first he could not endure the cold. But even after the soldiers had assembled at his command he would retire before addressing a word to them. And he took but very little food and that always at night.
>
> It was never his practice to eat during the daytime, unless it were some of the drug called theriac. This drug he took, not so much because he feared anything, as because his stomach and chest were in bad condition. And it is reported that this practice enabled him to endure both this and other maladies. . . .
>
> He could not display many feats of physical prowess. Yet he had developed his body from a very weak one to one capable of the greatest endurance. . . .
>
> As a result of his close application and study he was extremely frail in body, though in the beginning he had been so vigorous that he used to fight in armour, and on the chase would strike down wild boars while on horseback. . . .
>
> And not only in his early youth but even later he wrote most of his letters to his intimate friends with his own hand. . . . He was not strong in body.[50]

Clearly he was not, but what was the matter with him? Did he suffer from pulmonary tuberculosis? Of a gastric ulcer? Or migraine? Or some more obscure complaint of the blood? And at what stages of his life did these troubles become better or, more probably, worse? These are things that we shall never know. But we do know that he had a pain in his chest as a youth, that in later life troubles recurred, and that the physician Galen gave him, everyday, a drug from the imperial stores named *theriac*. This, normally, consisted of one part seed-clover, one of a species of the herb birthwort (Aristolochiacea), one of wild rue and one of pounded pulse, and was taken in pills with wine. The drug had been prescribed for Mithridates VI of Pontus and Nero ('viper's flesh') as an antidote to possible poisoning.[51] But it was also prescribed for various illnesses, and Aurelius probably took it as a pain-killer and sleeping-draught, since he found it difficult to sleep, and theriac made him drowsy. Galen probably put mandragora in it, or perhaps opium: to which it has been plausibly suggested that Aurelius may, in the course of time, have become addicted.

The physician Galen (Chapter 6) gives us a glimpse of one of the occasions on which Aurelius fell ill; it may have been not long after his return to Rome in 176. Galen administered a cure.[52] Aurelius himself, and the doctors who had accompanied him while he was travelling, were of the opinion that his illness was a violent attack of fever. On the previous day he had taken a dose of bitter aloes, Galen tells us, and then about five hours later his daily dose of theriac. Next, at sundown, he had a bath, and ate a little food, but was subsequently overcome by stomach aches and diarrhoea, which gave him a temperature. His doctors saw him at dawn, and advised him to rest. Later they gave him some porridge, or thick gruel.

As for Galen, he himself goes on to tell us that he was called in to spend the night at the palace and that, shortly after the time when the evening lamps were lit, a man came from the emperor to summon him to his presence. Three other doctors had already examined Marcus Aurelius, on two occasions, and had agreed that his symptoms pointed to the beginning of an illness. Galen, on arrival, said nothing at all, to Aurelius's surprise, and was asked why he had not, for example, taken the emperor's pulse. Galen excused himself on the grounds that the other doctors, who had accompanied him on his campaigns and journeys, were in a better position to offer a diagnosis than he was.

Nevertheless, when requested to do so, he did agree to take Aurelius's pulse. Having done so, he pronounced that Aurelius was not suffering from a fever at all, but that his stomach was merely out of order. The emperor was immensely impressed by this diagnosis, and praised it, thrice, in these terms: 'That's right! It's exactly as you said! I feel as if I'm weighed down, by some food that's rather cold.'

Then Galen spoke up. His prescription, he said, would normally have been wine flavoured with pepper, but 'for you monarchs, for whom it is customary to recommend the safest and surest remedies, it is sufficient to apply to the rectum a pad of red wool, smeared with warmed spikenard ointment.' Marcus Aurelius replied that this was the remedy that he customarily employed, and he requested the doctor Pitholaus to prepare and apply it. Then he had his feet massaged, and ordered some Sabine wine, which, after sprinkling pepper on it, he proceeded to drink.

In amplification of the many portrait-busts that have survived, the later emperor Julian (361–3) offers a haunting picture of what Marcus Aurelius looked like.

> He was careless of his appearance and unadorned by art. For he wore a very long beard, his dress was plain and sober, and from lack of nourishment his body was very shining and transparent, like light almost pure and stainless ... he looked excessively dignified and showed the effect of his studies in the expression of his eyes and his lined brows [Chapter 7]. He did not usually change his expression, in gladness or grief.[53]

How good a public speaker Marcus Aurelius was we cannot tell: he seems to have been straightforward, sensible and practical, but Fronto thought that, though he was not bad, there was room for improvement. He was, almost certainly, humourless; when he was still very young (and his name was Verus) Hadrian had been partly joking, as we saw, about the solemnity of this little boy when he called him 'Verissimus'. Aurelius did not, of course, escape criticism. Some said he was insincere, and not as simple as he seemed (not as straightforward as Antoninus Pius and Lucius Verus). Others considered that he was miserly. Others, again, accused him of keeping his friends out of social life and banquets.[54] But his strongest critic was himself, as his *Meditations* show. He realized that he had an impatient temper.[55]

His nature was complex and tense. Never forgetting his Stoic training, he continually admonished himself not to fall below the highest standards, and not to regard his imperial status in too glowing a light.[56] Although inflexible, he was probably too mild – as his attitude to the accomplices of Avidius Cassius showed. But he was aware that he could cause offence, and he found it difficult to talk to people in a friendly fashion: 'think of the characters of those whom you love: even the best of them can hardly be borne with.'[57]

In other words, he lacked a statesman's sympathetic understanding and tolerance of human nature. It has been fairly concluded that he was no judge of men, and lacked the constructive imagination which would have enabled him to infuse fresh life into the Roman world. And yet, his sense of duty being what it was,[58] he coped with his appalling problems with a conscientiousness that raised him into the top class of rulers.

> In addition to possessing all the other virtues, he ruled better than any others who had ever been in any position of power. ... Most of his life he devoted to Beneficence (*Indulgentia*). ... However, he did not meet with the good fortune that he deserved, for he ... was

involved in a multitude of troubles throughout practically his entire reign. But for my part I admire him all the more for this very reason, that amid unusual and extraordinary difficulties he both survived himself and preserved the empire.[59]

Nevertheless, this Roman rule (at least in the west) was destined to collapse in the future, and he could do, or did, very little to stop it. However, that collapse was still quite a long way ahead, so it is scarcely fair to brand Aurelius as the 'pathetic product and powerless actor in a great historic drama'.[60] On the contrary, most later commentators agreed with Dio's verdict, quoted above, that he had been an exceptionally good ruler. Indeed he was transformed into a golden legend, which lasted and was perpetuated by Julian the Apostate (despite Aurelius's mistaken promotion of Verus, and tolerance of his wife).[61]

# 4

# MARCUS AURELIUS AND COMMODUS

Marcus Aurelius, after his visit to the east to deal with the aftermath of the rebellion of Avidius Cassius, moved back to the <u>Danube front</u>, where a new war was now under way: it was described as the *Expeditio Germanica Secunda*. The main trouble seems to have come from the Marcomanni and Quadi, who were complaining of ill-treatment from the occupying troops; and the war spread to the Hermunduri, the northern neighbours of the Marcomanni. Marcus Aurelius established his headquarters at Carnuntum (Petronell), or on the Granna (Hrón, Gran), and crossed the Danube to put down the tribesmen.

The Romans began to move forward in summer 177. By exploiting the lack of unified purpose among the enemy, they had virtually concluded the war towards the end of the year. Aurelius, although neither he nor his son continued to employ the titles 'Germanicus' and 'Sarmaticus', felt that the occasion warranted the acceptance of a victorious acclamation. This he shared with his son <u>Commodus</u>, who, as we shall see shortly, was now his heir and destined successor.

In the following year, however, things warmed up still further. The brothers or cousins the Quintilii, Sextus Quintilius Condianus and Sextus Quintilius Valerius Maximus, who were probably governors of Upper and Lower Pannonia (Superior and Inferior), had in the previous year won a victory against somebody – it is not quite clear against whom – but were, in the words of Dio Cassius, 'unable to put an end to the war'.[1] Marcus Aurelius felt it necessary to lead the Roman troops across the frontier once again. This time he was accompanied by his son Commodus, whose departure with him was signalized by coins.[2]

The months that followed were occupied in collecting together a force consisting of detachments from the armies on the Danube and Rhine, and in summer 179 it went into action, under the command of the prefect of the praetorian guard, Tarrutienus Paternus. He won a resounding victory, for which Marcus Aurelius and Commodus were acclaimed.

It was at this juncture, perhaps, that Aurelius, establishing his winter headquarters for 179/180 at either Sirmium (Sremska Mitrovica) or Singidunum (Belgrade), decided to occupy the territory of the Marcomanni and Quadi with some twenty thousand Roman troops, so that the independent existence of the two peoples could be brought to an end altogether. And it may well have been now, in the light of this policy, that the Quadi attempted (in vain) to move bodily into the land of the Semnones, the central tribe of the great German group of the Suebi.

The intention of Marcus Aurelius was now clear. It was to extend the Roman frontier northwards from the Danube to the Carpathian mountains and adjoining heights, thus creating two new provinces, Marcomannia to the west and Sarmatia to the east. This policy was proclaimed by a medallion dedicated to Marcus and his son Commodus as PROPAGATORIBVS IMPERII, 'those who enlarge the boundaries of the empire'.[3]

Even if we accept Aurelius's conviction that, although wars were hateful, some wars could be just, it was a policy of dubious and arguable merit. In its favour it could be admitted that the Danube was an inadequate frontier, and that mountains served the purpose better – and were further from Italy; also that, since Dacia was now Roman, it was ridiculous that the deep reentrant between the Danube and the Pathisus (Tisza, Theiss) should remain outside the empire, as this meant that the frontier was unnecessarily long. It could also be argued that the policy of keeping the trans-Danubian Marcomanni, Quadi and Jazyges quiet as Roman 'clients' had not been very successful, largely because they had so often proved disloyal: so that it might be better to reduce them to provincial status, within the empire.

But the disadvantages of just moving up the frontier to the Carpathians were also manifest (see Introduction). It would need a tremendous and over-costly effort on the part of the Romans to find enough soldiers to garrison the new provinces permanently. The new frontier would still leave, and would indeed make more immediately threatening, formidable tribes outside it, to the north. Notable among these were the Gotones (Goths), who were migrating westwards and southwards, though their menace was probably not yet apparent.

Whether Augustus had realized that this must not be allowed, when he proposed to move the frontier forward to the Albis (Elbe), must remain hypothetical; but I think that he intended the new German province to reach northwards as far as the North Sea. It never came into existence, and Marcus Aurelius's solution, although it would stretch Roman capacity to the utmost, remained less ambitious. His plan, the creation of two new provinces, Marcomannia and Sarmatia, would extend the frontier northwards from the Danube but not as far as the North Sea. Subsequent history, in which the Goths played such a leading part in bringing down the empire, shows that his solution would not have been effective.

Marcus Aurelius had celebrated his earlier Triumph (against the Parthians) on 23 December 176, and afterwards had gone to Lavinium to rest. However, he had returned to Rome in order to be present at his son Commodus's inauguration of his consulship on New Year's Day 177. It seems to have been on the same day that Commodus – already Caesar – was also granted the tribunician power. Later, in 177, he was given the name of Augustus, and all the other titles and honours of an emperor (except the position of *Pontifex Maximus*, which only Aurelius held). Coins were issued to honour and commemorate each of these steps.[4] If Aurelius were to die, Commodus would need no further powers. His succession to the throne was now completely secure.

Lavish distributions and spectacles were arranged to celebrate the occasion, and before the emperors left Rome on 5 August 177 Aurelius had arranged for Commodus to marry Bruttia Crispina, with the intention of obtaining grandchildren who would solidify the succession still further. Thus, it was no accident or sudden whim that prompted the emperor, in presenting Commodus, by now Augustus, to the army, to have his son accompany him to the north in 178.

The severest criticism that was launched against Marcus Aurelius at the time, and that has been directed against him ever since, arose from his promotion of Commodus. The only harm that Aurelius ever did, it was said, was by being a father. But the evil son of a good father was a conventional traditional theme, and in fact Aurelius had no alternative. There has been much play with the notion that the three immediately preceding emperors, all 'good' rulers, owed their position not to heredity but to adoption 'of the best man': that Trajan, Hadrian and Antoninus Pius were all 'adoptive emperors', and that Aurelius fatally broke with this tradition. Yet his three predecessors were adoptive only because the emperors who came before them had no sons, or no surviving sons. The idea of hereditary, dynastic succession was deeply embedded, and it was out of the question that Marcus Aurelius should have deviated from it. There is no need to blame his wife Faustina for the choice; or to excuse it by his alleged ignorance of his son's character, or his supposed belief in the good that might be in the young man, or his trust that Commodus's counsellors would be strong enough to lead him.[5]

Certainly, there were other possible candidates, such as Avidius Cassius (before his disastrous revolt) and Tiberius Claudius Pompeianus (married to the emperor's daughter Lucilla). His later successor Julian thought that Marcus Aurelius ought to have designated Tiberius Claudius Pompeianus (who was disliked by his wife, and had bad eyes, but had vast experience) to become his heir and successor. He 'had an excellent son-in-law who would have administered the state better, and besides would have managed the youth [Commodus] better than he could manage himself'.[6] That was no doubt true, as far as it went, but the elevation of

Tiberius Claudius Pompeianus would have been contested not only by at least six other Roman notables but also by the Roman public in general, with its preference (especially among the army, and most of the provincials) for heredity: the result would unquestionably have been civil war.

The promotion of Commodus, the male survivor of a number of children born to Faustina, was therefore inevitable. Marcus Aurelius was said to have been aware of his son's deficiencies, and to have hinted at them in his dying moments. But, if so, this was irrelevant, since Commodus was unmistakably his heir who would succeed him.

Commodus had been born in 161, one of twins. (Rumours that he was not really the son of Marcus Aurelius[7] were spread only later, when it was clear that the two men were very different, and can be discounted; see above, p. 53). Twins in the imperial family were a sign of the 'happiness of the age'.[8] However, Commodus's brother died at the age of four, and other brothers and sisters died very young. Commodus survived, and it was the first time that the imperial position had been gained by an emperor born while his father was the ruler, *natus imperator*.[9] He assumed the *toga virilis* upon the day on which Romulus had become a god.

In 180, Marcus Aurelius died. He may have died at Vindobona (Vienna) or at Sirmium (Sremska Mitrovica) or at Bononia Malata (the Danube port of Sirmium, now Vidin). We do not know either the precise location or the exact cause of his death. It is best to suppose that he died from natural causes. Possibly he had caught the plague, which was still about. We can disregard the predictable rumour that his death was due to his son Commodus, or that he died at the hands of doctors who wanted to do Commodus a favour – although Dio recorded that he had 'clearly heard' this said.[10] More probably, as Edward Gibbon saw, the incessant winter campaigning in the north had taken its toll on his feeble health.

> War [Marcus Aurelius] detested, as the disgrace and calamity of human nature. But when the necessity of a just defence called upon him to take up arms, he readily exposed his person to eight winter campaigns on the frozen banks of the Danube, the severity of which was at last fatal to the weakness of his constitution.[11]

Aurelius saw his son Commodus just before he died, and after his death Commodus ensured that he was deified. His apotheosis was celebrated on an Arch at Oea (Tripoli), and at Rome Commodus may have built a temple in his honour (destroyed in the Middle Ages), as well as quadri-frontal arch, from which reliefs have survived. Commodus also issued coins to celebrate the deification.[12]

# 5

# COMMODUS

The friends of Marcus Aurelius accepted the wishes of the dead emperor, and presented his son Commodus to the army in the camp. The senate, though conscious that the selection of the 'best man' had ceased to have any reality, must very soon have been formally notified of the appointment which, in any case, it could have done nothing to prevent. Moreover, the new ruler began by showing tact, transmitting a gesture of respect to Rome and its institutions. The senate sent him every good wish for a rapid and successful homecoming (ADVENTVS AVG., FORT*una* RED*ux*),[1] and celebrated some trifling military success, which he could be said to have won, by issuing coins which displayed a figure of Victory and invoking, as responsible for it, the bravery of the new emperor (VIRTVS AVG*usti*).[2]

Almost the first thing that Commodus then proceeded to do was to reverse completely Marcus Aurelius's northern policy (as Aurelius had perhaps foreseen). Aurelius had intended to move the imperial frontier northwards from the River Danube to the Carpathians, creating two new provinces of Marcomannia and Sarmatia, and he had been on the verge of bringing this about. Commodus, it was said, had at first had the same idea, but then, almost at once, he abandoned the plan altogether, leaving the frontier on the Danube.

Within a short time after his father's death, and against the advice of his brother-in-law Tiberius Claudius Pompeianus, he made peace with the Germans and Jazyges. The terms bore a considerable resemblance to those which Marcus Aurelius had compelled them to accept in 175. Prisoners of war and deserters must be given back, and 'barbarian' soldiers were to be provided for the imperial army. Warfare between the tribes was banned; and they were not permitted to draw near the Danube. Moreover, the times and localities of their public assemblies had to be subject to regulation. In response to the acceptance of these conditions, Commodus undertook that the Romans should pay subsidies, and announced that he was prepared to evacuate all Roman troops from the territories across the Danube frontier which Marcus Aurelius had occupied.

These conditions, it must impartially be recognized, were not unsatisfactory to Rome, if they could have been enforced. The tribes, exhausted by the recent fighting, agreed to the restrictions that were imposed, although the prohibition to draw near the Danube was not strictly insisted upon. Land in Roman Dacia was assigned to 12,000 tribespeople who had been driven from their territories outside the empire and who seemed to pose a threat if they were left to roam.

Nevertheless, skirmishing continued in the 180s (and there was a minor rising of the Quadi in 188): existing fortifications on the advanced frontier, which had been established by Antoninus Pius, were enlarged. New fortresses and roads were also constructed, and mounted archers were raised from among friendly tribes in order to deal with any external people who might still make trouble. By and large, Commodus's arrangements remained effective for quite a long time.

Commodus, in reversing the policy of his father Marcus Aurelius, had decided not to attempt imperial expansion into Germany across the Danube. Although some, including most of the younger courtiers, agreed to this change of policy, there was also strong opposition to it. This was led, as we saw, by the new emperor's brother-in-law, Tiberius Claudius Pompeianus, and found its way into the works of the senatorial historians and their modern successors. They attributed the change to base motives on the part of Commodus, including cowardice and a desire to escape from military affairs and to return to the luxurious fleshpots of Rome. It was also pointed out that Commodus was under the influence of Aelius Saoterus, a reputedly degraded Greek from Nicomedia (Izmit) in Bithynia, who encouraged his desire to return to a life of dissipation in the capital.

As we have seen, however, such criticism may have been unfair, since it is very doubtful whether Marcus Aurelius's plan to expand the empire northwards had been either wise or practicable, from a military or financial point of view. In addition, Commodus's decision, even if it were prompted by an urgent need for economy and by the difficulty of securing sufficient manpower, may also have been stimulated by a further consideration, which was not entirely unreasonable: that is to say, by a desire to be in the capital so as to scotch any internal uprising against him that might occur.[3] In any case, Commodus's decision not to try to advance the northern frontier may have been possible to justify.

Meanwhile, trouble almost immediately broke out on another northern frontier altogether. In Britain there were raids, probably from the lowlands or central areas of Scotland, which Ulpius Marcellus put down in three campaigns. He may, temporarily, have remanned the Antonine Wall (Chapter 1). For some time after that, there was a danger of a mutiny among the Roman troops, who were perhaps disappointed by the lack of a donative and who did not like the appointment of commanders of knightly (equestrian rather than senatorial) rank. It was feared that they might proclaim a rival emperor. But a new governor of Britain, Publius Helvius Pertinax (the future emperor), ensured that this came to nothing, and coins honoured the Loyalty and Concord of the Soldiers (184–5),[4] while Commodus accepted the title 'Britannicus'.

There was also some trouble in Africa, where the imperial troops moved against the Mauri and developed further outposts beyond the African frontier. An imposing bronze medallion commemorated Victory in these not very important operations. In 186 a regular service of ships was instituted to convey the produce of Africa to Rome, and the emperor's coins stress the plentiful grain supply. They also mark general peace, security and happiness, which (with reservations about happiness, Chapter 8) no doubt existed, since the provinces continued to be well governed.

Throughout these years, Commodus resided in the capital, welcomed back there from the north by the senate and people, including many who genuinely welcomed his decision not to try to advance the northern frontier of the empire. (They dissuaded him from a further northern expedition.) His governmental administration was not entirely bereft of achievements: he was recognized as having done some acts of public service.[5] For example, he increased the exemptions and privileges of University teachers. And he usefully increased the functions of the equestrian class (the knights).

As an inscription found at Soukh el Khmis in north Africa shows, the tenants (*coloni*) of imperial estates in the Saltus Burunitanus in Africa complained to him in *c.* 181, because injustices had been inflicted on them.[6] In these estates, which lay in the Bagradas (Medjerda) Valley, the procurators were bound by regulations (the Flavian [?] *Lex Manciana*) governing the obligations, in cash, kind and labour, of the tenants (who cultivated the land) to the lessees of the imperial estates, i.e. the landlords who held the prime leases (<u>*conductores*</u>). A group of these tenants appealed to Commodus against non-observance of these rules, as a result of collusion betwen the procurator and the *conductores*. The tenants, describing themselves humbly as 'most unhappy men' and 'poor rustics' (*miserrimi homines, homines rustici tenues*), objected that more than the proper share of their crops and the prescribed number of days of labour services (six per year) had been exacted from them and that the procurator had sent in troops and had some of them seized and tortured, fettered or flogged (even though they were Roman citizens), simply because they had dared to make a complaint to the emperor. They appealed for a restoration of the proper rules, 'so that by the kindliness of your majesty we, your rural workers, born and raised on your estates, may no longer be harassed by their lessors'.

Before sending this lengthy protest they had already received one imperial reply (*subscriptio*), apparently from Marcus Aurelius and Commodus, which the procurator of the time had ignored. Now another such reply came from Commodus:

> In view of established tradition and my order, procurators will see to it that nothing more than three periods of two days' work per man is unjustly exacted from you in violation of established practice.[7]

What are we to make of this reply from Commodus? Some have considered it liberal (though prudent), others regard it as merely a brief restatement of an established rule and therefore unhelpful. It would seem, however, that it deserves to be neither particularly praised nor blamed. It is not so much an autocratic as a bureaucratic reaction: the procurators should obey the rules, and all will be well. The acid test, of course, was whether the abuses continued or stopped. The answer is that we do not know, although it seems likely that the petition of the *coloni* did more good than harm.

On the whole the governors who ruled the provinces of Commodus's empire continued to do a fair or adequate job. The Upper German, Raetian and Danubian frontiers were strengthened, and so were those in Britain, in Mauretania and Numidia, and in the east. Military roads along all of these borders, and elsewhere, were maintained and repaired. It was the vigilance of these governors, and their determination to keep the imperial administration going, that prevented a larger number of revolts from taking place and, when these did occur, prevented them from ending in disaster for Rome. The government kept up a flood of propaganda, displayed on the coinage, but it was the vigour of the *legati* and proconsuls that kept things working smoothly.

This was all the more noticeable because the central rulership, being somewhat rickety, tended to leave the governors alone – more than had ever happened before. True, recognitions of the role of the emperor were not lacking. Alexandria, Carthage, and certain cities of Asia Minor paid tribute to his personal care for them. There were dedications to him in various parts of the empire, even if they were somewhat fewer than in previous reigns. Something was always being done. A bridge was restored in Dalmatia, or a temple in Egypt (for which the government did not pay). The Roman garrison in Armenia Minor put up an inscription to celebrate a piece of construction. Frontier forts, and roads, and baths were constructed, in addition to the Baths of Cleander at Rome. But Commodus has been accused of having his name inscribed upon buildings that others had set up. And he has been charged also with failing to finish projects that his father had started.

We know very little about any of the laws that Commodus brought into force – with a few exceptions. This is partly because his *Acta* were cancelled, at least for the time being, after he died. Although as we shall see, he was subsequently rehabilitated by Septimius Severus, scarcely any jurist thereafter alludes to his activity in the legal field. This strongly suggests that he did not make any serious attempt to cope with the problems left behind by Marcus Aurelius, following all of the difficulties that had encumbered his reign.

As for Commodus himself, it is likely that he was not really fit to be emperor. His appearance, it is true, was impressive, although he suffered from what seems to have been an unsightly hernia of the groin.

> Commodus had something wrong with him in the groin, which stuck out so much that the Roman people could detect the swelling through his silk clothing. Many verses were written on this subject, and Marius Maximus [Chapter 6] prides himself on recording them in his work. . . . [But] physically, at least, he was well proportioned. His expression was vacant as is usual with drunkards, and his speech disordered. His hair was always dyed and made to shine with gold dust. He used to singe his hair and beard from fear of the barber.[8]

The *Historia Augusta* observes that he was debauched from his earliest years,[9] but the row of salacious anecdotes which it quotes in support of this assertion must be treated with caution. However, quite apart from the fact that he was a poor speaker, there were two flaws in his personality, both of them serious. First, like Gaius (Caligula) (AD 37–41), he was passionately keen on being a gladiator. Dio Cassius, among other senators, was obliged to watch him indulging in this taste.

> As for wild beasts, he slew many both in private and in public. Moreover, he used to contend as a gladiator; in doing this at home he managed to kill a man now and then, and in making close passes with others, as if trying to clip off a bit of their hair, he sliced off the noses of some, the ears of others, and sundry features of still others. . . .
> [In the arena] having killed an ostrich and cut off its head, he came up to where we [senators] were sitting, holding the head in his left hand and in his right hand raising aloft his bloody sword. And though he spoke not a word, yet he wagged his head with a grin, indicating that he would treat us in the same way. And many would indeed have perished by the sword on the spot, for laughing at him (for it was laughter rather than indignation that overcame us), if I had not chewed some laurel leaves (which I got from my garland) myself, and persuaded the others who were sitting near me to do the same, so that in the steady movement of our jaws we might conceal the fact that we were laughing.[10]

Certainly, this sort of behaviour, duly recorded in the *acta urbis*, was not appropriate for an emperor – but one wonders whether its unrestricted indulgence was not partially due to reaction against his father, who, in addition to disliking organized applause, had found gladiatorial sports boring, and had said so, as well as passing legislation to limit the expenses of Games of this kind (176/7). There was nothing new in the prowess of the hunt being regarded as an allegory of war, and a sign of imperial courage on the part of the Royal Huntsman (the counterpart of Alexander the Great and the Persians and Parthians). But clearly Commodus, by descending into the arena (in which he no doubt exhibited considerable skill) took this concept too far.

The second flaw in his personality, which was more alarming, was his tendency to idleness. This meant that he delegated a great deal to his personal friends.

> Commodus was not naturally wicked, but, on the contrary, as guileless as any man that ever lived. His great simplicity, however, together with his cowardice, made him the slave of his companions, and it was through them that he at first, out of ignorance, missed the better life and then was led on into lustful and cruel habits, which soon became second nature.[11]

The companions upon whom he thus so greatly depended were not drawn from the senatorial class that had traditionally collaborated with the ruler in the administration of the empire. This became apparent at the very outset of his reign – often regarded as a decisive moment for Rome – when he relied heavily on the unpopular Saoterus, as the historians disgustedly recorded.[12]

Before long, in 183, this anti-senatorial tendency was greatly intensified when Commodus blamed the senate for a plot against his life. The plot was initiated by his sister Lucilla, a woman of (it was said) less than impeccable virtue who had been married to Lucius Verus and was now, reluctantly, the wife of Tiberius Claudius Pompeianus. She was probably jealous of Commodus's wife, Bruttia Crispina (who may well have been believed to be pregnant, but who was now accused of adultery, banished to Capreae [Capri], and executed).[13] The plot did not go well.

> Since she was well aware that her husband Pompeianus was devoted to Commodus, Lucilla told him nothing about her plans to seize control of the empire. Instead, she tested the sentiments of a wealthy young nobleman, Marcus Ummidius Quadratus [probably the grandson of Marcus Aurelius's sister], with whom she was rumoured to be sleeping in secret. Complaining constantly about the matter of imperial precedence, she soon persuaded the young man to set

in motion a plot which brought destruction upon himself and the entire senate.

Quadratus, in selecting confederates among the prominent senators, prevailed upon Claudius Pompeianus Quintianus, a bold and reckless young senator, to conceal a dagger beneath his robe, and, watching for a suitable time and place, to stab Commodus; as for the rest, he assured Quintianus that he would set matters straight by bribes.

But the assassin, standing in the entrance to the amphitheatre (it was dark there and he hoped to escape detection), drew his dagger and shouted at Commodus that he had been sent by the senate to kill him. Quintianus wasted time making this little speech and waving his dagger. As a result, he was seized by the emperor's bodyguards before he could strike, and died for his stupidity in revealing the plot prematurely.

Thus found out beforehand, Quintianus brought about his own death, and Commodus was put on his guard by this forewarning. This was the initial reason for the young emperor's hatred of the senate. He took Quintianus's words to heart, and, ever mindful of what his attacker had said, now considered the entire senate his collective enemy.[14]

This Quintianus may have been a nephew of Tiberius Claudius Pompeianus or a son of another senator, likewise named Pompeianus, who married Lucilla's daughter (and was put to death by Commodus). Quintianus and his fellow conspirators may have intended to give the imperial throne to Tiberius Claudius Pompeianus, who was Lucilla's husband. It is uncertain how accurate he was when he proclaimed that he was acting as agent of the whole senate; but no doubt some senators supported him, though others were critical, and their criticisms were echoed by Ammianus Marcellinus.[15]

Commodus believed Quintianus when he ascribed the intended assassination to the senate as a whole, and for ever afterwards he regarded the senate as against him. This had disastrous results for the government of the empire, including a considerable crop of murders or executions, including the death (after banishment) of Lucilla herself, and the death of Marcus Ummidius Quadratus. Commodus was a somnolent, inactive man, but when roused, as he was by Quintianus's attempt, he turned vicious.

There was, apparently, a further plot against him (in 185?). This time it did not arise from among the ranks of the senate, but was led by a former soldier named Maternus, who was alleged to be a criminal. Some of the supposed facts have been rejected by modern historians, but the story, if it has any truth at all (and it probably has) is of interest as the prelude to a long series of peasant rebellions (Chapter 8), aided by impoverished townsmen and army deserters (so that this was sometimes called 'the War of the Deserters'). Such people, it seems, were the 'huge mob of desperadoes' who were gathered by Maternus (p. 149). They operated in Gaul (where destruction, notably at Juliobona (Lillebonne), has been attributed to these convulsions) and in Spain, and slipped 'unnoticed, a few at a time, into Italy, by a quick but different route'.[16] This having been done, Maternus decided to assassinate Commodus at the annual festival of the Magna Mater (Cybele) at Rome, when disguises were worn.

> This seemed to Maternus an ideal time to launch his plot unde-tected. By donning the uniform of a praetorian soldier and outfitt-ing his companions in the same way, he hoped to mingle with the true praetorian guardsmen, and, after watching part of the parade, to attack Commodus and kill him while no one was on guard.
>
> But the plan was betrayed when some of those who had accompanied him into the city revealed the plot. (Jealousy led them to disclose it, since they preferred to be ruled by the emperor rather than by a bandit chief).
>
> Before he arrived at the scene of the festivities Maternus was seized and beheaded, and his companions suffered the punishment they deserved.
>
> After sacrificing to the goddess and making thank-offerings, Com-modus completed the festivities and did honour to the goddess, rejoicing at his escape. The people continued to celebrate their emperor's deliverance after the festival came to an end.[17]

This was the kind of incident which made Commodus suspicious, not only of the senate – which in this case, as far as we know, was not involved – but also of the world in general. In consequence, he tightened up security measures, by leaning more strongly than his predecessors on the praetorian guardsmen. He suspended the restrictions that they had imposed on the guard, and allowed its members to engage in petty plundering which had not been permitted before. The most notable change was that he depended with a new intensity on a small number of personal friends. Certainly, he continued to seek official advice of his *consilium*, which included prominent figures, but, being an idle man who preferred gladiatorial activities to government, he relied more and more on a few individuals, both officials and servants. First was Aelius Saoterus of Nicomedia (Izmit), then Sextus Tigidius Perennis, and later, Marcus Aurelius Cleander. The last two became prefects of the praetorian guard on which Commodus so greatly relied.

Previous vice-emperors had been within the imperial family; this new set-up, on the other hand, was harking back to the time of the emperor

Tiberius (AD 14–37), when Lucius Aelius Sejanus had held so much authority. But Tiberius, although he had retired to Capreae (Capri), was a strong and determined man, whereas Commodus was not; so that he allowed Perennis and Cleander almost unlimited power.[18]

There has been much dispute about the use that Perennis made of his full personal charge of the empire. After the downfall of his colleague, Tarrutienus Paternus, all imperial messages passed through his hands. Probably he was a coldly efficient administrator and grand vizier, with an eye to economy, but also ambitious; and he became extremely rich. Yet he fell, all the same. Whether he was guilty of disloyalty must remain uncertain. He very likely was: Herodian's suggestion that this was so is circumstantial. Or, if Perennis did not aspire to empire, he was capable of doing so.

> Commodus was persuaded to put the prefect's sons in command of the army of Illyricum, though they were still young men. The prefect himself amassed a huge sum of money for lavish gifts in order to incite the army to revolt. His sons quietly increased their forces, so that they might seize the empire after Perennis had disposed of Commodus.[19]

His 'plot' to do so failed, and he perished. The ancient writers tell highly coloured but unreliable tales of what went wrong, and there are various other conflicting versions. The truth may well be that Perennis came under suspicion because of his sons' Illyrian military connections, and that he did not, in the end, enjoy sufficient support, partly because he had alienated a good many soldiers and senators (to whom he had shown continual hostility) by placing knights in legionary commands. Coins celebrating the Loyalty of the Army (FIDES EXERCIT*us*)[20] seem to have been issued on the occasion of an address to the troops by the emperor in January 186 reasserting the fidelity of the guards after the fall of Perennis.

Thereafter, as Herodian tells us,

> Commodus regularly appointed two praetorian prefects, believing that it was safer not to place too much authority in the hands of one man. He hoped that this division of authority would discourage any desire to seek the imperial power.[21]

Before long, in late 186 or early 187, the number of praetorian prefects was raised to three, to make room for Marcus Aurelius Cleander, who was given the unprecedented title of *a pugione*, Minister of Protection. (Or was this a joke, offered by his enemies?) From then on Cleander was the mighty power behind the throne.

He had formerly been sold as one of a group of slaves and had been brought to Rome with the others to be a pack-carrier. But in the course of time he advanced to such a point that he actually became Commodus's *cubicularius*, married the emperor's concubine Demostratia, and put to death Saoterus of Nicomedia, his predecessor in this office, together with many others. . . .

So Cleander, raised to greatness by the favour of Fortune, bestowed and sold senatorships, military commands, procuratorships, governorships, and, in a word, everything. . . . He was obtaining money from every source, and he amassed more wealth than any who had ever been named *cubicularii*. A great deal of it he gave to Commodus and his concubines, and he spent a great deal on houses, baths, and other works of benefit either to individuals or to cities.[22]

Cleander was said to have sold twenty-five consulships in a single day, partly to pay for Commodus's extravagances but also to line his own pocket. 'In his haughty madness', said Ammianus Marcellinus, 'he had ruined the fortunes of many men.'[23] He was generally hated. Thus, in 189 (more probably than 190), he too fell and perished. His fall was engineered by Marcus Aurelius Papirius Dionysius, the grain commissioner. There was a famine at Rome, as well as a recurrence of the plague (or the outbreak of a new and perhaps different strain), which caused two thousand deaths a day at Rome. The grain commissioner deliberately increased the severity of the food shortage, so that Cleander should receive the blame.

It was a risky enterprise, but it worked. There were violent demonstrations among the urban *plebs* (furnished, for the moment, with a revival of its political influence), against which Cleander sent 'some soldiers' without effect. It may be conjectured that the city cohorts (dependent on the *praefectus urbi*) or the imperial cavalry escort (*equites singulares*), both comprising units which were jealous of the praetorians under Cleander's command, sided against him.

Commodus apparently did nothing to save his imperilled adviser.

No one had kept him informed of what was going on, but [his mistress] Marcia . . . reported the matter to him. And Commodus was so terrified (he was always the greatest coward) that he at once ordered Cleander to be slain, and likewise his son, who was being reared in the emperor's charge.[24]

Others, too were put to death. Whatever splits the convulsion may have caused in the army's ranks were covered up by coinage celebrating 'The Joy of the Emperor' (LAETITIA AVGVSTI)[25] and by the distribution of a largesse (*congiarium*), which had been announced in 187 but not handed out until now.

One of the reasons why Commodus killed so many people was in order to confiscate their property and money.[26] He had become extremely short of funds. His eight *congiaria* were costly, and the magnificent shows which he gave and in which he personally took part (celebrated by MAGNIFICENTIA on his coins)[27] were very expensive; indeed, they were probably the biggest item of his expenditure. *Alimenta*, an important part of social services, had already been suspended in 184, legionary pay had risen from 300 *denarii* under Domitian to 375, and a general decline in coin-weights and purities suggests a serious rise in prices towards the end of the reign. In other words, there was a deep recession and inflation, which made the emperor's financial predicament even more acute, especially as the plague may not have disappeared, and in 192 there was a damaging fire at Rome.

Commodus, however, during these same last years of his reign, distracted public attention from such worries by taking steps in various directions. This he could do with increasing idiosyncratic freedom, since the division of power among his chief advisers after Cleander, combined with the cowering silence of a terrorized upper class, gave him more initiative in which to develop his own ideas.

One of them was the startling conversion of Rome into a colony, bearing the name of Commodus itself; henceforward it was to be called Colonia Lucia Annia Commodiana, or Colonia Lucia Aelia Nova Commodiana, or Colonia Lucia Aurelia Nova Commodiana. The last-named is the most likely, since in 191 Commodus abandoned his former name 'Marcus Antoninus' in favour of 'Lucius Aelius Aurelius': his coins are inscribed 'Lucius Aelius Aurelius Commodus Augustus Pius Felix'.[28] His abandonment of 'Marcus Antoninus' seems to show that he no longer wanted to seem the heir and follower of his father Marcus Aurelius, whose names these had been; he wanted to stand on his own.

He intended to be an absolute ruler. He wore gold embroidery permanently on his mantle and tunic. He employed a host of new titles for his own aggrandizement, including 'Amazonius', 'Exsuperatorius' and 'Herculius'. Indeed he had already, in 187, incorporated the same designations into the calendar, whose reform, symbolizing the Blessed Age, he celebrated by New Year medallions displaying the double head of Janus, looking both backwards and forwards (Patulcius and Clusius).[29]

The title of 'Amazonius' looks like a sidelong reference to his gladiatorial aspirations, and Amazons appear as part of the decoration on a bust of Commodus;[30] but the term primarily resulted from the emperor's love of his mistress Marcia, who was portrayed as an Amazon.[31] 'Exsuperatorius' was paralleled by the description of Jupiter as EXSVPER. (*Exsuperantissimus*) on the coinage.[32] Here was a Jupiter who transcended the idea of the god of a state or of one (even the chief) of the Olympians and became instead the centre of a universal system of divinities, to unify the divided world. The Roman world was moving in the direction of the monotheism that was currently taking an astral form and was now being taken over by Christianity (Chapter 6).

The proclaimed link of this same deity with Commodus himself must not be overlooked. This was clearly expressed not only by his title 'Exsuperatorius' but also by the description of Jupiter on coinage, designed for the seventh centenary of his temple, as SPONSOR SEC(*uritatis*) AVGVSTI and DEFENSOR SALVTIS AVGVSTI.[33] Jupiter had been named as the protector of emperors before, and even of Commodus himself, but never had this been said with such emphasis and with such a wide range of Jupiter coin-types. The implication was that just as Jupiter was the supreme, quasi-monotheistic god, so Commodus was his deputy as *rector orbis*, surpassing all the rest of humankind: he was *omnium virtutum exsuperantissimus*.[34]

Commodus did not go so far as to identify himself with Jupiter, but towards the end of his reign he definitely identified himself with Hercules,[35] following the example of Alexander the Great.

Rulers of the stamp of Gaius (Caligula) and Nero and Domitian, who wanted to be recognized as divinities in their lifetime, had chosen Hercules as their model, since he was reputedly the first man who had become a god. Second-century emperors had no such ambitions. Nevertheless, they greatly revered Hercules as a heroic personage who had dedicated his life to fighting for good against evil and who had always stood up for civilization, which it was their task as emperors of Rome to cherish and maintain.

Moreover, it did not fail to cross their minds that if they faithfully modelled themselves on Hercules, they too would eventually gain the reward of deification that had fallen to him. So they applied themselves to following whatever aspect of his career best matched their own capabilities and tastes. Thus, to Trajan, Hercules was the conqueror of the world. To Hadrian, he was the great traveller. To Antoninus Pius, he was above all the redeemer who had struggled on behalf of Italy, by battling against its legendary monsters. To Marcus Aurelius, Hercules was the hero of self-sacrifice and love of humanity: the martyr to duty.

It was the aim of Commodus, in his dedication to Hercules, to blend all of these various aspects into one: to make Hercules the mythical symbol of his rule. On his coinage Hercules appears not only as the mighty warrior and conqueror but also as the god of peace, who is the protector and companion of the ruler. But Commodus eventually came to feel that to be the protégé of Hercules was not enough. He wanted to be regarded as a divinity in his own lifetime, and so permitted himself to be celebrated as the incarnation of Hercules himself. Thus, on the coins of the last phase of his life (190–1), Hercules Romanus bears the name of Augustus: he is Commodus (HERC. COMMODIANVS).[36]

The stages of this process can be followed. Already in 183 Hercules had appeared on the coinage as protector from danger, and later he was not only HERCVLES ROMANVS (191–2) but also the Founder of Rome (ROM*ae* CONDITOR), like the emperor himself,[37] and Commodus's role as gladiator perfected his assimilation to Hercules. And so identification came easily to him: Hercules, as we saw, was defined as COMMODIANVS. There were very many statues of Commodus as Hercules: on a bust he is shown as his personification, wearing the Nemean Lion's skin and brandishing a club. In other words the emperor, like Hercules, was a god.[38] After claiming the gods as protectors, he became one of them – their double upon earth.

So, in spite of his almost revolutionary belief in his own godhead as a sort of monotheistic Jupiter, Commodus was not averse to displaying himself as the earthly counterpart of other deities as well. That these included a number of divinities of eastern origin was very much a sign of the times, as well as of his own personal tastes. Thus he appears as Mithras, wearing the cosmic skull-cap, on an inlaid bronze and gilt bust (which is in the Victoria and Albert Museum in London). The dying Aurelius had declared Commodus the Rising Sun, the Rising Sun of a New World,[39] and amid increasing Sun-worship Sol is given the features of Commodus.[40] This fitted in well with the cult of Mithras, by now the largest missionary force in paganism (Ostia had revealed its enormous popularity).

There are also unprecedented honours to the exciting eastern cults of Cybele, Serapis and Isis on the coinage of Commodus. It was at Cybele's festival that Maternus's attempt to murder him had been thwarted, and she, the Great Mother, was *salutaris*, the preserver of the emperor. She was not, of course, new to the imperial coinage, but Commodus's reverence towards her was special and personal. At the end of his reign Serapis and Isis appear with Commodus; and Serapis, too, is hailed as his preserver (CONSERV*ator* AVG*usti*).[41] All of this went down well with the public, which was not faring prosperously and felt strong discontent with the old Olympians and what they had to offer.

Commodus, representing and leading this type of emotion, quite early on called himself PIVS (183). To say that this was intended as a mockery by the senate, or a reference to his favour towards his mother's lover, is a misunderstanding.[42] He was PIVS, and AVCTOR PIETATIS,[43] not only to appeal directly to the memory of Antoninus Pius but also to stress his own personal, devout connection with the divine favour. With PIVS went FELIX: alluding not only to his happy escape from plots but also to his inauguration of a new Golden Age. From 190 coins associate the concept with the emperor's Genius.[44]

Thus Commodus struck out in many exuberant religious directions, some of which corresponded with the times while others were novel and prompted by his own tastes and aspirations. The coins present his policy with unusual, and indeed unprecedented, clarity and force. There was certainly a come-down, or at least a radical change, from the philosophical high-mindedness of his very different (and different-looking) father Marcus Aurelius. This has always been widely condemned as a lamentable development: the descent from philosopher-king to king-gladiator, so that Ernest Renan was able to describe Commodus as a 'stupid butcher's boy'. But a case can also be made for Commodus's peculiar type of vision, the vision of 'lord of the world, of space and time, of mankind and its happiness': eccentric megalomania, yes, but a megalomania that in some ways prefigured the future. 'However unworthily, Commodus represented new aspects of thought and emotion that were not without meaning and value.... He sinned against Roman discipline. But was Roman discipline too class-bound and conservative?'[45]

Wilhelm Weber's summing-up of Commodus in the *Cambridge Ancient History* in the late 1930s has been branded as too high-flown, emotional and explosively anti-democratic, but it is worth noting all the same.

> The youth with his fair hair and burning eyes, whose head seemed to the people crowned with divine brilliance, stirred in the old and the moralists horror and loathing. But why judge him by our standards? A Spanish visionary, mystical, handsome, pliant, strong, now lively now indolent, now intrepid now a coward, with spirit now soaring now sinking, a notable creature, he was in everything extreme, in obedience towards God, in power to take divinity on himself, in wild sensuality, in iron fearlessness, in animal passion.
>
> Unchecked by any laws of morality, without care whether fair boys or women serve his appetites, whether he shed the blood of strangers or his own kin, breaking any fetters that could enchain him, he yet felt himself without guilt or stain, the source of all piety and the creator of all happiness. His life was lived beyond the world of reason, compounded of the potencies of the body, of instinct and of imagination.
>
> To the kaleidoscopic variations of his personality was added the effect of the cosmopolitan group that surrounded him, bringing to play upon him the forces that were now young, now more than old, from the far corners of the empire....
>
> In the witches' sabbath that plagued Rome in these years the emperor stands a strange figure. He had grown out of an intellectualism that was breaking down. He guided life by instinct from its heights to its depths, gave to the forms of the old world a content of passion and enthusiasm born of a new life, and sought an empire of happiness to be guided by men of devout obeisance to piety and the supernal.

Rejected by the old, pioneer for the new, far removed from Hadrian, he was the 'rising sun' of a new world.[46]

Commodus's period of wild self-indulgence and quasi-mystical autocratic religiosity was making too many enemies, and could not last. After the fall of Cleander he had begun to act very much on his own initiative, but there were still powerful people around the court. They included the praetorian prefect Quintus Aemilius Laetus, the emperor's chamberlain Eclectus, who was a bold, quick-tempered man of action, and his wife Marcia, who was, or had been, Commodus's mistress. The two men became nervous, both for the welfare of the empire and for their own future, because they saw how often their predecessors had come to a bad end. They launched a serious plot against Commodus himself, enrolling the generals on the Rhine and Danube in support of their causes. Their action was precipitated by the discovery of a proscription list which spelt danger to their partisans. And so they took the decisive step.

They had felt it particularly necessary to enlist the help of the army because the soldiers, they feared, might not have liked the termination of the Antonine dynasty. What finally happened was described by Dio Cassius.

> Laetus and Eclectus, displeased at the things Commodus was doing, and also inspired by fear, in view of the threats he made against them because they tried to prevent him from acting in this way, formed a plot against him.
>
> It seems that Commodus wished to slay both the consuls, Gaius Julius Erucius Clarus Vibianus and Quintus Pompeius Sosius Falco, and on New Year's Day to usher forth both as consul and *secutor* from the quarters of the gladiators. In fact, he had the first cell there, as if he was one of them. . . .
>
> For these reasons Laetus and Eclectus attacked him, after making Marcia their confidant. At any rate, on the last night of the year, when people were busy with the holiday, they caused Marcia to administer poison to Commodus in some beef. But the immoderate use of wine and baths, which was habitual to him, kept him from succumbing at once, and instead he vomited up some of it. And thus suspecting the truth, he indulged in some threats. Then they sent Narcissus, an athlete, against him, and caused this man to strangle him while he was taking a bath.[47]

Dio's account may not be entirely accurate. It is uncertain, for example, whether Marcia (who had helped to bring down Cleander) was involved at all. The man who succeeded Commodus on the throne, Publius Helvius Pertinax, may have been an accessory to the plot; the later emperor Julian thought that he was.[48] Moreover, it is uncertain whether Commodus really intended to kill the two new consuls; Herodian says nothing about this. Yet Dio's version remains, on the whole, not unreliable. Certainly, if Commodus intended to emerge on New Year's Day from the gladiatorial barracks, the offence to public decency would have been enormous, and indeed intolerable. And so Laetus and Eclectus acted to bring the reign and life of Commodus to an end. Once he was dead, the voices of the senators, so long stifled, were released, and they produced a long statement of hatred.

> Senate and people demanded that Commodus's body be dragged with the hook and thrown into the Tiber (though subsequently, by order of Pertinax, it was transferred to Hadrian's tomb)....
>
> There were great acclamations by the senate after his death. In fact, so that the senate's verdict on him may be known, I have included the acclamations verbatim, from Marius Maximus, and the contents of the decree of the senate....
>
> 'Let the remembrance of the parricide, the gladiator, be wiped out, let the statues of the parricide, the gladiator, be dragged down! ... Let the executioner of the senate be dragged with the hook, in the ancient fashion! ... We have been slaves to slaves.... Spies out of the senate, informers out of the senate, suborners of slaves out of the senate![49]

Nevertheless, the acts of Commodus were not rescinded, although some modern historians have said that they were, and Laetus, although heavily involved in the murder, gave the body secret burial. Dio was right to say that the new emperor, Pertinax, transferred the body to the Mausoleum of Hadrian.[50] And the senators who had so violently denounced Commodus were obliged to think again when, some two years later, Septimius Severus, who had by then become emperor, declared, fictitiously, that he himself was the adopted son of Marcus Aurelius and therefore the brother of Commodus, who was consequently deified.[51] Dedications to *Divus Commodus* are particularly frequent in Africa.

# Part II

# THE ANTONINE AGE

# 6

# ANTONINE SPEAKING AND WRITING

There was a considerable number of important writers during this period, both in Latin and Greek, though it is easy to forget this because they are neglected in schools and universities, which prefer their students to study earlier, 'classical' writers in those languages.

In particular, some of the prose writers are very significant: in Latin, Apuleius and perhaps Fronto (though not enough of his work has survived to enable us to judge); and in Greek, Marcus Aurelius and Lucian. Various other authors are notable, either because they were highly regarded in their own time or later, or because they were specialists who constituted landmarks in their own fields.

It will be noted that there were many more Greek authors than Latin. This is one of a number of signs that the Greek part of the empire was asserting itself (Chapter 8), prompting, in particular, the Second Sophistic movement (see Polemo, p. 96). In addition, the Christian Apologists at this time, like the Gnostics, wrote mostly in Greek (see pp. 119ff).

## LATIN

### Florus

Florus was a Roman historian of the second century AD, who probably wrote in *c.* AD 140. The historical treatise that bears his name is an *Epitome of All Wars During Seven Hundred Years.* One of the manuscripts describes his work as an abridgment of Livy's *History.* Florus deviates sometimes from Livy, but resembles him in his ecstatically patriotic tone – which means that the foreign powers attacked by the Roman Republic are described as villains and rebels. Florus describes the wars of conquest of Trajan, which he presents very favourably, though not without occasional implied criticisms: for example, 'it is more important to keep a province than to conquer it.'

He constructed his narrative effectively and with a certain strength, but it is spoilt by repetitiveness, rhetorical exclamation and a taste for epigrams that are not lacking in obscurity. There are errors in his chronology and geography, and his depictions of individuals are sometimes misguided: for instance, Florus's indication of Marcus Aurelius's humble origins is inaccurate.

Yet a brief, speedy, chauvinistic survey of this kind met a characteristic need among his contemporaries, and continued to be widely read. However, Julius Caesar Scaliger (1540–1609) was too kind when he described Florus as 'a very fine writer' (*un très bel auteur*).

> The popularity of his works, says Moses Hadas,[1] is easy to understand. The books present all the memorable stories of Roman history, and yet are very short, because everything else which pertains to history is eliminated. The style is rhetorical and elegant, but not too turgid or difficult. . . . Rome is the special object and agent of destiny in operating through history, and 'those who read of Roman exploits are learning the history not of a single people but of the human race'.[2] It is axiomatic that Roman policy and Roman aims must always be successful; even their failures are part of a divine plan, either as rods of chastisement, or means of discipline, or as a trial.

## Fronto

Marcus Cornelius Fronto was born in *c.* AD 100 (or possibly somewhat later) and died in 166/7. His birthplace was Cirta (Constantine) in Numidia (eastern Algeria), of which he was a *patronus*, and to the ruling council of which he addressed a letter. He calls himself 'a Libyan (African) of the Libyans', but was presumably of Roman origin.[3]

He is notable, for two reasons. First, he was such an influential literary figure that the contemporary intelligentsia regarded him as the foremost orator of the age (and Lucius Verus wrote to him, asking him to write a History praising his eastern campaigns). He held the supreme position at the bar in an age of eminent jurists – and was a famous speaker in the senate. This is hard to imagine nowadays, when we have only a few fragments of his speeches to study. Even if we had more, tastes have changed so much that we probably would not appreciate them. However, we must try to place ourselves within the tastes and minds of his age.

Fronto's reputation, which has now gone so far down hill, stood high for at least fifteen hundred years. People echoed the view of those who lived in his time that he was the Cicero of his epoch, or at least not very far short of him: 'the alternative glory of Roman eloquence', as Eumenius still described him in the fifth *Latin Panegyric*, in AD 297.[4] About a century later Macrobius declared Fronto the master of the plain, precise, down-to-earth kind of oratory, in contrast with the copious kind, in which

Cicero had been supreme. Saint Jerome (*c.* 348–420), writing of the special qualities of various authors, indicates 'serious dignity' as the particular characteristic of Fronto. A little later Claudius Mamertus, likewise discoursing on the typical features of writers, singles out Fronto for splendour (*pompa*). Sidonius Apollinaris saw in him *gravitas*.[5]

Although Fronto's reputation for oratory was so great, so few fragments of his speeches have survived that they cannot be utilized to contribute to an assessment of the quality of his speech-making. It would be wrong, however, to deduce that such non-survival means that the speeches were bad. Too much that was good has failed to survive for any such conclusions to be justifiable. It is merely one of those unfortunate accidents with which the history of ancient literature is replete. And we cannot, therefore, dispute the unanimous verdict that Fronto was a very fine orator indeed, according to the judgment of his time. (Nevertheless, the particular character of his oratory may have been overrated by Marcus Aurelius, and might not have appealed to us today, because of his over-indulgent taste for similes.)[6]

Fronto's own view, however, was that eloquence was the only thing that mattered in the universe. He saw it as a vehicle of the highest ideals, and believed that an orator, although his task was to please, must do so without sacrificing the true, lofty principles of eloquence. In this balancing trick we must suppose that he was successful: although it is ironical that the first-hand evidence from which we ought to judge has been withheld from us.

What has survived however – it was rediscovered in 1815 – is a large collection of Fronto's letters. A poor view of these letters was taken by their early editors, and, although efforts have been made to produce arguments to the contrary, it must be concluded that they are, in general, feeble stuff. Not all fine orators are good writers of letters, and Fronto, clearly, was an orator whose letters were not very distinguished. It is only fair to add that he himself took the same view. He disclaimed the habit of writing letters and declared that no one could be a worse correspondent than himself.[7]

The trivialities that he penned in these letters, including a good deal of literary comment that scarcely deserves a higher verdict, are, on the whole, disappointing as historical sources. But they do include a few letters between Fronto and Antoninus Pius (whom Fronto praised in the senate), a few between Fronto and Lucius Verus, and many more exchanged between himself and his other imperial pupil, Marcus Aurelius, of whom he was made tutor by Hadrian in 138, the appointment subsequently being reaffirmed by Antoninus Pius.

These letters provide the second reason why Fronto remains a noteworthy personality. They are important not only because they display the Education of a Prince, Marcus Aurelius, but also because they asseverate the great love felt for him by Fronto and the reciprocal feelings of the young Marcus Aurelius, even if Aurelius's letters appear to us a little forced and unnatural. 'Like all your friends,' wrote Fronto, 'I take in deep draughts of love for you.' 'Your letter,' said Aurelius, 'had the effect of making me feel how much you loved me': and 'beyond question you have conquered in loving all lovers that have ever lived.' Aurelius himself is equally affectionate. 'So passionately, by heaven, am I in love with you. . . . I will love you while I have life and health.' 'I will love you more than anyone else loves you, more, in fact, than you love yourself.' 'I can never love you enough.' He quotes the poet Naevius (third century BC about *a love transcendent*.[8]

The expression of such unrestrained sentiments today would immediately prompt suggestions of homosexuality. But there is no evidence that either Fronto or Marcus Aurelius entertained any such feelings, on a sexual level. Aurelius found Fronto a liberating spirit, and declared that he learnt to speak and hear the *truth* from him.[9] It was an age when the love felt by man for man could be expressed more freely, without any such suspicions arising.

Their relationship was temporarily disrupted when Aurelius ultimately abandoned rhetoric as being unworthy of serious pursuit (in favour of philosophy). This went down very badly with Fronto.

> You seem to me, in the fashion of the young, to have deserted the pursuit of eloquence and to have turned aside to philosophy, in which there is no introductory section to be elaborated, no account of the facts, bringing them together with concision, clarity and skill. . . .
>
> You would read a book to your philosopher, listen in silence while your master explained it, and nod to show your understanding: would hear again and again: 'What is the first premiss? What is the second premiss?' And when the windows were wide open, the point that 'If it is day, then it is light' would be laboured. Then you would go away carefree, with nothing to think over, or to write up at night, nothing to recite to your master, nothing to say by heart, no search for words, no adorning of a single synonym, no translation from Greek to our language.[10]

Why not? Fronto does not seem quite fair; although it is clear that he did not care for philosophy (and especially the Stoic school of Athenodorus, under whom he had studied). Marcus Aurelius, on the other hand, never turned back from philosophy to rhetoric. He was curiously reticent about Fronto in the *Meditations*,[11] but he remained his very close friend, continuing to admire his character and goodness, if not his rhetoric.

The other main peculiarity about Fronto was his poor health, especially in the early 140s and then again in the years just before his death. In his letters to Marcus Aurelius he complains of pains in the elbows, feet, groin, neck, shoulders and stomach, and also mentions diarrhoea. In addition there is an allusion to a 'choleraic attack', whatever that might be (? AD 154–6).

> I have had such a choleraic attack that I lost my voice, gasped and struggled for breath. Finally, my circulation failed and, the pulse being imperceptible, I became unconscious. In fact, I was given up by my family as dead and remained insensible for some time.
>
> The doctors were given no time or opportunity to revive or relieve me even with a warm bath or cold water or food, except that after nightfall I swallowed a few morsels of bread soaked with wine. Thus I was gradually brought quite round.
>
> For three whole days after I did not recover my voice. But now by the help of the gods I am getting on very comfortably. I walk with more ease and my voice is stronger and more distinct. So I propose, please the gods, to take a drive tomorrow. If I find I can stand the flint paving well, I will hasten to you as fast as I can.[12]

Well might Fronto conclude (? AD 148–9): 'I have ... of pains and infirmities something more than enough to spare.'[13] He felt so bad that, when Antoninus Pius offered him the proconsulship of Asia (153–4), he considered that he had better decline the honour. His health deteriorated again after the loss of his wife and grandchild in 165. What was actually wrong with him has been disputed. Probably a good many things: gout and arthritis have been suggested and ruled out, but he may well have suffered quite badly from rheumatism.

Nevertheless, after holding a series of appointments – *triumvir capitalis* (praetor's assistant in civil and criminal cases), quaestor in Sicily (which gave him a place in the senate), plebeian aedile (an elective post originally created to assist the tribunes of the people, and later supplemented by the curule aediles), and then praetor – he was able, despite his later refusal of a major proconsular post, to accept a suffect (supplementary) consulship in AD 143, the same year in which Herodes Atticus was consul. The relationship between the two men was fraught by crisis, since Fronto led a legal battle against Herodes Atticus (140–3) – who was Marcus Aurelius's friend, hence an embarrassed correspondence. Later, however, Fronto and Herodes Atticus made peace. But it was his appointment by Hadrian (138) as tutor to the future emperors Marcus Aurelius and Lucius Verus that had given Fronto special significance.

Fronto loved the Games, unlike Marcus Aurelius, as he indicated in a letter to a certain Volumnius Quadratus, a Ciceronian scholar.[14] Yet the pursuit of learning was his greatest passion. It was learning of a specialized kind: excluding, as we saw, philosophy, and concentrating on style. He saw style as a competitor and contrast to philosophical themes such as ethics, and the winner of any contest between the two. And it is to matters of style and language that his interest in rhetoric is largely confined. This resulted in, or derived from, a certain poverty of thought.

Fronto was modest about his command of Greek, as he showed in a letter to Marcus Aurelius's mother, Domitia Lucilla, who was surrounded by Greek writers and scholars. He did not underrate Greek, and he could not escape the prestigious Greek literary world, but it was Latin that really attracted him. He was eager to make his own Latin vocabulary as pure as possible, hankering to return beyond recent corruptions to a less contaminated past; and (perhaps a little paradoxically) he enjoyed the refinements and artful simplicities that seemed to him to make this possible. Archaisms appealed to him, and he was fascinated by old Latin words no longer in use – provided, he insisted, that they were more expressive and more appropriate than words that were more up to date.

His most favoured model of speech and life was Cato the elder (234–149 BC). He also admired many other old Romans, down to Cicero and Sallust. He did not underrate Cicero, whose preeminence he recognized. But he disliked the Stoic writer and statesman Seneca (d. AD 65).

From the casual mention, in one letter, of *elocutio novella* it has been assumed that this is a technical term, meaning a 'new style', which was being advocated by Fronto and his friends. But the phrase may mean no more than 'novelty of expression', a fresher and more original and individual style which Fronto valued highly and reproved Marcus Aurelius for not using. The few rhetorical exercises of Fronto's which survive are in a vigorous and straightforward Latin, and it can be concluded that he left the language freer and more plastic than he had found it.

## Gaius

A Roman jurist (*c.* 129–*c.* 199), Gaius composed a number of treatises on the Law between the years 130 and 180 AD. His other names are unknown, and his identification is disputed. His writings refer especially to conditions in Asia Minor, which may suggest that he wrote there.

The most important among his various studies was the *Institutiones* (Institutes), which it has now proved possible to reconstruct almost completely. It is a textbook for beginners, divided into four books (perhaps by some later editor): (1) on persons and their varying legal statuses; (2) on objects and the methods by which rights over them may be acquired; (3) on intestate succession and obligations; (4) on actions and their kinds.

Gaius offers a pleasantly lucid and economical form of exposition. Another of his good features is his persistence in attempting historical explanations. Yet they are by no means always accurate. Indeed, Gaius hardly ever achieves any depth of interpretation: he was certainly not a first-class jurist. His influence, however, has been enormous. Our knowledge of Roman civil procedure relies almost entirely on what Gaius tells us. To take one example, he is aware that imperial pronouncements (*constitutiones*) now have the force of law.[15]

## Apuleius

Apuleius was born of wealthy parents in *c.* AD 123–5 at Madaurus (now Mdaourouch), a Roman colony in Numidia, which belonged to the province of Africa.[16] His father was a leading citizen of the town and had held office as one of its *duoviri*, the principal annually elected officials; he left Apuleius and his other son a considerable sum of money.

Apuleius was presumably given his elementary education at Madaurus. But thereafter he was taught grammar and rhetoric at the large metropolitan city of Carthage, of which he subsequently wrote with devotion. Then, at the age of eighteen, he proceeded to Athens for further studies – no doubt including courses in philosophy – and stayed there for five or even seven years, during which time he undertook several journeys, notably to Samos and Hierapolis (now Pamukkale) in Phrygia. Subsequently he went to Rome, where he received further training, and pleaded in the law courts.

After these and other travels he returned to north Africa – into the world of which he gives us our most vivid insight – and while on his way to Alexandria fell ill at Oea (Tripoli) in *c.* AD 155. This was the home town of Sicinius Pontianus, an old friend of his from his Athenian days, who proceeded to call on him. Pontianus had been studying in Rome, but had returned to Oea because his rich widowed mother Pudentilla (owner of a large estate, worked by slaves, at Oea) was proposing to remarry, taking her brother-in-law Sicinius Clarus as her second husband. Pontianus was afraid that this would mean that he and his brother would not inherit his mother's money. He proposed, therefore, that Apuleius should marry Pudentilla instead, in the hope, presumably, that this would keep the funds under his own control. Despite some opposition within the family, this was duly arranged.

Pontianus died soon afterwards. Clarus's brother Sicinius Aemilianus, who no doubt was also anxious about the money, arranged that Apuleius should be accused, first, of having Pontianus murdered, and, second, of having won Pudentilla's affections by magic. The first charge was dropped, but the second was tried at Sabratha (Sabrata) in *c.* 158–9 before the proconsul Claudius Maximus (possibly identified with a Stoic philosopher and teacher). Apuleius defended himself and was evidently acquitted, but he then left Oea for the more congenial surroundings of Carthage. There he enjoyed renown as poet, philosopher, rhetorician, public lecturer and valedictory speaker, making speeches in honour of departing

Roman governors. He was appointed chief priest of the province, and his statues were erected at Carthage, Madaurus and elsewhere.

The speech that Apuleius gave in his defence at his trial, the *Apologia* (*A Discourse on Magic*), has survived. It is brilliant, learned, surprising and outrageous, and deserves to be better known than it is. The *Florida* (literally 'flowers', but also meaning 'anthology'), which has likewise come down to us, comprises excerpts from his declamations on various themes, which vary in style from the trivial, extravagant and amusing to (occasionally) the beautiful. Apuleius also wrote on philosophical and religious subjects.

By far his most famous work was the *Metamorphoses*, 'changes of shape' (*The Transformations of Lucius*). This had always been a favourite theme of classical mythology – witness the numerous transformations of Jupiter – and became a fashionable topic among Hellenistic authors, who sometimes gave this name to their works. Then, in Latin, Ovid's *Metamorphoses* gained eternal fame. Apuleius's work, about the transformation of a man into a donkey, also became known as the *Golden Ass*, not later than the time of Saint Augustine, who employed the title.

Apuleius casts the work into the studiously discursive form of a Roman satire (*satura*). At what stage in his life the *Metamorphoses* was written is disputed. Some have argued for an early period in his own career, but on the whole it seems probable that all of the numerous jokes and parodies relating to legal proceedings indicate a date subsequent to his traumatic trial for magic in *c.* 158–9 – and there is evidence that the work might even be a good deal later still.

After a riddling introduction in which Apuleius drops a good many learned, mock-modest and misleading hints about his intentions, the *Metamorphoses* is told in the first person by its principal character, a young man called Lucius. Riding through the mountains of Thessaly, Lucius meets two other travellers, and is told the story of a murder committed by a witch at Hypata, the Thessalian town to which he is going. Once there he receives hospitality from Milo, whose wife, Pamphile, proves to be a witch. At a party given by his relative Byrrhaena, Lucius hears a further macabre tale of a man mutilated by witches, and on his journey back to Milo's house he kills three robbers who, however, after his mock trial at the Festival of Laughter, turn out merely to have been animated wine-skins.

He makes love to Pamphile's maid Fotis, who allows him to see her mistress transform herself into an owl. Lucius, too, wishes to experience a magical metamorphosis but, owing to a technical error, finds himself transformed into an ass (though retaining his human faculties, with the exception of his voice). To recover his human shape he must eat roses, but, before Fotis can bring any, robbers attack the house and take him away. In the robbers' den he listens to stories telling of the deaths of three of their number and sees them bring in a beautiful girl, Charite, who had been kidnapped for ransom on her wedding night.

To comfort her, the old woman who cooks for the robbers tells her the story of Cupid and Psyche. She recounts how a certain king had three daughters, the youngest of whom, Psyche, was so lovely that she was as greatly adored as the goddess Venus herself. As a result, the goddess became jealous and sent her son Cupid to make Psyche fall in love with some ugly wretch. Instead Cupid fell in love with her himself, and dispatched Zephyrus, the West Wind, to transfer her to a fairy palace, where he visited her as her unknown husband – always in the dark, so that she would not recognize him.

After a time she begged that her two sisters should be allowed to visit her, and he very reluctantly agreed. Her sisters, on learning that Psyche had never seen her husband, and suspecting him to be a god, became madly jealous of her. They persuaded her that her husband was in fact a fearsome monster, and they gave her a lamp and a knife to kill him. As he slept, however, Psyche saw Cupid revealed in all of his beauty by the light of the lamp. A drop of oil falling on his body woke him, and, rebuking her for her disobedience, he went away and left her.

Psyche then set out to look for him. After bringing her sisters to a bad end for their jealousy, she came to the house of Venus, who received her harshly and set her three tasks. Impossible though they seemed, she accomplished two of them, with the help of ants and an eagle. But then, after Venus had instructed her to go down to the Underworld to fetch a casket full of beauty from Pluto's daughter Proserpina, curiosity moved her to open the casket. It contained, however, not beauty but a deathly sleep, to which she succumbed. But now Cupid intervened to save her, having at last gained the consent of Jupiter to their Olympic wedding, the celebration of which brings the tale of Cupid and Psyche to a close.

After listening to this story, Charite is rescued by her lover, disguised as a robber. He is subsequently assassinated by a rival, and his death is violently avenged by Charite. Lucius, still in the form of an ass, passes into the hands of three further owners or sets of owners. During this period he beholds the indecent, effeminate orgies of priests of the Syrian Goddess (Atargatis), and listens to three sex-orientated anecdotes, 'The Tale of the Tub', 'The Lost Slippers' and 'The Laundryman's Wife'. He witnesses a fourth event, described as 'The Baker's Wife'. Next comes the tale of a wealthy young man and his savage treatment of his neighbours; the story of an amorous stepmother who tries to poison her unresponsive stepson; and the account of a brutal woman who commits five murders. As part of her punishment it is proposed that she should be publicly displayed having sexual relations with the ass Lucius. He finds the prospect so appalling that he runs away from Corinth to Cenchreae, where he falls asleep, exhausted, on the seashore.

91

The work then takes an entirely new turn. As Lucius sleeps, the goddess Isis, in all of her splendour, appears to him and promises her help. At the ceremonial spring festival for the launching of her sacred ship, her priest offers Lucius a wreath of roses, and he is restored to human shape. Resolved to dedicate the rest of his life to the service of his divine saviour, he undertakes the exacting preparations for initiation, during the course of which further visions are vouchsafed to him. Finally, alone in the shrine of the goddess at night, he is granted the experience of death, rebirth and revelation which is only permitted to the elect. Lucius then goes to Rome in order to devote himself to the service of Isis, and at her direction is twice initiated into the mysteries of her partner, Osiris, finally attaining a respected place in the hierarchy of the cult. And so the *Metamorphoses* ends.

Like most of the greatest 'original' literary achievements of all time, it is not entirely original, in the sense that its author drew quite heavily on earlier writings. We have a shorter version, *Onos* (*Lucius*, or *The Ass*), of unknown authorship – not necessarily by Lucian (see p. 106), to whom it has been attributed – which contains much of the material on which Apuleius drew (but not 'Cupid and Psyche' and his concluding chapters relating to Isis). To cut a lengthy controversy short, it seems that both Apuleius's *Metamorphoses* and the Greek *Ass* were derived, separately, from a lost Greek *Metamorphoses* about a certain Lucius of Patrae (Patras). This could, indeed, have been by Lucian, but there is no certainty. (Once again, it appears that Apuleius's Isis sections and his 'Cupid and Psyche' story, like many other features, did not figure in this work.)

Apuleius's story of Cupid and Psyche derives its form from a widespread type of folk-tale. No classical author had presented the account of the two lovers in this form before, although the pains of their love had become a common theme of Hellenistic writers and artists.

In his introduction to the *Metamorphoses* Apuleius refers obliquely to a further debt to the 'Milesian Tales', which were sexy short stories (owing their name to Miletus, near Yenköy [and the River Balat]) that had enjoyed a considerable vogue since the first century BC. But he had, of course, changed and amplified this genre beyond all recognition. The same applies to his debt to the Greek novel, of which several of the practitioners were his contemporaries (see pp. 117f.). These Greek romances were mostly starry-eyed affairs figuring boys and girls who were separated by various vicissitudes and who eventually enjoyed a happy reunion. Apuleius's *Metamorphoses*, on the other hand, although it has a happy ending of quite a different kind, is emphatically *not* starry-eyed. It echoes the Greek romances (which Apuleius may or may not have read) chiefly in order to guy them.

An earlier Latin novel in a similar vein was Petronius's *Satyricon*, written, probably, by a minister of Nero (*c.* AD 65). Its surviving portions (for it is incomplete) depict wittily and satirically an extremely sordid low life quite alien to the sentimentalities of the Greek romances.

However, three finds of papyrus fragments have also revealed small portions of previously unknown Greek novels which are far closer to the seedy, macabre low life that is depicted by Petronius and Apuleius than to the sugary type of morality that is portrayed in the Greek romances that were hitherto known. Here, then, was a genre, of which we now have Greek fragments, together with (in Latin) the incomplete *Satyricon* of Petronius and the complete *Metamorphoses* of Apuleius.

Apuleius was very well versed in a range of earlier classical writings. He liked to parade his learning, so that those who are interested may trace influences, echoes and parodies of many other types of literature, notably the epic (especially Homer's *Odyssey*), Platonic dialogue, tragedy, comedy, the pastoral, mime, and adventure stories of various kinds, as well as Egyptian and Mesopotamian literature (known from inscriptions).

In his Introduction to the *Metamorphoses* he announces his desire to entertain the reader. He succeeds. All the same, the statement is somewhat disingenuous, since he achieves a great deal more besides. True, the suggestion that the whole work is a gigantic moral allegory is now somewhat discredited. But nearly all of the proper names that he introduces have a self-descriptive significance, as frequently occurs in ancient writings. The story of Cupid and Psyche, at least, surely has some link with the progress of the soul (*psyche*), via various hazards, towards happiness; and this theme is further illustrated by Lucius's conversion to the religion of Isis at the end of the book – a religion which is shown not as an artificial survival but as a deeply felt faith (see also Chapter 5).

One of the most arresting features of the *Metamorphoses* is the progress from the squalid, brutal miseries of the earlier scenes to the sublimity of the Isiac initiations. On the other hand, Apuleius seems to have hated at least one other pagan, eastern deity, the Syrian Goddess (*Dea Syria*) Atargatis. This goddess was associated with the sun-god (Sol, Helios) of Heliopolis (Baalbek). She herself was essentially a goddess of fertility, and sometimes appears with fertility emblems of pomegranates and grain-stalks. On occasion, she is a fish-goddess; possibly that, too, is a fertility motif, though the dolphins that accompany her are a symbol of fair weather. As a fish-divinity, she had a sacred pool at Hierapolis-Bambyce (El Manbej) in Syria.

In spite, or perhaps because, of the current fashion for eastern religions, the supposedly debased devotees of Atargatis receive very severe treatment from Apuleius. Apart from Isis, his strongest religious belief – if it can be called such – is in Luck (Tyche), the blind Fortune that strikes random blows but is superseded in the end by a happy Fortune, which (like so many other deities) is incorporated in Isis herself – in the true spirit of classical novels, in which Fortune is a dominant concept (and it figures prominently on the coins of the Antonines).

As for philosophy, Apuleius, although his mind did not run very deeply in that direction, firmly believed himself to be a Platonist, as his other writings showed: his combination of Isiac devoutness with Platonism is typical of his times. That is to say, he subscribed to the Middle Platonism of his epoch (see Albinus, p. 103): and Psyche's pilgrimage includes echoes of Plato's pilgrimage of the soul in the *Phaedrus*. Apuleius was not only the conscious heir of the Alexandrian literary tradition (known to him directly and through Latin models) but also a typical example of a 'sophist' (of the Second Sophistic; see Polemo, p. 96). Sophists were rhetoricians and lecturers who travelled around during the second century AD giving public lectures and popularising philosophy, and earning themselves large fees and reputations to match. Apuleius's sometimes archaistic, peculiar Latin is not provincialism but deliberate affectation.

All of this emerges in the *Metamorphoses*, and much more besides. There is a lot of fairly lecherous sex in the book – based on the assumption that no woman's virtue is unassailable – and this has substantially contributed to the enormous renown, or notoriety, of the work throughout the centuries. It is a type of sex that very easily takes a nasty and sadistic turn, to which Isis provides a welcome change and relief.

There is also a great deal of magic in the book. As we have seen, magic constituted the burden of the charge against Apuleius at Sabratha; indeed, Saint Augustine, among others, was quite prepared to see him as a magician.[17] From this miasma, too, Isis rescues him. Or does she, for was she not believed to be a magician herself? Augustine condemns Apuleius for his interest in magic, and this damaging, unsatisfied, lethal curiosity (*curiositas*) about the unknown runs right through the *Metamorphoses*. What happens to Lucius and Psyche are but two conspicuous examples of such trends – reflecting the spirit of the age, which was intent on *curiositas*. But Apuleius is at pains to show that indulging this trait can lead one along perilous paths and bring evil results.

Is the *Metamorphoses* a unity, and to what extent? Apuleius is determined to confuse us. He leaves loose ends, and does not seem to mind. And nothing is quite what it seems; it is not always clear, or meant to be clear, what has really happened. Nor is it certain how far Lucius is to be identified with the author. Certainly, Madaurus, and no longer Greece, is named as Lucius's home.[18] How can we make our way through this magical atmosphere, in which *aporia*, puzzlement, abounds? It is precisely this prevalence of ambiguous, contrasting fantasies, this original, experimental synthesis of the comic, romantic, macabre, tragic and edifying, this dream-land atmosphere of mystery and unreality, that intrigues us and keeps us thinking.

## Gellius (Aulus)

We do not know where Gellius was born, and the dates of his life are not certain (*c.* AD 130–*c.* 180). Nor is it sure whether he was primarily a Roman or a north African. He wrote the *Attic Nights* (*Noctes Atticae*). This consisted of twenty books, of which the beginning and the end, and all of Book 8 except for the chapter headings, are now missing.

As a young man he studied literature at Rome, above all with the grammarian Gaius Sulpicius Apollinaris, and he knew Fronto (see p. 84), whose salons he attended as an earnest hanger-on. Then Gellius went to undertake further work at Athens for at least a year, attending lectures and visiting Herodes Atticus. His work includes descriptions of his student days at Athens. It was possibly after his return from that city that he was appointed a judge (*iudex*), for the conduct of private cases, though we have no reason to believe that his application to legal practice continued for very long. He married and had children.

The *Noctes Atticae* consists of a collection of chapters (mostly brief) concerned with a wide variety of topics, including philosophy, history, literary criticism, textual questions, grammar and law. Gellius started collecting his material in Attica,[19] and assembled it later in order to entertain and instruct his own children. It has been argued that it cannot have been published much before 180.

Gellius shows that he possessed a strong enthusiasm for learning (including translation), although he is not the possessor of an acutely critical mind, and offers little more than an epitome of the sources that he had studied. He thus provides a prime example of borrowed, second-hand erudition, though the identification of these sources is often impossible. His arrangement of his material, he tells us, is intentionally haphazard. But individual chapters are usually constructed with some care, often with picturesque (if imaginary) settings to enhance their vividness. Despite the only moderate ability of its author, the *Noctes* is not unattractive, but its continued usefulness is derived, for the most part, from its author's preservation of numerous passages from earlier writers, both Latin and Greek.

Gellius's Latin is a curious mixture, involving an attempt at old-world classical purity. His literary tastes are very much those of cultural personages of his time, with a strong and somewhat affected preference for archaic writers. But he is sensible enough to appreciate Virgil as well as the earlier Ennius in verse, and Cicero as well as the elder Cato in prose. Moreover, Gellius also wanted to appeal to readers who knew Greek as well as Latin.

## GREEK

Greek poetry was not dead: a recent effort has been made to resuscitate some of its exponents, but they are pretty dim. The following list will therefore concern itself with writers of prose: it was in the writing of prose that the growing supremacy of Greek over Latin literature was mainly apparent.

### Polemo (Marcus Antonius)

Polemo was born in *c.* AD 88 and died in 144, so that he just deserves to be mentioned in a book devoted to the Antonines, whose epoch started in 138.

His birthplace was Laodicea on the Lycus (Eskihisar) in south-western Phrygia, but he was a citizen of Smyrna, where he was taught by Scopelianus and Timocrates and later founded a school of his own.

Polemo became a prominent sophist who enjoyed the friendship of Trajan, Hadrian and Antoninus Pius (although he once expelled the last-named, before he became emperor, from his house). In addition, he did useful work in reconciling city factions in his own country. He was selected to deliver a speech at the inauguration of Hadrian's Olympieum at Athens (AD 130). The speech has not survived, but two of his short declamations are extant. Their topic is 'the fathers of Cynegirus and Callimachus contest their sons' claims for the prize of valour at the battle of Marathon (490 BC)'.

Polemo's oratory was in the grand manner, his delivery passionate and excited: Fronto described him to the young Marcus Aurelius as a Ciceronian. Polemo was one of the teachers of Herodes Atticus (who influenced him), and had bad, competitive relations with Favorinus (see p. 98). He dreamed about the Athenian orator Demosthenes (384–322 BC), and set up a statue proclaiming the fact. He also wrote on history, and compiled a treatise *On Physiognomy*, which is known to us through an Arabic translation and a paraphrase by the physician Adamantius.

Visitors flocked to Smyrna to hear Polemo. He was a benefactor of the city, and diverted Hadrian's generosity to it, and he exercised large influence over its population. When he went on a journey, he rode upon a horse with a silver bridle, and was followed by a train of luggage carts and extra horses, accompanied by slaves and several packs of hounds.

Polemo was an early leader of the influential rhetorical movement known as the New or Second Sophistic, to which most of the writers discussed in this section either belonged or owed extensive debts. The movement is described in detail in Philostratus's *Lives of the Sophists* (*c.* AD 230), which looks back on this second century AD as the 'classical' age of these personages (the original sophists had lived in the fifth century BC). For knowledge of Polemo we are indebted to Plutarch (died after AD 120).

In general, the Second Sophistic authors endeavoured to be Attic in their vocabulary and syntax, although they were often by no means Attic in the rhythm of their language, nor in the spirit that animated their work. Their principal aim was to entertain their listeners by a firework display of eloquence. But they were prepared to instruct and edify them as well, and, for that matter, to educate the young. They ambitiously claimed the titles of rhetor, sophist and even philosopher, and jealously refused those titles to men of whom they did not approve. But there were, in fact, numerous gradations of status between them – so numerous that they would defy any attempt to divide them into categories.

The success of these latter-day sophists resulted from their fulfilment (although not in a very glorious form) of the antique ideal of combining intellectual, artistic and practical activity in the work of a single person. This success, and the power that went with it, were amply confirmed by their capacity to win applause and remuneration from their listeners. Sometimes they displayed their talents in the law courts, or upon the local political scene. More often, and more willingly, they revealed them in exhibitionist speeches – adorning festival assemblies, revering the gods, consoling those in distress – in which they sought to excite their audiences.

Although these sophists often claimed, as we have seen, to be philosophers, they were not serious philosophers at all, but merely their competitors as popular figures. Most of the sophists were quite rich Greeks from the cities of Greece and Asia Minor, particularly Athens and Smyrna and Ephesus. They frequently travelled abroad, not only to make speeches on their own account but also as ambassadors for their province and city, which they were also expected to assist by holding office in its administration and by making munificent benefactions (as Polemo did to Smyrna). Their eminence in these local circles brought them and their families and dependants into close touch with the Roman governing class, with whom they developed close connections, which extended even to the imperial palace and to the emperors themselves. They remained, it is true, very strongly aware of their Greek past, but they mixed easily with the new cosmopolitan world of their own times. By so doing, they played a significant part in the economic, social and governmental life of the Roman empire.

But their prime contribution was, of course, of a literary character. Since they set out to be Atticists, all of these men employed, publicly, a form of speech which was very different from the Greek language that was current at the time. As already noted, they were deliberately, consciously, copying, or endeavouring to copy, the literary language and style of three or four hundred years before. This makes it difficult for us to love them today. True, all art has an artificial component, and it is not easy to find, or employ, a natural style. Nevertheless, there is a strong, and perhaps predominant, modern school of thought which holds that the best literary manner is the one which most effectively looks as though it were natural, even if great powers of artifice are needed to attain that effect. The Greek authors of the Second Sophistic in the second century AD took an entirely different view. In their opinion, the best literary style had been determined and firmly fixed by the supreme writers of the long-past classical age – and the only way to do well oneself was to imitate their manner and idiom as exactly as possible.

The writings of the Second Sophistic are often second or third rate. But they illustrate the cultural aspirations of a whole age, so that they play a vital part in the history of the Roman empire.

### Favorinus

Favorinus was typical of the clever literary figures known to Marcus Aurelius in his youth: he was a rhetor with philosophical interests of the period of the Second Sophistic (see Polemo, p. 96).

A eunuch, born at Arelate (Arles) in southern Gaul, perhaps in the early 80s, he received a Greek education at Massilia(Marseille), and seems to have written and spoken Greek by preference. Although sceptical by disposition, he admired the Stoic philosopher Epictetus (c. AD 55 – c. 135); and he was the teacher of Herodes Atticus and Fronto (to whom he owed a procuratorship) and Gellius. After prolonged speaking tours (during which, in Ionia, he became the rival and enemy of Polemo), he went to Rome, where he pursued a successful career under Hadrian. But in c. AD 130 he fell into disgrace and was exiled to Chios. However, Antoninus Pius allowed him back to Rome, where he died in about the middle of the century.

The titles of nearly thirty of Favorinus's works are known. They included many speeches, some autobiographical and others of more general character. He also published two miscellanies, his *Memoirs* (*Apomnemoneumata*) and *Miscellaneous History* (*Pantodape*), which show how widely he had read.

### Appian

Appian was born at Alexandria, probably during the last years of the reign of Domitian (AD 81–96).[1] He was still there during the Second Jewish Revolt (115), and in the following year moved to Rome. There, in the reign of Hadrian, he took up the legal profession, becoming an advocate. Among his friends was Fronto, through whose influence Appian occupied the post of imperial agent (*procurator Augusti*), probably in the province of Egypt. He suffered from gastric troubles, but the date of his death is uncertain. He lived at least until *c.* 180, having finished work on his *Romaica* some time earlier.

The title of the work suggests that it is a straightforward history of Rome, but it is actually somewhat different – a survey of the conquests that the Romans had made. It contained twenty-four books, as follows:

| | |
|---|---|
| 1 Kings | 11 Syria |
| 2 Italy | 12 Mithridates VI of Pontus |
| 3 Samnium | 13–17 Civil Wars |
| 4 Gaul | 18–21 Egypt |
| 5 Sicily | 22 The first century of the empire |
| 6 Spain | 23 Dacia |
| 7 Hannibal | 24 Arabia |
| 8 Carthage and Numidia | |
| 9 Macedonia and Illyricum | |
| 10 Greece and Asia | |

Eleven of these books are extant, but thirteen survive only in fragments or in Photius's epitome.[2]

The *Romaica* provides insight into how a historian of the second century AD considered that the vast agglomeration of the Pax Romana, under which he lived, had been brought about. In regard to external policies Appian is loyal to Rome, even if very well aware of the realities of class strife (though efforts have been made to play this down).[3]

He writes as a Greek who seeks to inform his fellow-countrymen, in their own language, about their history and the history of the Romans, and about how the two peoples interacted and created the world of the future.

Appian had read widely, drawing his material from a number of earlier writers. He is able to interpret and discriminate for himself and to control a complex narrative, and his writing can be 'concise, lucid and vigorous'. Moreover, he is able to lay claim to 'an original, not badly contrived, arrangement'.[4] Unfortunately, however, when he is drawing on his sources, he reveals a lack of critical acumen – and on occasion he indulges in unashamed imaginative fiction. Moreover, his ethnographical arrangement, though enterprisingly novel, means that chronology is weak. And he is all too ready to call in divine revenge as a cause of events.

He was conscious, and proud, that he himself came from Egypt. To him the Ptolemies, who had ruled that country from the fourth until the first centuries BC, were 'my kings': and his narration of the civil wars of late Republican Rome culminate in Egypt's annexation by Rome. (Egypt was the subject of four books, which are unfortunately among those that have been lost.) Indeed, as a dweller in the Roman empire, his approach is distinctly provincial; unless one prefers to say that it perpetuated the cosmopolitan tradition of Herodotus. Appian took the view that the traditional annalistic handling of Roman history prevented an accurate assessment of Rome's dealings with the states that it had conquered, and of the qualities of the two sides on those various occasions. In consequence, he took the conquered peoples as his fundamental themes, allotting to each of them a book relating to its initial encounter with Rome (though a different treatment is sometimes necessary).

Appian's story, once we have pieced it together from its regional sections, is our only continuous account of the period from the Gracchi (Tiberius Sempronius Gracchus, d. 133 BC; Gaius Sempronius Gracchus, d. 122 BC) to Augustus. Despite a tendency to cram too much into too narrow a space, his narrative is usually believable, and often gripping. His choice of sources was intelligent. Although his style is somewhat depressingly sober and bare, indifferent to literary form, he was capable of lucid, vigorous writing, which is not overblown. His language (like his frequent employment of speeches) echoes his knowledge of the classical historians. But he steers clear of the worst excesses of Atticism, even admitting Roman technical terms in transliteration.

### Arrian (Flavius Arrianus)

Arrian was an approximate contemporary of Appian, born in c. AD 95.[5] Like Appian, he was a Greek. He came from Nicomedia (Izmit) in Bithynia (north-western Asia Minor), where his family was prominent. He also obtained the citizenship of Rome, under the name Lucius Flavius Arrianus, and occupied important state positions, about which recently discovered inscriptions have added to our knowledge. Under Hadrian he became consul (in the 120s) and later, in the 130s, *legatus Augusti propraetore* (imperial governor) of Cappadocia in eastern Asia Minor, where he had to repel the Alans (described by himself; see below). He also undertook extensive official journeys, for example in the Danubian provinces. Subsequently he retired to live at Athens, where he was appointed to a civil office in 147–8. He was also honoured by a priesthood for life in his native Nicomedia. He was a provincial who achieved worldly success among the Romans without feeling ashamed of his Bithynian origins.

Many of his writings, on philosophy, biography and history, have not survived.[6] But his *Indica* is extant and it offers much information about the Indian sub-continent. We also have by far the most famous of Arrian's works, the *Anabasis* (*Expedition up Country*, or *Up from the Coast*), describing the campaigns of Alexander the Great. The work serves as an invaluable, consciously demythologizing, corrective to the mass of fictitious romance, slander and absurdity that obscured the events of Alexander's career. It is also of interest to see what an intelligent servant of another, later, huge empire could make of the stirring events that were wrought by that archetypal conqueror half a millennium earlier.

Arrian writes with an attractive plainness, devoid of unnecessary rhetorical embellishments. He is capable of weighing contradictory or unsatisfactory versions and of producing an opinion of his own; although he cannot be regarded as wholly unbiased, since his authorities were Alexander's own officers. Nor, any more than Appian, did he try to liberate himself from the ancient historians' taste for inventing speeches. Furthermore, Arrian is guilty of carelessness and omissions. Some of these omissions were deliberate, but it also becomes evident at times that he was more of a practical soldier than a professional historian. Yet he hoped to be able to compare himself with eminent historians of the classical Greece that had existed before Alexander.

There were contemporary testimonies to Arrian's wisdom: he was hailed as a *philosophos*. That is to say, he was considered to be one of the most eminent representatives of an epoch when Greek civilization was believed to be experiencing a kind of revival. Nevertheless, his writings do painfully demonstrate the lack of originality of the literary conceptions of the age, which were all derived from the past. This is illustrated by his literary style. It was admired for its clear language and sound arrangement, which was held to strike a happy medium between exaggerated simplicity and over-ornamentation. Yet, even if this is conceded, it is clear that in most of his works he adhered closely to the language of previous epochs. In particular he employed Xenophon (*c.* 458/7 – *c.* 354 BC) as his model. But whereas in the *Anabasis* Arrian employs an old-fashioned sort of Attic, in the *Indica* he endeavours to reproduce the Ionic dialect of Herodotus (d. before 420 BC). In both cases he avoids using the language of his own day, which evidently was regarded as a laudable achievement. This helps to explain his own boastful assertion that he was a masterly exponent of Greek.

Nevertheless, Arrian does at the same time illustrate the current taste for mitigating attention to the past by exhibiting a concern for the present. In addition to his classic *History of Alexander* he wrote about the *Expedition against the Alans* (*Expeditio contra Alanos*) of which he himself had been in command.

### Ptolemy (Claudius Ptolemaeus)

Ptolemy, Greek astronomer, mathematician, musicologist and geographer, came from Ptolemais Hermiou (El Manshah) in Upper Egypt, and probably lived from *c.* 100 to *c.* 178.[7] He resided at Alexandria.

The most famous of his writings was his astronomical work, the *Mathematical Collection* (*Mathematike Syntaxis*), which was later known as the *Great Astronomer*, and described as *megiste*, 'the Greatest', hence its more generally employed Arabic title, the *Almagest*. It contains thirteen books, of which the first outlines the geocentric system of the universe and rejects the heliocentric theory, which was not revived until the sixteenth century. The *Almagest* is a lucid and well-ordered synthesis, compiled by a practising astronomer who knew how to make good use both of his own observations and of the conclusions reached by other astronomers before him. It rapidly became a standard work. Ptolemy also wrote a number of other monographs on astronomical themes. In addition, he was a geometrician of impressive calibre; and in the field of music his *Harmonica*, in three books, expounds the mathematical theory of harmony. Of his *Optics* we have a substantial part, in a Latin version translated from the Arabic.

Ptolemy's renowned *Guide to Geography*, largely based on the works of an earlier Greek geographer Marinus of Tyre (late first to early second century AD), is divided into seven books. References are given to no less than eight thousand locations, but only a small proportion of these are founded on exact observation. The work contains many fundamental mistakes, including a number of internal contradictions.

Nevertheless, no one in the ancient world ever wrote a more comprehensive geographical survey or one that achieved greater accuracy. In consequence, the work remained canonical until our own times, and is the foundation of modern cartography. This profound influence on later generations is where its importance lies. And yet, taken in their entirety, Ptolemy's geographical studies do not warrant the highest praise. Of the countries that he describes, he gives no special attention to their particular features, their inhabitants, their products, or their climate. Whereas, earlier, Strabo had appreciated the geographical significance of mountain ranges and rivers, Ptolemy is negligent of them, and what he says is not really very useful.

## Herodes Atticus
### (L. Vibullius Hipparchus Ti. Claudius Atticus Herodes)

Herodes Atticus (*c.* AD 101–77) was an Athenian of the deme Marathon, and consul at Rome (143). He was extremely wealthy by inheritance – his father having discovered a treasure – and spent much of his wealth on enormous building projects in Greece and elsewhere (Chapter 7). He deserves his place here because of his literary activity as a sophist (see Polemo, p. 96), which gained him primacy among his contemporaries and comparison with the classics. The teacher of Aelius Aristides, he was the jewel in the crown of Philostratus, who wrote about the sophists in *c.* AD 230.

Unfortunately, however, his reputation has to be taken entirely on trust; apart, perhaps, from a single speech (of questionable attribution), no example of his works has survived. His writings included not only 'discourses' (*dialexeis*) and 'stories' (of one of which a Latin translation is extant) but also diaries and letters. These works reflect the fact that Herodes Atticus owed his reputation both to his expertise in sophistic rhetoric and to awareness of philosophy.

He was a friend of successive emperors. When Hadrian came to the imperial throne, Herodes Atticus – inarticulate 17-year-old student of rhetoric – was dispatched to the Danube camp to congratulate him. Subsequently he grew up to become the tutor of the emperors Marcus Aurelius and Lucius Verus; and Marcus Aurelius always stuck up for him, even in embarrassing moments (such as an unsavoury lawsuit).

Herodes Atticus was one of the most unpopular men of his time. The gateway of his property near Marathon was inscribed 'Gate of Eternal Harmony'. But this Herodes failed to attain. His life was damaged not only by the widespread dislike that he attracted but also by charges of partial responsibility for the death of his wife Annia Regilla (159/60), and by an accusation that he had bribed the archons of Athens (174). The loss of members of his family grieved him. But he was also worried by the stupidity of one of his sons, who could only master the alphabet by having twenty-four slaves, carrying sandwich-boards inscribed by Greek letters, parade repeatedly in front of him.

## Albinus

Albinus, a (Middle) Platonic philosopher, was a pupil of a certain Gaius, an expounder of Plato in the early second century AD. Albinus taught at Smyrna (Izmir), where Galen heard him lecture in AD 151–2. Albinus's work (in Greek), *On Incorporeal Qualities*, perhaps owes its preservation to the belief that it was a work by Galen rather than himself.

Albinus's other extant writings include a brief preface to Plato's writings and a summary of the latter's works, the *Didascalicus* or *Epitome*. His version of Platonism (Middle Platonism), which contributed largely to a Platonic Renaissance, reveals the eclectic tendencies of his time, notably by its incorporation of Stoic and, especially, Peripatetic (Aristotelian) doctrines, and by its dislike of the Scepticism of Pyrrho (d. 275/270 BC).

Albinus is important not only because he led the revival of Platonism in the Antonine period but also because he pointed the way towards the future Neoplatonism of Plotinus, of which much of the raw material (though not the mysticism) is present in his works. This Middle Platonism was, very often, as much a religion as a philosophy. Its principal objective was mastery of the truth about the superhuman, divine universe. As for its adherents, their attitudes exhibited considerable variations. Their approaches could be somewhat emotional and mystical, such as those of Apuleius or Maximus of Tyre (see p. 115). Or they could be less religious and more scholarly, and rational; and that was the viewpoint of men such as Albinus.

## Aristides (Aelius)

Aristides, Greek speech-writer and man of letters, was born in Mysia (north-western Asia Minor) in AD 117, of a landowning family, and died in *c.* 189.[8] He was taught Greek literature by Alexander of Cotiaeum (Kütahya), who was also one of the teachers of Marcus Aurelius, and then he studied rhetoric at Athens under Herodes Atticus (see p. 102), of whom he was the most eminent student. There are signs of oblique criticism of the emperor Hadrian; but not of Marcus Aurelius, whom Aristides met at Smyrna (Izmir) in 176.

Aristides himself had already been active and productive in the 140s. His lecture tours carried him through large regions of the Greek world and then to Rome, where at the age of twenty-six he was struck down by the first of a prolonged series of illnesses. These, probably psychosomatic in character, put an end to his public appearances and caused him to spend much time thereafter as a patient in the Temple of Asclepius (Aesculapius) at Pergamum (Bergama) in his native country. But it was at Smyrna that he passed most of the rest of his life, and its people regarded him as their next most important citizen after Homer (who was believed, doubtfully, to have come from that place).

Throughout this period, lacking the capacity either to teach or to make extempore speeches, Aristides devoted himself to writing orations, of which fifty-five (some in the form of letters) have come down to us. They are composed in the elegant, but somewhat bland, Attic prose of the high Second Sophistic manner (see Polemo, p. 96), of which he was one of the principal exponents. One of the greatest literary hypochondriacs of all time, he wrote six *Sacred Discourses* offering elaborate discussions of the treatment that he had received from Asclepius for the illnesses from which he believed he had been suffering. These descriptions not only are illuminating in regard to the ancient practices of temple medicine but also provide the most comprehensive record of personal religious experiences that has come down to us from any pagan author, combining extreme superstition with inflated personal vanity.

Aristides' important speech *To Rome* (or *The Roman Oration*) – the main basis for history's favourable verdict on the Antonines (Chapter 8) – was delivered in the imperial capital in 143, or not very long afterwards. The speech is a eulogy of Rome (where his Greek friend, Herodes Atticus, was one of the consuls of the year) as seen by a provincial – the only work in which the power and generosity of Rome are systematically expounded by one of the Greeks (who would mostly have agreed with him). The orator praises the blessings of universal peace and free communications, amid which the Greece cities were able to prosper in a mighty world-state. A further oration, *To the Monarch*, which was ascribed to Aristides but subsequently reattributed to the third century instead, has now been reassigned to him, and declared genuine:[9] perhaps it was delivered before Antoninus Pius at Puteoli (Pozzuoli) in 140 or 143. Aristides's *Aegean Sea* gives a vivid picture of his pleasure in the sea and the islands, and of the fishing-boats setting out on their expeditions.

He was also a deeply religious man, as his *Sacred Teaching* (*Hieros Logos*) shows: five of his extant speeches are usually described as 'hymns'.

## Galen (Claudius Galenus)

Galen, Greek physician, psychologist, philosopher and literary critic, was born in *c.* AD 129 and died in *c* 199.[10] His birthplace was Pergamum (Bergama). His mother was said to be a shrew who bit her maids.

Between the ages of 14 and 16 he studied various schools of philosophy: Platonism, Aristotelianism (the Peripatetics), Epicureanism and Stoicism. In 146, however, he began to study medicine, and after two years went to Smyrna (Izmir) to work under the eminent physician Pelops. Then he set out on extensive educational travels in Asia Minor, Greece and Egypt, where he visited the famous medical school at Alexandria. In *c.* 157 he became the gladiators' doctor in his native city, but after four years moved to Rome, where he won a considerable reputation as a physician and gained many distinguished pupils and friends. In 166 he returned to Pergamum.

Three years later he was recalled by the emperor Marcus Aurelius to serve in the German wars. This Galen contrived to avoid, although he did treat Marcus Aurelius himself (Chapter 3), thereby gaining the emperor's warm praise as 'first among physicians and unique among philosophers', and securing the appointment of medical attendant to Aurelius's son and heir, Commodus. Later Marcus Aurelius made him his physician-in-ordinary. Galen was apparently in Sicily at the time of his death.

Galen himself enumerated 153 works which he had written, contained in 504 books. The extant medical works which are attributed to his authorship (complete or surviving in large part) number more than 150. They cover, in their gigantic range, practically all of the specialist fields existing at the time. His anatomical studies were unequalled in the ancient world for their thoroughness and accuracy. His physiological researches were likewise of pioneering character. As an epidemiologist and pathologist and pharmacologist, he also came to original conclusions. His acumen in the field of neurology is particularly impressive. He also left several psychological studies of considerable interest.

He believed that every physician ought to equip himself with an adequate education before he began to study medicine at all. In addition to studies of grammar, rhetoric and comedy, his own bibliography mentions no less than 124 philosophical treatises. Like many of his contemporaries, too, he possessed a firm, deterministic, monotheistic belief in a supreme creator of the entire universe, which earned him enormous later popularity. However, his opinion of both Judaism and Christianity was not high, since he considered that they made too much use of faith instead of reason.

The tone of Galen's writings suggests that he was not an easy person to get on with. He indulges in copious and aggressive vituperation which is directed against men whose opinions and systems have incurred his disapproval. At all times he seems thoroughly pleased with himself. And yet we can see behind the boasts 'a man who was genuinely concerned with imparting knowledge'. He came to be revered for his systematization of much of Greek medical theory, and for his establishment of common concepts of medicine which rise above sectional differences and which provide common ground where all scientists can meet and agree.

## Lucian

Seventy-one prose pieces by Lucian survive; and a mock tragedy (*Podagra*) in iambics and other metres.[11] His prose works comprise four sophistic declamations (*Phalaris* 1 and 2, *Tyrannicide*, *Disinherited*); nine *Protaliai* (addresses: *Dionysus*, *Electrum*, *Harmonides*, *Heracles*, *Herodotus*, *Prometheus in words*, *Scythian*, *Thirsters*, *Zeuxis*); five epideictic pieces or orations for display (*Hippias*, *The House*, *Praise of Fatherland*, *Praise of the Fly*, *Defending a Lapse in Greeting*); seventeen narrative or argumentative pieces in epistolary or pamphlet form; and thirty-six dialogues. On the doubtful authorship of *Onos* (*Lucius*, or *The Ass*), see Apuleius (p. 92).

The two towering Greek writers of the age were Marcus Aurelius and Lucian. As far as we know, they never met. But, if they had, how they would have disliked one another! Lucian would have considered Aurelius over-solemn and humourless, while Aurelius would have thought that Lucian (who was likewise content to remain undecided about life, but in quite a different way) was flippant, cynical, satirical, and careless of his social duty.

Lucian was born at Samosata (Samsat) (*c.* AD 120 or 125?), which had formerly been the capital of Commagene on the Euphrates, in an area where the Semitic language, Aramaic, was the popular tongue and Greek the language of its more cultured inhabitants. His family was of limited means. He was apprenticed to an uncle, but probably went to Ionia (in western Asia Minor) for his higher rhetorical education.

We are left in the dark about a great deal, however. It is sad that a writer so eloquent on the subject of his contemporaries should tell us so little about himself, and that when he does so it is often in a way that makes biographical fact hard to distinguish from fictional posture. The only contemporary mention of him, recently noticed in an Arabic translation of a work by Galen, is a valuable indication of Lucian's delight in debunking. We are told that he 'discovered' a writing of the philosopher Heraclitus – and only revealed that it was a fake, after all, when an eminent philosopher had been persuaded to furnish the work with an erudite commentary!

Lucian says that he had a dream of a 'choice of Heracles' between the ladies Education (*Paideia*) and Sculpture, just at the moment when his family were trying to choose his career. This, however, is not authentic, but merely a piece of learned invention to entertain his fellow-citizens when he came back home a distinguished man and delivered *The Dream* (*Enhupnion*) at Samosata. The report that he was a barrister at Antioch may be correct, but this could, alternatively, be a misunderstanding of Lucian's own allusion to abandoning a career in the law courts. He very probably delivered sophistic declamations, though whether he actually practised as a sophist remains equally uncertain.

However, in his other major work which contains autobiographical features, *Twice Prosecuted*, Lucian states that the dreamed promises of Education were realized when he took up Dialogue.[12] We are told that Rhetoric, in prosecuting her now renegade disciple, complains that she found Lucian at a loose end in Ionia, gave him training and embarked him on a successful series of enterprises which moved him from Ionia and Greece to Italy and even Gaul. Elsewhere Lucian claims that he did well as a sophist in Gaul, but this must remain dubious, since Philostratus, in his *Lives of the Sophists*, says nothing about any such phase.

If *Twice Prosecuted* were to be accepted literally, Lucian abandoned Rhetoric at the age of forty and took up with Dialogue, the second of his 'prosecutors'. But the age of forty is proverbial for maturity, and reappears in the *Hermotimus* (*c.* 165) as the age of Lycinus (Lucian's spokesman), who is described as a man who mocked philosophers. Lucian's own attachment to serious philosophy cannot have lasted very long; indeed, more probably, it never existed at all. He is scathing about conflicting philosophical doctrines. Although he did not object to Epicurus (*c.* 341–270 BC), he particularly disliked the Stoics. However, Platonic dialogue provides the pattern for more than half of his major works, and the 'diatribes' of the Cynic school, which was founded by Diogenes of Sinope (*c.* 400–*c.* 325 BC; see p. 112), also play a part. The *Nigrinus*, a dialogue in which Lucian describes how the (Middle) Platonist of that name persuaded him of the pointlessness of ordinary ambition and the rewards of plain, honest goodness, is the nearest approach that Lucian makes to serious philosophy. Probably he tackled the theme under the influence of some impressive philosophical personality (perhaps Albinus:

see p. 103). He sees Herodotus as a compulsive liar, in a tradition inaugurated by Homer's Odysseus.

In most of the dialogues of which Lucian's authorship is certain, he commits the very offences of which Dialogue accuses him: 'He took from me that tragic, restrained mask and made me put on another which was comic and satyric and all but ridiculous.' The trips to heaven and Hades which he describes offer ample opportunities for these humorous qualities. We may reasonably doubt that Lucian's exploitation of the dialogue form began with a new life at forty. 'He gathered his roses where he could': thus, in addition to the Cynic diatribe which was just mentioned (and which produced the satire of Menippus of Gadara [Umm Keis; early third century BC] – 'a dog with quite a bite, it turns out, as well as a bark'), the Old Comedy of the fifth century BC must also (as Lucian himself claimed) be partially credited with his mixture of keen questioning, humorous exposure and vigorous though never vulgar abuse.

These qualities are strongly to the fore in his attack on imposters in the *Parrhesiades* (Mr Frank) and in his denunciations of *Peregrinus* (*c.* 165) and *Alexander* (of Abonuteichus; Ionopolis, Inebolu). Peregrinus of Parium (Kemer) was a Cynic who burned himself on a pyre at the Olympic Games. In the *Alexander* Lucian tells how Peregrinus greeted Alexander, not by kissing his hand but by biting it, whereupon Alexander plotted unsuccessfully to have Peregrinus drowned at sea. Lucian also gives an account of the various hoaxes by which Alexander, in his view, was fraudulently amassing wealth as a seer and a priest of Asclepius (Aesculapius); though the question has been raised of whether Alexander was, in fact, a deceiver or sincere.

Lucian's attitude to all religions is satirical (see p. 124f. regarding what he had to say about the Christians).

Paganism does not emerge any better: Lucian fully shares the current view that the oracles, and with them the Olympian gods, had been discredited.

Most of Lucian's writings cannot be dated. However, some works, besides the *Hermotimus* and *Peregrinus*, can be grouped together and attributed to the 160s. Thus two dialogues, *Twice Prosecuted* and *The Ship*, are plausibly associated with Lucius Verus's presence at Antioch in the period 163–6. There is also evidence that Lucian attended the Olympic Games in 165.

In the 170s he accepted a post on the staff of the prefect of Egypt, which was a step towards a professional career. This was in spite of his earlier satirical dismissal of such jobs as a prostitution of professional talents. However, as far as we can tell, he did not pursue public office any further. Our last fixed point is the reference in the *Alexander* to the emperor Marcus Aurelius as divine (i.e. dead),[13] showing that this scurrilous biography was not published until after 180: even if it may be suspected that it was composed nearer 170, when Aurelius was still alive. Lucian was not an admirer of Rome. But he was not anti-Roman either, although he displays signs of the conscious opposition to Romanization that Greek intellectuals were showing (Chapter 8).

Lucian made known his satirical dialogues by apparently following the pattern that was established for the display rhetoric of travelling adherents of the Second Sophistic (see Polemo, p. 96). He clearly achieved fame, and acquired some important friends, and the works that he delivered must soon have been circulated in book form.

Many of his writings transform the conventional, short treatise into epistolary or near-epistolary form, in order to launch a series of amusing onslaughts (making fun, for example, of the manners of parvenus, and of superstitious beliefs) which might equally well have been handled in dialogues. The contents of the dialogues themselves vary between amusing and comparatively harmless caricatures of various philosophical schools to the remorseless torpedoing of other human aspirations. Freedom of speech, and of behaviour, is the only virtue that Lucian respects. Although some of his writing is not satirical at all, his principal image is that of a satirist. But his primary purpose is to entertain and, like more conventional sophists, he must have done so as much by the techniques of his orations as by their contents.

Lucian's inexhaustible inventive genius is nowhere more striking than in the *True History*. This parody of a traveller's tale, which extends over two books, derived much of its impact from its clever development of themes from older narratives which were familiar to everybody. Much of the fantasy, however, is recognizably Lucianic. Even without its parodies of past writings, *True History* is a masterly piece of funny, imaginative story-telling. This capacity for telling stories forms a significant part of Lucian's literary personality as a writer.

He was a literary artist, and literary critic, with a light and delicate touch, a ready wit, and a versatile range. He appeals usually, perhaps, to the less reflective side of human nature, but does so with a keen sensitivity towards his readership and audience.

His own generation, and those that immediately followed, say little or nothing about his works. But they enjoyed enormous influence, for instance, during the equally zestful Renaissance, when they were widely read in a Latin translation and were admired by Ben Jonson and Dryden. Nowadays, once again, they are not extensively known, being neglected in schools, for example, because their Greek is considered 'too late'. That deserves to be rectified, if only because of Lucian's fearless sponsorship of commonsense at a time when it was not all that common. Even in translation the quality of his writings is sufficiently perceptible to make them classics of European literature.

Lucian thought of himself as a Syrian: was he Semitic? At all events he was 'an Asiatic who out-Greeked the Greeks', and Syria, in his day, had been Hellenized for a very long time. Although 'he learnt his Greek at school, and it has the curious purity of the kind of French that used to be spoken by educated people in the Balkans, a beautiful and sinuous, but slightly refined, unidiomatic language',[14] his dialect is not as much affected as that of a cultured Syrian of his time; and his style is not merely borrowed, but truly original.

When he seems to be pedantically sophistic, he is probably making a joke; and his apparent simplicities bear watching, because they contain shafts which are as sharp as the sting of a wasp. Translators, in particular, have to take care, because Lucian is never quite as obvious as he may at first appear to be. On the contrary, no one ever exceeded him in the use of rhetoric (and sophistry) as entertainment.

Today the perennial argument about Lucian is whether he was a continuous and true observer of his own times or a throw-back who took refuge in the past, and concentrated his utterances on its study. Certainly he did the latter, including as much material from bygone ages as he could; even if his contemporary influence remained incidental and peripheral, he wanted such readers and listeners as he could mobilize to join the affirmation of their past inheritance. His passion for Greece and the classics is genuine and obsessive; he revered the lost greatness of Greek literature.

Yet, he was also very much of his own age, an age which existed in its own right and of which he was a citizen. 'He is not', writes Peter Levi,[15] 'living in the twilight of the west where the bat cries to the owl, nor in a mellow after-glow invented by Gibbon.' Moreover, within this epoch of his own, he shrewdly characterized not only timeless stereotypes but also contemporary individuals. However, he hated the religiosity and philosophical posturing and hysterical obscurantism that he felt was engulfing his world.

What had he to offer in exchange? That, perhaps, is the only potent criticism that can be launched against Lucian: he was predominantly negative.

## Marcus Aurelius

Against the ills and anxieties of the age, the remedy of novelists such as Apuleius was to note their existence obliquely and to ride triumphantly over them in the imagination; the remedy of Lucian was to make fun of them. For the emperor Marcus Aurelius (121–80),[16] on the other hand, as we saw in Chapters 2 and 3, the remedy was to do all in his power to put them right, with utter conscientiousness.

Marcus Aurelius had once intended to write a *History of the Greeks and Romans*,[17] but the project, if it ever materialized, did not prove significant.

The dramatically intimate disclosures of his deepest thoughts and the admonitions to himself (perhaps written down in odd moments of leisure, unless the passages that we have are the scattered elements of a lost, coherent original or of what was intended to become one) were entitled by editors 'his writings to himself' and were later called his *Meditations*. They comprise the most famous book ever written by a monarch.

The *Meditations* have a literary cast, because Marcus Aurelius had a literary training, but they were private notebooks not designed for publication (cf. above): a cross, perhaps, between a diary and a commonplace book. Nor do the *Meditations* form a connected unity. Even if they are, for the most part, in chronological order, there is a case for putting Book I at the end.

The *Meditations* are a work of self-consolation and self-encouragement, an unparalleled self-scrutiny, each separate passage reflecting its own mood, hardly to be defined as philosophy, but a sort of personal creed, sometimes poetically expressed. The unpretentious and mundane letters which Marcus Aurelius had written to his friend and tutor Fronto (see p. 84) contain his thoughts from the age of seventeen. The *Meditations* take up the story, with greater profundity, during the last ten or fifteen years of the emperor's life. The intensity of their imagery (resulting from the wars in which Marcus Aurelius was engaged, although they are only once mentioned in the *Meditations*) seem to have become increasingly bleak and gloomy. There is much reference to age and death, and it is ironical to recall that Fronto had once urged him: 'Smile and be happy all your life.'[18]

Marcus Aurelius wrote in Greek, which was not his mother-tongue. Perhaps he felt that he needed its technical terms. He was writing at a time when bilinguality was becoming unusual, even though the interests of the Greek and Roman cultures were tending to converge, as the eastern provinces more and more asserted themselves (Chapter 8). His Greek was not incoherent or ungrammatical, but it shows a certain inelegance and awkwardness, betraying a sense of effort which occasionally reveals itself in an uncommon phrase.

Nevertheless, his writings convey the difficulty of moral and social effort with a more comprehensible urgency than had ever been used before to clothe such ideas. This, in terms of decent behaviour, is the climax of ancient Rome. But it is an austere creed, without consolations except its own performance. Man must just strive onward, and continue his unremittingly laborious efforts as best he can. When Marcus Aurelius gratefully praises his predecessor and adoptive father Antoninus Pius, what emerges is the patient, long-suffering endurance of Antoninus. The central, practical point of Marcus Aurelius's demands upon himself and others is the same: turn inward and strengthen yourself, find the courage to complete your job (his was almost intolerably burdensome). Life is short, he says, and all that is required is that you should think and act responsibly and unselfishly, 'like a Roman and like a man . . . always adhering to strict Reason'.[19]

Here Marcus Aurelius was echoing Greek philosophy. Perhaps as a boy he may have been attracted to the Cynic school (founded by Diogenes of Sinope, *c.* 400–*c.* 325 BC), which preached the gospel of simplicity and independence, and comforted many in troubled times by demonstrating that a person who needs next to nothing and keeps aloof from all entanglements can live happily when all around him is disordered.

But Antoninus Pius brought the Stoic Apollonius to Rome to teach Marcus Aurelius, and he was definitively converted to Stoicism by Quintus Junius Rusticus, a descendant of the Domitianic martyr Quintus Junius Arulenus Rusticus (died *c.* AD 93). Stoic, of a kind, Marcus Aurelius remained, but the nature of his Stoicism has been open to debate. Galen described him as 'the most scientific of the Stoics', and in modern times he has sometimes been called the greatest of them – or the last; he certainly did much to maintain Stoicism as a living force in subsequent centuries. But his *Meditations* show him to have been a very selective, eclectic sort of Stoic; indeed, that is what he had to be, since he was also the emperor of Rome. What he liked about Stoicism, surely, was that it strengthened and nerved him to perform that task.

'Only seek', he said, 'in each passing action a conformity with nature.'[20] That is Stoic doctrine. Conformity with nature (as well as with the divinity inside oneself) is an ideal which goes back to Zeno of Citium (Larnaca) in Cyprus, the founder of Stoicism in *c.* 300 BC. 'Nature' is the providential deity that governs the universe. According to the Stoics, drawing in part upon the idealism of Plato, a spark of that divinity is present in each of us. Such is the religion of Marcus Aurelius, who would have liked, perhaps, to adhere to some religious faith, but there was no acceptable one at hand. 'This intelligence in every man is God, an emanation from deity. . . . To be a philosopher is to keep unsullied, unscathed, the divine spirit within oneself.'[21]

Marcus Aurelius was also a pious worshipper of the Roman gods, because such ritual was necessary for the survival of the state and the cohesion of its people. But he saw these divine powers as aspects of a universal deity. He himself believed, like the Stoics before him, that this deity is immanent in the world in such a way that it and the world make a single whole, like the soul and the body. That is why man must be true to himself – to the highest part of himself, the heavenly force which has lodged this spark in his soul. Call this god or gods, it does not matter. Occasionally, twice for example when he was giddy or spitting blood, Marcus Aurelius felt their strength help him. 'It is experience which proves their power every day, and therefore I am satisfied that they exist, and I do them reverence.'[22]

Accordingly Marcus Aurelius believed that there was something infinite in human experience itself. His is a more sombre version of the joyful resignation to transcendent Divine Providence which had been the creed of that other Stoic missionary and physician of the soul, the Phrygian slave Epictetus (died *c.* AD 135). Marcus Aurelius, introduced to Epictetus by Quintus Junius Rusticus, owed a very great deal to him (much more than he owed, for example, to Seneca, for whom like Fronto he did not care). Aurelius was more gloomy than Epictetus, but both stressed the utter instability of the human condition, and Epictetus's lectures (*Diatribes*) were Marcus Aurelius's favourite book, and quoted by him more often than any other writing.[23]

On the other hand he owed nothing to the hopes of salvation that were conferred by a host of contemporary religions and were referred to by many contemporary paintings (Chapter 7). He did not share those hopes. Death, to him, is an unanswerable riddle; it is impossible to see where any consolation or remedy for it can be found. And yet, failing in health and facing the enemy, Marcus writes and thinks often of dying, and advises that each day should be lived as if it were your last.[24] He needed all of his Stoicism to prevent such thoughts from overcoming him. Nor, even if the divine power occasionally seems present, did there appear to be any hope of influencing it by prayer.

For these reasons, the *Meditations* have been called the saddest of all books. Dedicated but far from optimistic, their writer looks for heavenly guidance but is only rarely conscious of receiving it, and tries to do his best though more than doubtful of a reward in the hereafter, let alone in this world.

He was not a free-thinker (there were none) or an unbeliever or, according to the modern atheistic use of the word, a humanist. But Marcus Aurelius did not share the irrational, unprovable assumption, common to all major religions, that the supra-sensible can be influenced by the activities of man. The rhythm of the universe is monotonous, meaningless and predestined. 'Whatever may happen to you was prepared for you in advance from the beginning of time. In the woven tapestry of causation, the thread of your being had been intertwined from all time with that particular incident.'[25]

Nevertheless, he believed that very much still *does* lie within our power, and inside the bounds of our own strength and capabilities. Although much is predestined, much else is determinable by our own will. So the prime duty of the soul is to realize its moral perfectibility by arduous discipline. Even if there are no posthumous rewards, men are capable of behaving well. And indeed, because of the divine spark which they share, it is natural and right for them to do so.

For Marcus Aurelius there were no oriental sensualities, but a rigorous asceticism which was typical of the age. He questioned the classical principle of a link between physical and moral beauty, and nowhere can one find a more relentlessly destructive analysis of the pleasures of eye, ear, food and sex. The last password of Antoninus Pius had been Equanimity. To guide one's will successfully through the batteries of Fortune is possible only by avoiding what are supposed to be pleasures, and indeed by maintaining absolute calm. 'Never flustered, never apathetic, never attitudinizing – here is the perfection of character.'[26]

These ideals, and Marcus Aurelius's manful endeavours to live up to them, are more noteworthy because he had to fight continuously, with melancholy resignation, against tortured convictions of his own personal shortcomings and those of the entire world. In such a fog and filth, what can be respected and pursued with enthusiasm he often no longer knows. Hellenism's bright incentives encouraging material achievement have now been left behind. True, man remains the measure, since he must and can forge ahead. He is still to that extent captain of his own spirit, but with no sunny, classical sense of unlimited power. Not only is life disgusting, but it is also transient.[27] Marcus Aurelius saw life as a temporary visit to an alien land.

So what can be done except to withdraw into one's own resources and draw strength from the inner life, that little domain that is the self? Therein is the only chance of a more reassuring reality. Preoccupied with this introversion in a transitional age – 'had he lived a century or two later, he doubtless would have ended his days in a monastery' – Marcus Aurelius felt that you should 'leave another's wrongdoing where it lies'.[28] Such a suggestion has been criticized for carrying tolerance to the point of becoming anti-social, but that is not his intention. On the contrary, 'men exist for each other. Then either improve them, or put up with them.'[29] However difficult this may be, we must be kind to our fellowmen and tolerant of their faults. Not to work with other men is against nature.

The exceptional significance of the *Meditations* of Marcus Aurelius lies in the lofty standard which he undogmatically proposed and attained without the insistent prompting of any personal kind of religious inspiration or encouragement. Because he believed that there are things in life which we can change, human life, to him, has a meaning. It is up to us to realize all of our potential worth and dignity. Marcus Aurelius, as seen in his *Meditations*, is the noblest of all the men who, by sheer intelligence and force of character, have prized and achieved goodness for its own sake and not for any reward.

## Maximus of Tyre

Maximus (*c.* AD 125–85) was a rhetorician who lived the life of a travelling lecturer. Athens was one of the cities in which he lectured, but some of his forty-one surviving lectures (*dialexeis*) were delivered at Rome towards the end of his life.

Maximus was keen on Homer, but called himself a Platonist, and together with Albinus (see p. 103) played a leading part in Middle Platonism. Although he was not unacquainted with Greek literature in general, his lectures in that language do not display any philosophical originality. They are simply well-expressed, though not unaffected, exhortations to virtue laced with ample quotations, placing philosophy in a sophistic mould. Numbers 18–21 of his lectures are collectively entitled *What was Socrates's Art of Love?* Maximus had much in common with the sophists of the Second Sophistic (see Polemo, p. 96), although he claimed to be more of a philosopher than most of them were.

As for his self-proclaimed philosophy, although quotations from Plato predominate, it nevertheless exemplifies the manner in which the frontiers between the different systems were becoming blurred in his time. Maximus was able to adjust his (Middle) Platonism to almost every other philosophical school (with the exception of that of Epicurus). Nor was he wholly averse to demonism, despite his overall belief in the transcendence of divinity.

His *dialexeis* were mainly written on trite and popular themes, and they were designed to achieve an interesting and successful impact, easy on the ear and mind alike. However Maximus, although he knew the raw materials about which he was speaking, is an expounder rather than a thinker, and does not seem to us to be very inspiring or very inspired. He is perhaps at his most interesting when he suggests how to distinguish a flatterer from a true friend, quoting his own profession as an example. 'Even the fake informer', he says,[30] 'flatters the rhetor, setting word against word, and putting up a fortification of justice against injustice, and evil against good. And the sophist flatters the philosopher: he is the most accomplished flatterer of all.'

### Hermogenes of Tarsus

Hermogenes was born *c.* 160 and admired (at the age of fifteen) by Marcus Aurelius, probably when the emperor was in the east after the revolt of Avidius Cassius. He failed to fulfil his early promise as an orator, but started quite early to write a set of rhetorical textbooks which were widely employed and annotated in the Byzantine epoch (as, also, in the later Renaissance), giving rise to *Commentaries on Hermogenes* which amount to an entire literature in themselves.

Although some of the works that have been ascribed to him are of (more than) doubtful authenticity, we have two writings that are certainly his: *On Issues* and *On Types of Style*. The former deals with kinds of argument to be used, particularly for the defence. The latter offers a systematic treatment of the forms and medium of speech, and lists seven qualities of style, all of which contributed to the unique forcefulness and variety of Demosthenes (384–322 BC).

Hermogenes' classification is not original, and does not constitute worthwhile literary criticism. Yet he offers quite a sensible (though sometimes too discursive) analysis, inserting subdivisions and distinguishing between the styles of different authors with some subtlety. He was the most important writer of imperial times in the field of rhetorical theory. Despite his lack of originality, he held certain strong views of his own, castigating the style of Isocrates (436–338 BC), for example, as senile and pedantic. Hermogenes was ready to include speakers of his own second century AD among the models for imitation.

### Pausanias

Pausanias was a Greek travel writer who wrote in the latter part of the second century AD.[31] He came from somewhere near Magnesia (Manisa) beside Mount Sipylus in Lydia (western Asia Minor).

He is the author of a *Description (Periegesis) of Greece*, in ten books, which seems to have taken about a decade and a half to complete. His descriptions of religious buildings and works of art are still indispensable today. During his travels, Pausanias utilized the service of guides (*exegetai*) and was able to observe personally many of the places that he describes (and admires; for example, the buildings of Herodes Atticus at Athens), though inaccuracies creep in. To call him 'the Baedeker of Antiquity', as has sometimes been done, is misleading, since he is writing not for travellers but for readers. His style remains almost wholly without distinction, but the book is extremely well adapted to the requirements of the armchair tourist, who will be further pleased because Pausanias airs few personal prejudices about politics or philosophy. And indeed he has been continually used throughout the ages.

The profoundest interest of Pausanias was in the local cults and traditions and legends of various parts of Greece. He was a religious man, and a believer in the most deeply revered of these religious institutions. Moreover, although prepared (like so many of his contemporaries) to accept warnings that were supposed to come from dreams, he possessed the capacity to offer sophisticated philosophical solutions of the problems that these institutions offered.

Indeed, it has been suggested that the entire range of his curiosity, which expressed itself in scholarly topographical and encyclopaedic descriptions, was founded upon a more profound obsession, which had its origin in religious terms and preoccupations. He was aware that the ancient religion had crumbled, and he felt that some even graver crumbling was involved and was taking place. Had he not been obsessed by this deep-rooted anxiety, the archaeology to which his patient and erudite journeying contributed so much would have suffered significantly.

## Iamblichus

Iamblichus was a writer of Syrian origin who wrote in the reign of Marcus Aurelius, and perhaps later under Commodus. Although his mother tongue was Aramaic, he wrote in Greek, showing familiarity with the canons of the Second Sophistic (see Polemo, p. 96). He was said to have predicted Lucius Verus's victories against the Parthians.

Iamblichus was the author of a novel entitled *Babyloniaca* or *Rhodanes and Sinonis*. The work is lost, but an epitome or abstract of its contents was made by Photius.[32] This, and a few fragments presented by the lexicon known as the *Suda* (or *Suidas*), suggest that the story incorporated all of the customary ingredients of the Greek romantic novel (although a more astringent type also existed, see p. 93): a pair of lovers (already married, in this case) are separated by events, and after suffering numerous adventures are finally reunited.

The somewhat disjointed plot seems to have contained an even richer crop of exciting happenings – persecutions, bloodthirsty deeds, mistaken identities, a man-eating robber, and a good deal about ghostliness and sorcery – than most extant Greek novels provide. There are also short stories. The couple, Rhodanes and Sinonis, flee from the salacious Babylonian monarch Garmis in a series of melodramatic incidents. They are estranged from one another, temporarily, by the jealousy of Sinonis, after Rhodanes has rewarded the kindness of a country girl with a kiss. They are brought together again only when Garmis dispatches Rhodanes as commander-in-chief against the Syrian king whom Sinonis has permitted herself to wed out of pique. Thereupon Rhodanes wins the war and becomes king of Babylonia – and wins back Sinonis.

The setting of the novel, therefore, is Mesopotamia, before Persian times; Iamblichus seems to know quite a lot about eastern lore, as he reveals by digressions on various customs. His characterization, however, was apparently not very strong.

## Achilles Tatius

Achilles Tatius was a Greek novelist from Alexandria, who lived and wrote, as papyrus discoveries have now shown, in the second century AD – probably during its last quarter – and not several hundred years later as had hitherto been believed.[33] About his life nothing is known.

His chief extant work, *Leucippe and Clitophon*, in eight books, is a romance of love and adventure told in the first person by Clitophon himself. It contains many melodramatic happenings, including the customary disasters and frustrations of true love, which are described in breathless succession.

A series of blatant exaggerations makes it possible that Achilles Tatius is not entirely serious, but is making fun of well-worn themes. Clitophon's willingness, in the absence of Leucippe, to go to bed with another woman (admittedly under coercion) seems to show a new, ironical tolerance of human weakness, implying criticism of impossibly high standards of sexual restraint. Towards the sufferings of love, Achilles Tatius is unusually sympathetic.

For the most part, blind Fortune is more prominent in his fiction than religious intervention. Yet, like contemporary Platonists, Achilles Tatius compared the amorous passion with religious Mysteries: Serapis, one of the gods of his native country in whose honour such mysteries were celebrated, plays an important part in the work. Achilles Tatius is a writer who loves marvels, and he devotes all of the inquisitive, encyclopaedic credulity of his age to building up digressions on a great variety of curious subjects. But the possibility that he is not wholly serious has been mentioned; and he mocks the current taste for imaginative anthropology. Furthermore, although his main story, for all its exuberance, is told lucidly enough, with characters more human than in previous Greek novels, the language, when not pseudo-naïve, is sometimes artificial to a degree that may well have been found laughable.

Achilles Tatius's *Leucippe and Clitophon* was much read and imitated in Byzantine times; he was said to have become a Christian and a bishop. Translations of the work influenced the development of the European novel.

## Pollux (Julius)

Pollux, of Naucratis (Kom Gieif) in Egypt, was a rhetorician who became professor of his subject at Athens (not before 178), and his ten-book *Onomasticon* was composed in the lifetime of Commodus, to whom forewords of each of its books are dedicated. The work (like his others) does not exist in its original form; but extant manuscripts are derived from four imperfect copies of an early epitome.

The *Onomasticon* bears some resemblance to a rhetorical handbook. However, although it is principally concerned with the collection and definition of terms rather than with other sorts of information, a wider interest is denoted by citations from literature and by discussions of music and the theatre. Besides these, the subjects of Pollux include religion, ethics, the sciences, war, human anatomy, law, trade, houses, ships, cookery, agriculture, arts and crafts, and children's games. Special attention has focused on his treatment of the Athenian constitution and of Greek serfs, 'between free and slaves'.[34]

# CHRISTIAN

## Justin (Saint Justin Martyr)

One of the earliest Christian 'Apologists', and the most voluminous of them, was the Greek-speaking Justin, later known as Saint Justin Martyr, who was writing at a time when Christianity was beginning to assert itself as a religious and cultural force in the empire (Chapter 3).[1]

Born in *c.* AD 100 of pagan parentage, Justin died between 163 and 167. His birthplace was Flavia Neapolis (Nablus on the west bank of the Jordan). After wandering from place to place and familiarizing himself with the various philosophical schools that he encountered – Stoics first, Aristotelians (Peripatetics), Pythagoreans, and finally Platonists – he concluded that they were all unsatisfactory. Then, after meeting by chance an elderly Christian at Ephesus (Selçuk), he became a convert to that faith. He was inspired by the courage that had been shown by its martyrs, whose sufferings and supposedly miraculous acts attracted the widest attention, and he identified Christ with the highest Reason.

Justin continued his travels, with his philosopher's cloak on his back, and during the reign of Antoninus Pius moved to Rome, where he lectured to small classes on Christian themes. Thereafter, he directly addressed Marcus Aurelius (and Commodus), offering a prayer for imperial power. However, a denunciation of his other proceedings reached the authorities: it was said to have come from an adherent of the Cynic school named Crescentius, who disapproved of his teaching. Justin was arrested and executed. This is recorded in the *Acts* of his martyrdom, the earliest authentic document in this category.

His surviving works include two *Defences* (*Apologiae*), nominally addressed to the emperor but aimed at a wider public. The first was composed in Rome in *c.* 155. It begins by defending his fellow-Christians against the current charges of atheism and disloyalty to the Roman state. In the course of these arguments, the author presents a positive justification of his faith, paying special attention to rituals of worship and providing the fullest accounts of baptism and Sunday services and the Eucharist that we possess from this period. Justin takes a relatively hopeful view of relations between state and church (unlike, for example, some of the Judaeo-Christian *Sibylline Oracles*, Chapter 8). His *Second Apologia*, a kind of postscript to the first, cites the recent trials and executions of three Christians by the prefect of Rome under Marcus Aurelius (Chapter 3), arguing that the prosecutors themselves proved the innocence of their victims.

The *Dialogue with Trypho*, whether based on an actual discussion or not, purports to provide an account of Justin's conversation (over a period of two days) with an erudite Jew, and is valuable as the first known example

119

of anti-Jewish theological argument by a Christian. The *Dialogue* is also significant because it recognizes Greek philosophy, and especially Platonism, as a preparation for the truths of the Christian religion; Justin was the first in the long line of those who sought to harmonize and reconcile the two ways of thinking.

Although Justin was a poor writer, a confused thinker, and no philosopher, and was very imperfectly abreast of the culture of his age, he was trained in logical exposition, and his extensive works give a good picture of the attitude of second-century Christians towards their opponents. His life and thought reveal the interest which Christianity was beginning to arouse among educated people in the eastern portion of the empire in the time of the Antonine emperors.

### Differing viewpoints

In *c.* 165 Justin's pupil **Tatian 'the Syrian'** (although he really came from Assyria) wrote an *Address to the Greeks*, whom he disliked, though he knew the arts of Greek rhetoric.

**Melito of Sardes** (Sart), who died *c.* 190, was a Christian who was full of praises for the imperial regime. He addressed to Aurelius a defence of Christianity (of which fragments survive), declaring as providential the coincidence of Christ's birth with the *Pax Romana* of Augustus.

**Athenagoras of Athens**, too, wrote in Atticizing Greek (?*c.* 177), with some pretensions to literary style, in order to disprove current calumnies against the Christians. As far as we know, he was the first Christian to have distinguished (too simply) between 'bad' emperors, who persecuted Christianity, and 'good' emperors, who did not.

A few years later **Theophilus of Antioch**, in his *Ad Autolycum*, wrote the longest and most ambitious of second-century Apologies. Meanwhile the ex-Stoic **Pantaenus** was founding his Christian school at Alexandria, which tried to improve on the simple programme of Justin.

There were also the **Montanists**, a prophetic movement which emerged in Phrygia in AD 171–2. Montanus and two female prophets proclaimed the approaching New Jerusalem, stressing the glory of ritual purity and martyrdom, and freedom from the encumbrances of daily life. The movement was strongly opposed by the Christian bishops of Asia Minor, but it spread widely there and in many other lands. Its popularity indicates how the apparent silence of the rustic near east in the Antonine age was often underlaid by apocalyptic desires and hopes.

### Gnosticism

The Gnostic Christian writers, 'heretics', also produced notable and enthusiastic personalities. The Gnostics deserve eternal fame because of their consideration of the problem of evil. Epicurus had restated what became the Gnostic problem in timeless terms: is the divine power impotent or malevolent? If neither, where does evil come from? In later Greek and Roman times the dilemma was restated in the terms of the two powers, of good and evil. Within this dualist framework the restatement assumed a thousand different forms, which added up to dualist Gnosticism, a dominant religion of the age. It was stimulated by the manifest failures that were to be seen all around. Marcus Aurelius stressed the precarious nature of the human condition; other writers described it as a horror. They all saw that not only good but also evil prevailed: and explained this by distinguishing between a Divine Being (Unknowable) and a derivative Demiurge, who created the imperfect world.

Throughout this variety of dualist ideas ran the general hypothesis that the world, brought into being by this evil power, must be condemned, and that human beings, to escape the imprisoning vileness of the body, must purge the degrading elements within them. That is to say, the purpose of all of these doctrines was to rescue and raise up beings who are good but fallen, the world around us being an evil prison from which it is necessary to escape.

How was this to be done? How could the element of spirit be saved from the evil material body? Escape can be achieved only by *Gnosis*, knowledge. But this is not the sort of knowledge which most men and women would define by that word. It is neither science nor commonsense: it is irrational. Lucian deplored the ever-increasing irrationality of the times (see p. 108), but he was fighting a losing battle. Daylight reality was no longer to be trusted. This *Gnosis*, this 'knowledge' of the secrets of the universe − which gave its recipients special privileges not only here but also hereafter − is nothing that intellectuals would recognize: it requires piety, conferring a special sort of vision. This is the illumination that comes not from dialectical struggling but from proclaimed revelation. What reasoning was to the philosophers, revelation, intuition of the mystery of the self, was to the dualists.

Nevertheless the Gnostics, even though not working on the basis of philosophical reason, were not afraid to incorporate concepts from Platonism, Zoroastrianism and Mithraism. Many of them, too, drew heavily upon Christianity, and believed themselves to be Christians: much better Christians than anyone else, because evil seemed to be a problem which they alone, among all of the adherents of Christianity, had contrived to solve.

One celebrated Gnostic was **Basilides**, who was probably a pupil of a certain Menander at Antioch and taught at Alexandria in the time of Hadrian and Antoninus Pius. He was variously held to have received secret instruction from Glaucias, an interpreter of St Peter, or from St Matthew. Basilides wrote a *Gospel* and a lengthy comment on its contents, entitled the *Exegetica*, as well as psalms and odes. Since these writings have not survived, it is not possible, any longer, to gain a clear idea of his doctrine. It would appear that Basilides was a Gnostic teacher in Alexandria during the years following 130. He and his successors, in spite of their invention and deification of the mystic prophet Abrasax (Abraxas; called upon in many pagan papyri), stood somewhat closer than other Gnostics to orthodox Christianity. However, their views continued to deviate from it, especially as their teaching tended to be 'docetic', that is, to involve denials of the humanity of Christ upon earth.

Another eminent and influential Gnostic was **Valentinus**, who was born in *c.* 100. Originating from the Nile delta, he received a Greek, Platonic education in Alexandria, where he became a Christian and a religious teacher. He went to Rome in *c.* 136–*c.* 140, and left in the 150s or 160s, possibly for Egypt. He was at first a member of the Christian church at Rome and a candidate for its vacant bishopric. When this went to someone else he broke with the church, and was excommunicated at Rome. He founded the most frequented, profound and influential Gnostic church of the second century. It was during his stay in Rome, or perhaps rather later, that he wrote, or more probably inspired, the meditation entitled *The Gospel of Truth*. Valentinus was motivated either by an early current of Gnosticism or by coming into touch, at a later date, with one of its existing forms.

The dualism of Valentinus, although complicated and scholarly, was daringly speculative. It had a psychological, indeed almost psychoanalytical, freshness and originality of its own. In his world-order Jesus played a part but was little more than an incident. Evil had originated, he maintained, when the Fall took place, before human beings existed; it was a Fall of Wisdom (Sophia). (The *Poimandres*, doubtfully attributed to Valentinus, stresses instead that it was man who had fallen.) The theme of *The Gospel of Truth* is humanity's deliverance from its plight.

Another of the most influential of all of the Gnostics was **Marcion**. Born in *c.* AD 85, the son of the Christian bishop of Sinope (Sinop) on the Black Sea, he was a rich shipowner and businessman whose operations carried him all round the Mediterranean. Quite early, however, he quarrelled with the churches of Asia Minor, suffered violent attacks from Polycarp of Smyrna (Izmir; Chapter 3) as the 'first-born of Satan', and departed from his own country in order to go to Rome. There he was at first accepted by the Christian community, to which he presented the considerable sum of 50,000 *denarii*. But after he had written a work entitled the *Antitheses*, of which fragments are still extant, excommunication was inflicted upon him (*c.* 144), as upon Valentinus. For the remaining two decades of his life, Marcion founded a series of communities (the first of them in his native Pontus) in opposition to the church with which he was now at odds.

Alone among Christian writers of his time, he rejected the Old Testament, which he envisaged as merely the religious history of the Hebrew people and nothing to do with Christianity. The faith, with which he backed up this and his other, more characteristically Gnostic beliefs, was based on strong personal feeling. Marcion had the strength of character that was needed to make people accept what he put forward. He was an outstanding person, who amply merited the terrified opposition that orthodox Christians of the second and third centuries marshalled against him.

## Gnosticism rejected

In the first instance, Marcion and other deviants, notably Valentinus, were denounced by **Irenaeus**, who rejected Gnosis and Gnosticism. Irenaeus (*c.* 130–*c.* 202) was born in Asia Minor, had contacts as a boy with Polycarp, and later went to southern Gaul as a missionary. In 177–8, now a priest, he was sent on a mission to Eleutherius, bishop of Rome. He took with him a letter from the church in Gaul interceding for ecclesiastical peace, which was at that time disturbed by the Montanist controversy (see p. 120). On his return he was consecrated bishop of Lugdunum (Lyon), in succession to the martyred Pothinus. There is no secure foundation for the tradition that he, too, suffered martyrdom.

Irenaeus wrote a book *Against Heresies* (*c.* 185), portions of which exist in the original Greek and the whole in a Latin translation. In this work he stressed the reality of the incarnation and the work of Christ. It was under his auspices that Christian theology took on a coherent and consistent shape. For Marcion's rejection of the Old Testament he had nothing but disapproval. To him, the Old and New Testaments were a manifest unity, evident in the solid chain of Christian fulfilments of ancient prophecy. Moreover, by his presentation of revelation as a gradual process, he refuted Marcion's demonstration of the moral flaws in the Old Testament. And he triumphantly stressed the parallel which Saint Paul had drawn between Adam and Jesus Christ.

All of this, he emphasized, needed to be rammed home by faithful teaching. The tradition of correct and continuing instruction must be dutifully maintained. Dangerous, revolutionary speculation had to be meticulously avoided. This was achieved only by keeping to the path set by the scriptural tradition that was handed down by the apostolic churches.

As for heresy, Irenaeus concluded, it arose out of the urge for innovation: out of 'curiosity', which meant delving into questions which human beings had neither the ability to understand nor the authority even to consider. In this spirit, Irenaeus sketched the history of the various kinds of Gnostic heretics and compared them, most unfavourably, with the one and only true church. This he saw as unchangeable, subject to mutation neither in time nor in space, guaranteed to be genuine not only by its capacity to trace an unbroken succession of authoritative exponents right back to the founding Apostles but also by the emphatic, unified consent of believers in every land.

Irenaeus employed the language of educated Greeks, which marked the full elevation of Christianity to intellectual and cultural maturity and status, and which has earned him the title of 'the first systematic Christian theologian'. By *c.* 180, Pantaenus's school had also been founded at Alexandria. He and his followers deplored the fear that Christians felt for pagan culture and philosophy, belittling it, just 'as children are afraid of a scarecrow'.

### *The pagan view of Christians*

Pagans nevertheless remained sceptical about the faith of the Christians. They disputed the latter's claim that the alleged Rain Miracle, which was said to have saved the Roman army from the Quadi (or Cotini) in 172 (Chapter 3), was the work of the Christian God. Within quite a short time after the event many Christians had come to believe that it was the prayers of their soldiers of the Twelfth Legion that had brought the saving rain. Xiphilinus, the Byzantine monk who compiled the epitome of this section of Dio Cassius, offers this Christian version of what happened. Unhappily, however, one of the principal pieces of evidence that he brings forward is erroneous. The Twelfth Legion was called the 'Fulminata', or thunderous. Xiphilinus and other Christian writers alleged that it was because of this very battle of AD 172 that the legion received the name of Fulminata. However, the legion had borne this title, probably because the thunderbolt of Jupiter was its emblem, more than a hundred years.

Eastern legionaries were more likely than others to have been Christians at this time. The Twelfth, Fulminata, Legion was indeed a legion of Cappadocia. It may have been fighting in the northern wars at this time, but there is no certainty that it was doing so. There may have been Christian soldiers engaged in the battle, but, if so, it is evident that Marcus Aurelius did not give them any credit for the Miracle. A letter alleged to have been written by him ascribing the Miracle to their prayers, and supposedly addressed to the Senate and People of Rome, is a forgery.[2]

Marcus Aurelius, while accepting the Miracle (at least for public consumption), took the view that it had been provided by a pagan, and not the Christian, divinity. As we saw, the *Meditations* mentioned the Christians only briefly. Marcus Aurelius disapproved, it would seem, of their spectacular martyrdoms as playing to the gallery. They did not fit into his picture of imperial unity.

Lucian, on the other hand, wrote about the Christians at greater length.

In the *Alexander*, he bracketed them with the Epicureans as the chief opponents of the fraudulent Alexander of Abonuteichus (Ionopolis, Inebolu). In the *Death of Peregrinus*, he mentioned them as the innocent victims of the charlatan of that name; people who were very easily led up the garden path.

> They still worship that great man, the fellow who was crucified in Palestine, for bringing this new cult into the world. . . .
>
> When Peregrinus was put in prison, the Christians thought it a terrible disaster, and did everything they could to try and get him out. . . .
>
> They are always incredibly quick off the mark, when one of them gets into trouble like this – in fact they ignore their own interests completely. . . . For the poor souls have persuaded themselves that they are immortal and will live for ever. As a result, they think nothing of death, and most of them are perfectly willing to sacrifice themselves.
>
> Besides, their first lawgiver has convinced them that once they stop believing in Greek gods, and start worshipping that crucified sage of theirs, and living according to his laws, they are all each other's brothers and sisters.
>
> So, taking this information on trust, without any guarantee of its truth, they think nothing else matters, and believe in common ownership – which means that any unscrupulous adventurer who comes along can soon make a fortune out of them, for the silly creatures are very easily taken in.[3]

Lucian, although not positively hostile to the Christians, and apparently unaware of the charges of immorality against them, did not think much of their faith. But it remained for Celsus to deliver a sustained and detailed attack on their beliefs and doctrines.

### Celsus

Celsus, who wrote in *c.* 178 and who illustrated the pagan opposition to Christianity, was an eclectic Middle Platonist (see Albinus, p. 103). He may have lived in Rome or Alexandria. He is known only through the fragments of his work *Alethes Logos* (*The True Doctrine, Word, Discourse*) that are preserved in the reply of Origen, *Contra Celsum* (*Against Celsus*), written in 248.

Celsus's principal belief is that Christianity constitutes a lapse from the antique cultural and religious tradition of the human race, which reached right back to the remote past of the Golden Age. The 'true doctrine' – provided by polytheism – had already, he believed, been impaired and degraded by the Jews, with their social and religious exclusiveness directed against everyone but themselves, and their interpretation of monotheism to mean the rejection of all faiths other than their own. But he conceded that Judaism, however eccentric, endures because it is prompted by nationalism. Christianity, on the other hand, while based on similar exclusiveness, possesses no such justification, and displays the additional fault of claiming converts from all races. Its missionary progress is a menace to the Roman empire, not only because the gods, embittered by the neglect of their rule and existence, may not continue to display favour to Rome, but also because the Christians are failing in their duty to the state owing to their reluctance to serve in public life and the army.

As regards doctrine, Celsus chiefly attacks the Christian arguments based on Jesus's alleged miracles and the prophecies which were said to have been fulfilled in his life. The miracles ascribed to him, he maintains, are unreliably attested: the Virgin Birth is nothing but a cover-up of bastardy; the Resurrection story is based on the tenuous evidence of a hysterical woman. The supposed prophecies in earlier scripture are so unclear that one cannot be certain of any reference to Jesus – and if they *were* as clear as the Christians claim, why had the Jews not accepted them? Moreover, even if both miracles and prophecies are regarded as acceptable, it is impossible to see how they are superior to the healings of Asclepius (Aesculapius), or the predictions of Delphi.

The centre of Celsus's attack lies in his criticism of the Biblical doctrine of God, as seen from the viewpoint of the eclectic Middle Platonist that he himself was. In matters of religion, that is to say, he is a conservative: the 'true' faith must be the faith that has been the tradition of his forefathers. Of Jesus, he takes a very poor view. He sees him as illegitimate, as a man whose teaching was a degraded mish-mash derived ultimately from Plato and other Greeks, as a 'miracle-worker' whose miracles were just foreign conjuring, as the victim of an execution which he tried to escape but failed to, and as someone who could not even control his thirst when he was being crucified.

Celsus does not wish, however, to be wholly destructive. He is prepared to concede that the Christians have some good ideas, but is convinced that they were derived from misunderstandings of what wise Greeks had said. Apart from this, he seems to have three main reasons for disliking Christianity. First, he regards Christians (and the Jews) as intolerably small-minded and parochial. He finds them like ants or worms or frogs or bats staging a debate as if they alone were the centre of the universe. Second, he deplores their lack of patriotic feeling and behaviour. Third, he regards the doctrine of the 'incarnation' as disgraceful: it seems to him preposterous to imagine that God could 'descend' from a state of perfection to the all too imperfect world in which we ourselves live.

While Celsus was explaining why, like so many other educated pagans, he disliked Christianity, he incidentally provided us with important historical evidence about its characteristics as they manifested themselves in the Greek world, including references to matters about which we should otherwise know nothing.

## GENERAL

The authors of the Antonine period are of varying quality. Marcus Aurelius and Lucian in Greek, and Apuleius (and possibly Fronto) in Latin, were writers of distinction. It may be protested that to categorize the literary figures of the age into first and second/third class is a purely subjective procedure, depending upon the taste of our own time and upon what I myself think. So be it. That is true.

Nevertheless, the second/third-class writers ought not to be neglected for a variety of reasons. First, because of the very subjectivity that has just been mentioned. The classification that we would offer today may not be at all the classification that was thought of in the Antonine Age itself. To take one example, we may regard the rhetorical movement of the Second Sophistic as boring and unconstructive, but the cultured population of the Antonine period did not. These are writers who are of importance to the historian, because they reflect the age in which they lived.

Second, some of these lower rated writers not only attracted a following in their own time but also exerted an influence on subsequent generations. This was true, for instance, of Hermogenes, whose rhetorical definitions enjoyed an almost Biblical authority in Byzantine times. It was true of Galen, whose medical works were widely studied and admired for century after century. It was true of Pausanias, whose geographical and topographical descriptions have been carefully noted throughout the ages and are still registered today. In Latin, too, Gaius was perhaps not a juristic writer of enormous distinction, but he enjoyed long-lasting admiration.

As for the Christian writers, they represent an age of transition. The greatest Christian authors are still to come, but the Apologists of the Antonine epoch have made a decisive and significant start.

Indeed, to revert to the first-class pagan writers who are the glories of the age, they too are especially notable because they stand for transition. Lucian has rejected old-fashioned paganism with satirical humour. Anyone who reads Marcus Aurelius has a feeling of leaving behind the ancient world and of entering a different kind of epoch. Apuleius, too, evokes similar thoughts, and points the way to the novel of the future. We are coming into a new world: these are writers of the age in which it was being created.

# 7

# ANTONINE ARCHITECTURE AND ART

At Rome itself, although the emperors were keen on construction as an element in social welfare, most of the new buildings under the Antonines were not very interesting or original, owing to the intense enthusiasm for monumental traditionalism.

To Antoninus Pius, however, were attributed a number of buildings. In memory of his predecessor Hadrian, he built a Hadrianeum, on a huge podium, with a frontal porch of eight marble columns. Eleven columns from the temple as a whole, as well as remains of the *cella* (long believed to belong to a 'Temple of Neptune'), are still to be seen flanking the Borsa, in the Piazza della Pietra. The Roman taste for ornamental exuberance is to be seen in the building's bold decorations, including the depiction of provinces on the stylobate,[1] in faithful recollection of Hadrian's imperial tours. Antoninus Pius also completed Hadrian's rebuilding of the Pantheon, built a circular temple of Bacchus, restored the temple of Augustus, and constructed a Temple of Jupiter Dolichenus (Baal) on the Aventine.

From the time of Marcus Aurelius, is a hexastyle temple of Antoninus Pius and Faustina the elder beside the Forum Romanum. Standing on a tall podium and with a six-column porch-façade, it has owed its survival to conversion into the church of S. Lorenzo in Miranda. Apparently the Temple of Jupiter Heliopolitanus (of which nothing remains) on the Janiculum Hill was reconstructed in *c.* 176–180. Fronto planned new Baths, and in the time of Commodus, too, Cleander built baths (the *Thermae Commodianae*) on an unknown site.[2]

The reconstruction of the port of Ostia (which had now eclipsed Puteoli [Pozzuoli]) was completed under Antoninus Pius, in whose reign, also, the town acquired new Forum Baths. Their design is more adventurous than that of any of the other Baths in the town. The various rooms of Ostia's Forum Baths were heated to a range of different temperatures, displaying, we are told, 'a sophistication in the use of radiant heating well beyond what modern engineers have achieved'.[3]

Yet the glazing of windows was dispensed with. Some of the windows of the Forum Baths were large; holes in the walls suggest that on the coldest days a canvas could be rigged up to keep out much of the chilliness. With assistance of this kind, an unglazed room at the Baths could be occupied for 98 per cent of the time: so that glazing would scarcely have been economical. Besides, as today, it was considered desirable for the bathers to acquire a tan, and this would not have been so easy if the windows had been glazed. Even without such a measure, the floors and walls of the Baths radiated a sufficient quantity of warm air to keep their occupants comfortable even when the air was cool outside. Moreover, light and heat were reflected by the mosaics with which the courtyard of the Baths was paved.

There was also a good deal of private architectural enterprise at Ostia. In the same city is the House of Diana and the *schola* of Trajan (so-called because of a statue of that emperor found there). The Imperial Palace at Ostia, with baths, courts, peristyle, apartments, Mithraeum and a mosaic (now in the Vatican), seems to date from the time of Antoninus Pius. It has also been suggested that the Ostia lighthouse was restored by Antoninus. At Ostia, of the time of Marcus Aurelius, was the Campo della Magna Mater (Cybele, a goddess much honoured by the Antonines). It was a large enclosure housing temples not only of Cybele but also of Attis (her consort) and Bellona, the goddess of war. At Ostia one can study how the new Roman architecture affected the ordinary citizen – who lived in the new, large, brick apartment houses, and who benefited from the *Horrea Epagathiana* (warehouse), and from the reconstruction of the large Claudian *horrea* by Commodus. It was a very rich man, on the other hand, who lived in the House of Fortuna Annonaria (remodelled in the fourth century).

Eugenie Strong wrote about Antonine buildings in other sectors of the outskirts of Rome:

> Many of the fine family mausolea that border the Via Appia, the Via Latina and other great Roman roads were constructed at this date. The building material was usually red brick, not infrequently relieved by the use of white marble for the columns and other architectural details. . . .
>
> The *Triopion* was a memorial temple erected by Herodes Atticus [see p. 102] to the memory of his wife Annia Regilla, who had died in AD 160, and who, having held the high office of priestess of Demeter (Ceres), could be associated in her temple with the empress Faustina I, who herself figured here as the new Demeter. The *Triopion* is generally identified with the little church of Sant'Urbano, in the Valley of the Caffarella. . . . Six Caryatids found not far from Sant'Urbano . . . probably adorned the interior of the temple. One of the finest is in the British Museum. . . .

Not far from Sant'Urbano stands a temple, long misnamed that of the *Deus Rediculus*, now generally recognized as the actual tomb of Annia Regilla. . . . Similar in character is the tomb, misnamed 'Tempio della Fortuna Muliebre', at the fifth milestone of the Via Appia Nuova. A fine domed tomb, on the left of the Appian Way (long falsely given a first-century date), is, to judge by the brickwork and the style of the architecture, purely Antonine. . . . At the second milestone on the Via Latina stands yet another tomb, with engaged brick columns on the façade, and engaged columns supporting the cornice in the interior.

The wealthy suburban villa of Sette Bassi, six miles from the city, on the Via Latina – built in three phases, *c.* 140–160 – is impressively monumental. Its third phase witnessed the construction of a huge buttressed *cryptoporticus* (covered gallery), with round towers at either end: it enclosed the peristyle garden, a set of baths, and two large, high reception halls.[4]

During this epoch, however, many of the most beautiful buildings were in the provinces. Thus, in north Africa, at Thamugadi (Timgad), an open triple arch, possibly of the time of Antoninus Pius, replaced the functional west gate of the Trajanic colony, and a theatre with 3,500–4,000 seats, cut into a low hill and supported on arches, was completed in 161–9, during the opening years of Marcus Aurelius's reign. From the last few years of the same decade dated another free-standing arch at Thamugadi; there was also a third.

There were many other arches in north Africa, including a fine example at Lepcis Magna (Lebda), a wealthy town where there was also a small porticoed shrine of Antoninus Pius. Sabratha (Sabrata) had a temple of Marcus Aurelius, dating from his lifetime (166–9), as well as another erected a few years later; a Temple of Hercules incorporating a monumental dedication to a certain Messius Rufinus of the time of Commodus; and a very large theatre dating from some time during the last quarter of the second century, which was the outstanding monument of the place. A quadrifrontal Arch at Oea (Tripoli) displayed a relief of the apotheosis of Marcus Aurelius. At Lambaesis (Tazzoult) a temple of Aesculapius (162) was planned on baroque lines, and three dedications relating to the construction of the city's amphitheatre in 169 and its repair in 176–80 have come to light. At Thugga (Dougga), said to have been the second richest city in Roman Africa, a Capitolium was dedicated in 166/7.

At Volubilis (near Moulay Idriss) a strong wall was built in 168/9, and a big altar received its dedication in 173/5. At Carthage there were Antonine Baths of an original character (143), epitomizing the convergence of Italian and eastern Mediterranean architectural currents in this region. At Cuicul (Djemila) in Numidia, the Arch of Crescens was dedicated to Antoninus Pius and Mars and the Genius of the Colony, and later there were Baths (183–9), displaying a diamond-shaped scheme of oblique vistas which adapted curvilinear forms to a narrow site. Antonine buildings at Thuburbo Majus (Henchir el Kasbat) include a Capitolium (168) and one or more temples. An inscription of 144 from Sala (near Rabat) shows how deeply Romanization was taking hold in the region. At Cyrene (Shahhat), the huge temple of Zeus (Jupiter), dating back to the fifth century BC, was restored in the time of Antoninus Pius.

Behind the northern frontier, at Augusta Treverorum (Trier), it would seem that the St Barbara Baths may well be of the Antonine period, though their exact dating has been disputed. The forerunner of the even larger Imperial Baths in the same city, these symmetrical St Barbara Baths were reminiscent of the Baths of Trajan at Rome, though by no means an exact copy. The earlier river bridge at Augusta Treverorum was replaced in c. 140, nearly a century after its initial construction, and altered again in c. 185.

On the Upper Rhine, the whole complex of central Augusta Raurica or Rauricorum (Augst, Basel) – including basilica and Forum temple – dates, in its enlarged form, from just before the middle of the second century AD. In Gaul Antoninus Pius not only built many roads but also restored the Baths at Narbo (Narbonne). The triumphal arch (Porta Nigra) at Vesontio (Besançon) may celebrate the German victories of Marcus Aurelius.

In the Danube region, an amphitheatre was built at Aquincum (Budapest) in c. 150. Across the river, in Dacia, the camp at Porolissum (Moigrad) was reconstructed in stone in 157, with walls five feet thick, and the stone-built amphitheatre at Ulpia Trajana (Sarmizegethusa, Várhely) was repaired in c. 158. These arenas in frontier areas, which later suffered severely in Marcus Aurelius's wars, were no doubt primarily intended for the training of troops, although they could also be used for civilian shows.

In Greece, at Eleusis, Marcus Aurelius built the Greater Propylaea, the replica of a monument in Periclean Athens. Also at Eleusis was a temple of Faustina the elder. At Corinth, the sanctuary of Asclepius (Aesculapius), dating back to c. 300 BC, was remodelled in the time of Marcus Aurelius, and an Odeon with 3,000 seats was constructed in c. 175. In addition, Corinth's fountain Pirene was rebuilt by the millionaire Herodes Atticus in honour of his wife Annia Regilla.

Herodes Atticus, a quarrelsome and tyrannical man (see p. 103; whose friendship with Aurelius helped him to get away with what appear to have been criminal actions, though he was abused by the vociferous Peregrinus, showered donations and buildings on the cities of the region, including Athens, with which Aurelius, too, was deeply concerned for philosophical reasons (Chapter 6). The first of Herodes Atticus's many munificent donations to his city of Athens was a complete reconstruction of the Panathenaic Stadium.[5] Initiated in *c.* 138, the work was completed in 143/4, the year in which Herodes Atticus became consul at Rome. The marble of Mount Pentelicon was employed for the task; the enterprise was so enormous that for the time being it exhausted the quarries. The new Stadium could house 50,000 spectators, much like a football stadium today. There were resemblances to the Colosseum at Rome, notably a tunnel at one end for wild animals, and a grille to keep the spectators safe from them. At the other extremity of the stadium there was a monumental passage providing access from outside, by way of a bridge crossing the River Ilissus. The entrance portico possessed side rooms with mosaic floors, which seem to have been the dressing rooms of the athletes. The turns on the race-track were marked by herms (marble pillars topped by a bust), and the entire structure was surrounded by a lofty and spacious Doric colonnade.[6]

On the hill to the west, Herodes Atticus constructed a Temple of Fortune (Tyche), a goddess to whom he felt that he owed a great deal. The hill which flanked the Stadium to the east may have been the site of his tomb, although there are rival claimants in the Athenian suburb of Cephissia and his estate near Marathon. Before he died, he had built a temple and tomb for his wife Annia Regilla.

His ultimate gift to Athens was his roofed theatre or Odeon, which was constructed in 161 on the south slope of the Acropolis and was able to house an audience of 5,000. An Odeon was traditionally intended for musical performances, but Herodes Atticus is likely to have been principally interested in its function as a lecture-hall, in which he himself would perform. Although the materials which were used to build his Odeon were Roman brick – *opus incertum*, that is, largish stones set irregularly in cement – and the entrances were barrel-vaulted in the Roman manner, the location of the Odeon was in accordance with Greek tradition. It was inserted into the side of the hill, instead of resting on foundations made by human hands. The roof of the building was of cedar-wood, and buttresses strengthened the walls against its weight. The façade of the stage-building (*scaenae frons*) was an architectural composition and backdrop which was no less than three storeys high. The pavement of the *orchestra* was of white and green marble from Carystus in Euboea (*cipollino*, 'onion-stone'), arranged in a chess-board pattern.

Herodes Atticus also provided marble seats for 7,000 spectators in the stadium at Delphi. And in 153/4 he built an *exedra* (semi-circular recess) at Olympia to mark the end of an aqueduct. It was adorned by twenty-four statues of members of the imperial family.

He was not the only rich man who erected and restored monuments. Others did the same, if not quite as palatial a scale. Town councils, too, did what they could to help such private citizens meet their expense, although in Greece the towns were less well off than those across the Aegean.

Asia Minor, for example, was predominant in the supply and handling of marble, which was such a popular building material, and it is not surprising that construction within the area itself was extensive. However, the Temple of Asclepius Soter (Aesculapius) at Pergamum (Bergama), dating from just before the middle of the second century AD, not only employed marble but also made extensive use of brick. The temple was modelled on the Roman Pantheon but it graphically blended Roman and Asian ideas. In the same period, a temple of Demeter and Kore was built at Pergamum. A propylon was commissioned by Claudius Charax in the reign of Antoninus Pius, during which, also, the site was restored by Claudius Silianus Aesimus. There was a temple of Faustina the younger on the acropolis of Pergamum.

At Ephesus (Selçuk), Publius Vedius Antoninus constructed a council-chamber (*bouleuterion*), with room for 1,400 people, which was the gift off his wife to the city. He was also the builder of Baths, which incorporated an Odeum (?) and a gymnasium and wrestling-school (*palaestra*), and which were dedicated to Artemis and Antoninus Pius (who was a friend of Vedius). The scale, elegance and sophistication of the Baths are equal to those of the finest of the later thermal establishments at Rome or, indeed, anywhere else in the world. Statues of river-deities poured water from urns into the swimming pools. The dressing-rooms were furnished with hooks for clothing and lockers beneath the seats. Underground, there were at least fourteen furnace-rooms, which were required to provide heating for more than 10,000 yards of floor space. In the same city a grandiose temple behind the Library of Celsus dates also from the latter half of the second century AD, a little later than the library itself.

Following an earthquake, many restorations were undertaken in Asia Minor. Despite financial stringency owing to the wars, Marcus Aurelius practically rebuilt the centre of Smyrna (Izmir), probably in 178, including the large complex based on the *agora* (market-place). The temple of Artemis (Diana) at Sardes (Sart) was divided into two, and the eastern half dedicated to the deified Faustina the elder; it was probably her younger namesake who gave her name to the Baths of Faustina at Miletus (Yeniköy, Balat), with gymnasium attached, and stadium close by. In the same city, the Great Gate of the southern Agora probably celebrates Lucius Verus's Parthian campaigns. One of the buildings damaged by earth tremors was a huge, tall temple of Hadrian at Cyzicus (Balkiz), which had been completed in 139, and was subsequently reconstructed and rededicated in 167. The theatre at Olbia-Diocaesarea (Ura, Uzunca Burç) dates from the reign of Aurelius and Verus, and another theatre, at Aspendus (Belkis), was designed by a certain Zeno (the son of Theodorus) at the same time or a little later.

133

A major architectural triumph was the Temple of Zeus (Jupiter) Heliopolitanus at Heliopolis (Baalbek) in Syria. This displays the Syrian adoption, with variations, of the Italian formula of combining temple with extensive precinct. Its date has been disputed. Probably Malalas's attribution of the temple to Antoninus Pius was wrong. Its construction may have been begun in the first century AD, although the completion of the project may well be dated to Antoninus, who was known to have helped cities, at a time when construction or reconstruction could be adjusted to the more sophisticated second-century taste.[7]

Malalas's ascription of the whole project to Antoninus Pius should perhaps more correctly be applied to the adjoining Heliopolitan so-called temple of 'Bacchus' (or was it a temple of Aphrodite [Venus]–Atargatis?), which is generally (although not universally) ascribed to the middle of the second century AD, or a little later. This was riotously ornate, with great intricacy of detail, and was perhaps the richest of all temples in the Roman world. It is one of the best preserved. The enlargement of the Heliopolis precinct, to which this temple contributed in so singular a fashion, was a truly ambitious and memorable enterprise.

This temple of 'Bacchus' at Heliopolis stands on a lofty podium. The colonnade surrounding it consists of Corinthian columns, which have been left unfluted, although there are six fluted columns which hold up the spacious porch. The portico enveloping the whole complex had a roof and a ceiling of monolithic blocks of stone elaborately adorned with busts, in frames, of Ares (Mars), Demeter (Ceres), Hephaestus (Vulcan), a city-goddess, and Ganymede, as well as others.

But it is upon the interior of the shrine that most attention has been lavished, as a departure from the antique, austere Greek tradition. The heavily decorated entrance is flanked by a pair of towers which carry staircases up to the level of the roof (a phenomenon also found in temples elsewhere). The *cella* is framed in colossal fluted Corinthian pilasters, augmented by Corinthian half-columns set on pedestals. The pilasters provided a space for two storeys of niches, the higher with pediments of triangular shape, and the lower with round tops; these niches – or at least the upper one – originally contained statues. At the western extremity of the building, a grand stairway led to a highly ornamental altar platform (on which stood a cult statue; round it performances of Mysteries were enacted), surmounted by a canopy, above an underground crypt which resembled that of a Christian church.

It is not surprising that the magnificent extravagance of this edifice has aroused comment. The stone, observed Alphonse de Lamartine (1790–1869), 'groans beneath the weight of its own luxuriance'. 'It is a very singular building,' commented Mortimer Wheeler: 'As the most nearly complete surviving example of its kind, it holds a unique place in the history of architecture.'[8]

At Gerasa (Jerash), too, which was not uninfluenced by Heliopolis, there were important new edifices. They included a Temple of Zeus, ready for dedication in 163; a later and less conventional temple; the north Theatre of *c.* 161–6; finely vaulted West Baths; and a rich fountain building of 191. There was also a festival sanctuary at Birketein, one mile outside the town. The 'palace' at Shakka, of 191 or possibly earlier, seems to have been erected in awareness of the developments of Gerasa.

Although little can be said about ancient Antioch itself, because it is mostly buried under the deposits of the River Orontes (Nahr el-Assi), there were many other buildings of the period in the Syrian and Hauran regions, notably temples at Dmeir (149; two-façaded, with pairs of angle-towers), 'Atil (151), Hebron (155), Burdj Bakirha (161) and Es-Sanamen. At Phaena (Mismiyeh) the so-called 'Praetorium' dates from 161–9. At Palmyra (Tadmor) the western colonnade of the precinct may belong to the reign of Antoninus Pius, while the Propylaea date from Marcus Aurelius or Commodus. The artistic talent of the Nabataean Arabs also found architectural expression, for example in the sanctuary of Seeia (Si'; *c.* 150–75) in the mountains of the Hauran, north-east of Bostra (Bosra Eski Sham). It reveals the influence of the Nabataeans' capital city of Petra.[9]

In Egypt, also, construction took place. A Roman temple at Medamüd, near Thebes (Luxor) – rebuilt on the site of Pharaonic sanctuaries – is approached through a large courtyard, with graceful columns, which was constructed by Antoninus Pius. He also began (but did not complete) additions to the so-called 'small temple' at Thebes itself, comprising, once again, a courtyard, flanked by a columned portico. The restoration or enlargement of a temple near Lake Moeris, in the Fayum, has been attributed to the reign of Commodus.

By this time there were magnificent private villas throughout most of the Roman world (not only in Italy, where one has already been mentioned). There was a luxurious example at Kolarovgrad in Lower Moesia. Some of the villas in Pannonia, for instance at Baláca, Tac-Forenypuszta (Gorsium) in Hungary and Eisenstadt–Gölbesacken in the Burgenland (Austria), may well have been Antonine, or possessed features of Antonine date. A large suburban villa at Ulpia Trajana (Sarmizegethusa) in Dacia was burnt down during Marcus Aurelius's Marcomannic Wars.

In the Spanish peninsula, as in many other regions of the empire, villas were numerous. In about the time of Commodus there were magnificent mansions outside Conimbriga (Coimbra). The huge house at Els Munts was probably run by a certain Gaius Valerius Avitus.[10] Another was at Cuevas de Soria, in country full of pine-trees thirteen miles south of Soria, not far from Numantia.[11] It seems to have been in use from at least AD 161. The simpler west part of the mansion contains the rooms where the day-to-day jobs of the farm were conducted. The remaining

135

portion was the accommodation of the owner and was on a more luxurious scale. There were thirty rooms in the building altogether, and twenty-two of them possessed mosaic floors; so did the corridor, framed in columns, off which the rooms branched. A large apsed hall in the centre of the north wing contained a particularly impressive mosaic. The baths and lavatories are to be found in the south-eastern part of the edifice, at a higher level. The complete villa is 260 feet long and 195 feet wide. Some of the rooms, it was found, had been subsequently divided into two by partition walls. This would have had the effect of keeping what were now the inner parts of the villa excellently protected from cold, and it has been conjectured that, at whatever date this took place, the establishment was serving as a *valetudinarium*, or nursing home.

In Gaul, however, palatial country houses were almost new at that time, because the villa as an institution in that country did not flourish until the middle of the second century AD.

Physiognomy, it was believed by the ancients, often possessed moral implications. Polemo had recently written a textbook on the subject (Chapter 6). The art of making portrait busts attained remarkable heights under the Antonines, especially in relation to the emperors themselves and their wives. Antoninus Pius was personally sceptical about beauty, but that did not prevent the existence of fine busts of him, displaying his quiet observant glance, and the triangle of hair growing low above his brow. Perhaps the best of these heads is in the National (Terme) Museum at Rome. Another is to be seen in an *imago clipeata* (portrait in a round frame, resembling a shield) upon the pediment of the Outer Propylaea at Eleusis. Perhaps the best portrait of his wife Faustina the elder, with coloured marble drapery, is in the National Archaeological Museum at Naples. The Hellenized softening of features, so noticeable in the Hadrianic portraits of Antoninus, was being abandoned, and facial expressions became livelier; this has been described as a sort of 'enlightened classicism'.

Marcus Aurelius provides the most significant Roman series of lifetime portraits, ranging from his early to his later years. We can detect the efforts of at least two generations of artists to portray these successive phases of his arduous career. To his youthful period belongs a bust in the Capitoline Museum in Rome. It is a psychological achievement, displaying a prince whose thoughtful, melancholy air represents a distinct abandonment of the somewhat impersonal idealisms of much of the past. There is also a fine, youngish Aurelius from Tarraco (Tarragona). By way of contrast, a portrait projecting from a relief in the Conservatori Museum, which shows him sacrificing on the Capitol, displays a ruler in his troubled, tired, reflective last years, physically changed and worn down by age and hard work and war. It is a rendering which penetrates deeply into the character of this sensitive and suffering man.

In between, there are imposing representations of Aurelius's maturity. By far the most famous is the bronze statue on horseback, which stood on the Capitoline Hill and which has been removed (temporarily or permanently?) to escape air pollution. The earliest complete example of an imperial equestrian statue, it was dedicated by the senate in 175 to celebrate the emperor's victory over the Jazyges, one of whom originally lay huddled under the raised front hoof of the horse. It is probable that this statue first stood on the Arch of Marcus Aurelius. The head, like so many of his portraits, shows an almost mask-like impassivity which was, it seems, true to life.

It was also commented that there were many bad portraits of Marcus Aurelius in existence: which is hardly surprising, since the emperor himself was sceptical about physical looks. A terracotta equestrian statue of him at Singidunum (Belgrade), made in the workshop of Pacatus, is an example of something that is thoroughly bad. Nevertheless, his statues proliferated, and for centuries there remained many in private houses, among the household gods.

There is a good likeness of his wife Faustina the younger in the National (Terme) Museum at Rome. Her heads 'moved openly from young beauty to softened, matronly petulance, evident in both numismatic and sculptural portraits'.[12] But the person who best lent himself to this art of portraiture, which at its finest showed such a high degree of sophistication, was Marcus Aurelius's colleague Lucius Verus. His sensational good looks, and individual character veering from playboy to man of culture, are reflected in numerous portraits, which characteristically display a slightly distrustful glance. Colossal busts of Marcus Aurelius and Lucius Verus were made and erected at Lepcis Magna (Lebda).

There is a full, heavily sensual portrait of Verus's wife Lucilla in the Capitoline Museum at Rome. However, one of the finest female heads of the same period is that of a non-imperial woman in the same city's National (Terme) Museum. Employing a new ideal of womanhood, more tender and more spiritual, it was described by Eugenie Strong as 'probably the most perfect Roman figure in existence'.[13]

This art of portraiture reached its climax under Commodus. The somewhat disturbed sensual beauty of the young man, so very different from the looks of his father, is evoked by a head in the Louvre. In London's Victoria and Albert Museum, a small gilt-bronze head, inlaid with silver, shows him wearing a cosmic skull-cap. The famous Commodus–Hercules bust in the Conservatori Museum at Rome (c. AD 180) was intended to be seen gleaming in the penumbra of a shrine. It displays an exaggerated use of the drill, and emphatic eye-pupils. 'The transformation of stone from a clearly defined solid form into a drilled, twisted, hollowed, foamy substance represents the maximum of optical effects attainable in marble sculpture . . . the virtuoso refinement is carried to extremes.' By the elaborate drilling of the hair and beard, the sculptor is deliberately presenting a contrast with the face which is as polished as porcelain. The bust shocks Hellenists, who have described it as 'the worst piece of sculpture extant from antiquity'. But that is wrong. It is a brilliant achievement, perfectly evocative of the transition from ancient classicism to the world of later Rome and the Middle Ages.

This bust of Commodus in the Conservatori, wrote Mortimer Wheeler (d. 1976) somewhat imaginatively, is

> one of the familiar masterpieces of Roman sculpture, enlivened by that conscious touch of the grotesque which has again and again characterized the most vital portraiture, from Augustus to Augustus John.
>
> The smooth and effeminate emperor with his weak arms, his flaccid feeble face in its aureole of drilled and over-barbered hair, reeking of pomade, the property lion-scalp and club and the tiny 'apples of the Hesperides' in that tenuous manicured hand, is delicate but brutally expressive charade.
>
> No doubt it delighted, as it revealed, the sadistic pervert whom it has so faithfully immortalized. The sculptor must certainly have felt very sure of his ground, armed by the blind vanity of his subject.[14]

There are also interesting busts of male private citizens at this period, notably Tiberius Claudius Pompeianus (so it is supposed) on the Column of Aurelius, and a head of Aelius Aristides in the Vatican. A portrait of a woman has already been mentioned. Antonine heads of children, too, are full of charm, though not all are private persons. 'Their likeness to the ruling family', observed Eugenie Strong, 'is enough to prove that many of them, including the boy's head at Arelate (Arles) once thought to be the "young Marcellus", and the young prince in the Capitol [the Capitoline Museum at Rome], are members of the imperial family.'[15] The god Mithras was also depicted in some very fine sculptures, including one from his sacred cave at Igabrum (Cabra) in Spain.

Palmyra (Tadmor) had a school of portraiture of its own, which produced excellent busts of people of the region and of Parthians during the years c. 140–60. There is, for example, a remarkable head of a camel-driver. Palmyrene portraiture often displays the local taste for frontality (first seen in c. AD 32) which confronts the viewer with an unblinking stare and locks him or her in a spiritual link; this liking for frontality spread to Rome. There is also a fine statue of a king of Hatra (El Hadr) of about this period, in the Mosul museum.

Certain reliefs also belong to the period. Those in the Hadrianeum built by Antoninus Pius at Rome personify the provinces, in a manner not very enthusiastically recalling the provincial interests of Hadrian. A panel in the Museo Albani records a scene in which Antoninus (whose figure has been restored) is seen distributing grain, in the presence of Abundantia and Roma. To the same epoch belong two reliefs in the Palazzo Rondanini or Sanseverino (Banca dell'Agricoltura). One of them, reproducing a scene which also appears on one of Antoninus's medallions, shows a river-god, presumably the Tiber, holding out a cup to catch the water which flows from an urn, while a bearded serpent darts forward from a rock towards this stream: the group seems to be an allegory of the cult of Aesculapius (Asclepius). Another monument, in the Vatican, showing a sow and her young, is likewise paralleled on the coinage of Antoninus Pius,[16] and may be linked with his prospective celebration of the Secular Games in 148.

These reliefs, which seem perhaps a little arid, are in keeping with Antoninus's deliberate revival of some of the more solemn Augustan art forms. Arid, too, are some of those from the Column set up by Marcus Aurelius and Lucius Verus in Rome to celebrate the consecration of Antoninus Pius, whose body had been cremated on that spot. The column was made of pink granite, and has not survived. It stood on a tall cubical base, one side of which bore an inscription. This has endured and it tells how the column came to be employed as the monument to Antoninus. It was fifty Roman feet long, we are told, and was one of a pair which had been extracted from the ground in AD 106, when Trajan was the emperor. The inscription bears witness to the pride which was felt in the successful excavation of this massive piece of granite. It also testifies, indirectly, to the large quantity of stone which must have been available at Rome, in order to make it possible to find this enormous block more than fifty years later.

The other three sides of the base display reliefs, which are likewise extant. The design at the back of the base (now in the Giardino della Pigna of the Vatican) depicts the apotheosis of Antoninus Pius and his wife Faustina the elder. They are shown in the likenesses of Jupiter and Juno, swept upwards by a youthful winged spirit, with eagles on either flank symbolizing their deification.

Heinz Kähler observes that, at the foot of the spirit

who carried the globe of earth encircled by a serpent, rests the personification of the Campus Martius, with the obelisk which Augustus had put up to serve as the pointer of the great sundial. Rome, enthroned on captured weapons and leaning on the shield with the she-wolf and twins, bids farewell to the ascending emperor and his wife.

The calm, emblematic forms . . . and the somewhat empty beauty of line are all characteristic marks of classicism. . . . The academic precision and beauty of this composition, though they have earned

139

praise, are empty of any tension. They are even a little boring, like life and death themselves.

If we move round from this relief to the sides of the base, both of which show the solemn funeral procession, we suddenly arrive in a completely different world. A number of details, such as the care with which the arms and armour are represented, make it likely that these reliefs are the work of the artists who produced the ascension. But behind the formal beauty of their classicism something is beginning to happen which may be regarded as a protest against the traditional and the usual. The situation bears a striking resemblance to that which arose in pictorial art at the beginning of the twentieth century.

In contrast to the conscientious rendering of the ascent to heaven, the funeral procession is curiously abstract. The background, that is, the wall of the base, has suddenly become a perpendicular surface, and the soldiers – infantry in the middle, cavalry in a circle round them – are distributed over the surface without any regard to point of view or to the spatial relations between the various elements in the composition. . . .

Illusion is replaced by a new objectivity. A flat surface becomes a flat surface again and the figures are disposed on it more or less as they would be on a plan seen from above. There is no attempt to integrate them into an imaginary scene.

It is the end of an artistic convention which had lasted for over five hundred years. . . . It is the first flash of that revolution in artistic values which we describe as 'late antique'. . . . The classical ideal of beauty lost its hold on people's imagination because it no longer expressed their experience, their aims or their hopes.[17]

After these surprising innovations on the Column of Antoninus Pius, which defy all of the classical ideas of accurate anatomy and so on, and which prefigure the end of old artistic conventions, the relief adorning the Temple of Antoninus and Faustina, even if it is a virtuoso achievement, seems a little dull (and was condemned by Ruskin). The relief depicts griffins (on the significance of which see p. 144) and candelabra and acanthus scrolls.

Important panels of Aurelian date have also been preserved at Rome. They symbolize the imperial virtues of Clemency, Victory and Piety. Richard Brilliant argues that these, at least, do not deserve the same condemnation as unduly stiff and conservative.

The Aurelian panels in the attic of the Arch of Constantine and in the Conservatori were taken from a triumphal Arch or Arches of Marcus Aurelius, probably commissioned in the 170s.

The sculptors responsible were aware of current developments in the compression of space, the heightening of hieratically orientated schemes of distinction, and the increased patterning of the surface by dark–light contrasts. Perhaps they moderated their adoption of these features because they felt still bound to the old conventions established in such official, allegorical programmes under Trajan and even before.

Nevertheless, some genius, possibly influenced by the renewed interest in texture and attracted to the functions of the drill as a creative instrument, explored the possibilities of negative modelling, that is to say the removal of stone. . . . Therefore this artist and his fellow-sculptors abandoned the traditional vocabulary of plastic sculpture, which relied on the positive modification of surface by the shaping of material, and instead came to rely on negative model-ling, which used sharp differences in light to transform a surface, suggesting that what was not there at all appeared to be.[18]

Other reliefs of the reign of Marcus Aurelius, from Ephesus (Selçuk) and now at Vienna, depict Aurelius and his colleague Lucius Verus, in commemoration of their Parthian victories. Another, of about the same period, shows the Battle between the Gods and Giants (Gigantomachy), in a blend of Hellenistic and Asiatic styles.

Sarcophagi, which had for some time been of major artistic importance, now became increasingly ambitious. A fine example at the Palazzo Ducale, Mantua (Mantova) depicts a marriage. A sarcophagus showing the Judg-ment of Paris, from the Garden of the Villa Medici (French Academy) at Rome, has abandoned the realistic spatial relations between figures in the same way as the parade scene on the base of the Column of Antoninus. In the Museo Civico at Velitrae (Velletri), another sarcophagus with a gabled lid and two zones of figure scenes (though it may be of slightly earlier date)[19] depicts the Labours of Hercules, to symbolize man's earthly life and life after death, and displays rich ornateness. A scene of fighting between Romans and Germans on a sarcophagus from the Via Tiburtina, in the National (Terme) Museum at Rome, displays contorted poses and emotional expressions with unsurpassed technical skill. On another sarcophagus with an energetic battle scene (170–80), which was found at Farfarus (or Fabaris; Farfa), the figures are still distinct, but are patterned in 'rhythmically fluctuating intensities of light, progressively turning the description of action into a series of flickering forms'.[20] The Portonaccio sarcophagus in the National Museum likewise displays a bubbling inter-lace of writhing shapes. A discovery of the period was the sarcophagus adorned with niches. This is represented by a specimen in the Museo Nazionale del Melfese at Melfi, which adapts Greek and oriental motifs to the Roman manner.

The most important reliefs of the period, however, are those on the

Column of Marcus Aurelius in the Piazza Colonna at Rome. It appears to have been executed during the later years of the reign of his son Commodus, since an inscription recalls its completion in *c.* 193,[21] although the scenes depict the German wars of Marcus Aurelius, and particularly those of the years 172–5. (Some would also detect references to the campaigns of 178.)

The reliefs on the column depict 116 happenings from Aurelius's German and Sarmatian wars (Chapter 3). Comparison with the Column of Trajan is inevitable and was intended: in order to show that Aurelius was as great a conqueror as Trajan, or greater. Execution (in several styles) is as careful and accurate as ever, but much has changed – partly because of the growing influence of popular (folk) art. Amid deep-drilled grooving and hard, disturbing transitions, abstraction prevails, modified by exaggeratedly violent poses. Outlines are sketchy; vivid isolated episodes are hammered home with monotonous, almost Assyrian iteration, and the compactly grouped figures (short-hand indications of the setting) do not interrelate with one another. Illustrative detail is concentrated on essentials, and the pictures leap out at the viewers. So do the portraits of Marcus Aurelius himself, who turns repeatedly to the spectators, recalling the frontality that was encountered at Palmyra, and creating a new sort of spiritual link between those who were gazing at the reliefs and the ever more imposing figure of their emperor. All of these changes, even if not caused by the harrowing crises of Marcus Aurelius's reign, were probably accelerated as one followed another.

This was an age of haunting miraculous events, and the Column of Marcus Aurelius depicts the Lightning and Rain Miracles which allegedly saved the Roman army (see p. 42). These two peculiar incidents seem attributable to 172. In the former episode, Marcus Aurelius was said to have elicited by prayer a thunderbolt from heaven and, by means of it, to have demolished one of the enemy's military engines. A series of coins of 172 display the emperor, in military uniform, being crowned by the goddess Victory who holds a palm. He is carrying, in addition to his reversed spear, the thunderbolt of Jupiter,[22] which appears to be a deliberate reference to the Lightning Miracle.

The other alleged marvellous event is even more striking. This is the renowned battle at which the Rain Miracle was said to have occurred. The Quadi (or Cotini) had surrounded the Romans, who were fighting back, their shields forming a continuous line of defence. The Romans were wearied by heat and parched by thirst and were in danger of their lives, so that the enemy expected an easy and early victory. But then, suddenly, there was a mighty amassing of clouds, and a huge storm of rain burst over the combatants, whereupon the Romans were able to quench their thirst, while the eyes of the barbarians were dazzled by lightning and blinded by hail.

On the Column of Aurelius there is a vivid picture of this occurrence. An exhausted Roman legionary points to the sky, and, on the right, rain is shown coming down. One Roman gives his horse a drink, another drinks himself, and others hold their shields aloft to collect the water that is descending. Meanwhile dead barbarians and their injured horses are to be seen, as the rain-spirit plunges forward. This winged, shaggy, lowering spirit looks almost more medieval than classical. Marcus Aurelius, despite his general aversion to such supposed supernatural manifestations – indicated by a rescript in which he ordered relegation to an island for anyone who alarmed fickle minds with such fears (Chapter 5) – seems to have accepted the miracle, or to have found it politic to seem to do so.

What is most remarkable about the Column is that it depicts an age when war and the enemy are observed in an entirely new way. War is no longer a matter of extrovert triumphs, but is a tragic and painful affair, a grim and sordid necessity of burnings and executions. Faces and poses are contorted by pathos; the enemy are not just barbarians who are fit to be squashed, but people who are objects of sorrow and who suffer the miseries, anguishes and raw horrors of brutality and defeat. In this atmosphere of sombre, careworn realism we seem to see a scathing, if not wholly conscious, commentary on man's inhumanity to man: a counterpart to Marcus Aurelius's own resignation and sympathy.

The Column shares its key motifs with Trajan's: the emperor addressing troops, receiving embassies, performing sacrifices, leading attacks. But the emphasis is different. The emperor is more isolated, aloof, absolute; and the horrors of war are more crudely stressed. The message is beat, club, drag, burn, kill: villages are destroyed, prisoners taken; barbarians flee, are exiled. Turncoat barbarians behead loyal ones on Roman orders. Tribesmen are assassinated in a pit, speared by Romans from above. Their women are dragged by the hair, transported, and butchered.

The violence and anguish on the Column reflect the fragility of an age in which a philosopher is forced to make war. Roman art here conveys ideas which its Hellenistic antecedents were not created to express. This is a novel sort of originality, veiled and constrained until now, when it started to burst the serene but fixed equilibrium of classical humanism.

Besides the Column, Commodus commemorated his father at Rome by raising an Arch or Arches. Triumphal Arches were not of course new; they were a traditional branch of Roman architecture. In the time of Marcus Aurelius an Arch in his honour had been erected at Rome.

This Arch, which later provided the eight reliefs for Constantine's Arch . . . was erected in 173, when Marcus Aurelius interrupted his stay in the north to see his two sons-in-law entering on their year of office as consuls. As Marcus Aurelius did not celebrate a triumph on this occasion, but only four years later, The Arch was not at first topped with the triumphal quadriga, but with a statue of the emperor on horseback. . . . This statue must have looked like the one in the Piazza del Campidoglio[23] – or perhaps it was the very same statue (see p. 137).

The Arch/Arches which Commodus erected in honour of his father Marcus Aurelius is/are no longer extant, but certain panels (in the Conservatori and Torlonia Museums at Rome) have survived. One, in the former museum, includes a head of Aurelius which has already been mentioned (p. 136). Others were re-employed on the Arch of Constantine. These reliefs do not display identical styles (which has prompted some to support the view that there was more than one Arch). Although they have sometimes been condemned as ponderous and inert (even if restless), they have also been described as 'probably the most successful Roman attempt to relate figures to their environment'.[24]

Meanwhile, private citizens, too, were commissioning reliefs. For example, wealthy landowners in the Mosella (Moselle) region made use of the soft sandstone that was locally available. This prompted relief sculptors to evolve a bold style, which produced, in one instance, an effective school scene.

Painting and stucco included work of very varying quality. Some of the bad portraits of Marcus Aurelius, of which Fronto complained, were painted. There were good traditions of painted portraits in certain parts of Egypt, notably the Fayum and Antinoopolis (Sheikh Abade) in the middle of the country. The frescoes at Dura-Europus in Mesopotamia uniquely illustrate the fusion of Greek and oriental elements which were leading towards medieval art.

As regards Italian examples, chiefly interesting are the trends towards new varieties of religious thinking. For example, the tomb of the Valerii and that of the Pancratii (as it is generally called) on the Via Latina not only display much artistic decoration but also show what people were thinking about the immortality of human beings, and the rewards and punishments that await them after death. The tomb of the Valerii (AD 160) is an underground chamber with a barrel-roofed ceiling which is totally covered with elegant white stucco ornamentation, upon alternating round and square panels. We see Nereids riding sea-monsters, Nymphs ravished by Satyrs, and other mythological happenings. But the picture at the centre of the whole pattern, a woman riding on a griffin, symbolizes the transportation of the soul to other realms by the agency of the mythical griffin which was Apollo's sacred animal. Within the lunette in front of the entrance is a painting of a standing female figure, *Tellus* or *Terra Mater*, who holds up a panel on which the Seasons are shown. These are emblems of the passage of time (turned to imperial use on the coinage of Commodus).[25]

The double-chambered so-called Tomb of the Pancratii offers another treatment of contemporary religious themes, in the same combined range of painting and stucco. The inside chamber has a ceiling covered by mythological scenes in relief, which are varied by 'idyllic' landscapes depicting shrines, religious enclosures and pillars honouring cults. In the middle of the ceiling is the theme of an Apotheosis of Jupiter, which stands for the Apotheosis of the human soul. A similar allegorical significance lay behind the selection of the various events that adorn the lunettes on the walls, including, for example, the reception of Hercules into heaven. The artistic standard is high. The modelling is subtle, and the outlines firm and precise.

The Tomb of the Nasonii on the Via Flaminia presents a somewhat similar spiritual message. Here again we encounter mythical topics which have all been selected to illustrate the progress of the soul; for example, Orpheus and Eurydice. These are tombs that belong to the second half of the second century AD. So does another, not far from the same main road, in which the imagery, depicted in elegant stucco, is once more symbolic. And there are stuccoed and painted tombs elsewhere.

Moreover, the religious concerns of the period reappear in a large wall-painting of the same epoch in a tomb below the church of SS Giovanni e Paolo on the Caelian Hill. What is shown here is the *Ver Sacrum*, the Sacred Spring. The divinities of fertility, tentatively identified as Venus with an attendant (Libera?) and Liber Pater (Bacchus, Dionysus), appear upon the shore of a sea, on which boats containing miniature Cupids are to be seen. The painting depicts the reawakening of the world after its long winter sleep; that is, an attempt is being made to give visual, allegorical shape to the new ideas of resurrection that were in the air.

In another room of the same tomb, known as the *triclinium*, a painted podium is surmounted by a frieze in which there are not only figures of divinities but also birds, one of which is the peacock of immortality. Above there is a view of a garden, in which Cupids are picking fruit or flowers: it is evidently the pagan paradise.

As for the magnificent mosaics from Antioch and its suburb Daphne, which are now in the museum at Antakya, a number of them are of second century AD date, but it is not absolutely certain that they belong to the Antonine period.

Coins continue to provide ample, unequalled illustrations of the emperors' points of view, often put forward with a twofold meaning, so that both the cultured and not so cultured would be equally impressed. Even the coinage of the serene Antoninus Pius is full of questions and mild surprises. Coin portraits are often impressive, and their reverses offer a great deal of evidence for the artistic and architectural developments of the time.

The production of <u>medallions</u> in all metals increased vigorously during this period, reaching its peak of quantity and spectacular quality under Commodus. The medallions were intended, for the most part, for presentation to individuals, for instance at New Year and other ceremonials. On these pieces, portraiture is even more effective than on coins, and the reverses offer room for complex and elaborate scenes, replete with religious and allegorical and traditionalistic allusions. As time went on, the types became fussier and heavier.[26]

*Figure 1* Antoninus Pius (AD 138–161). Courtesy of the Ancient Art &
Architecture Collection.

*Figure 2* Bronze medallion of Antoninus Pius, showing Horatius Cocles swimming for safety after defending the Sublician Bridge against Lars Porsena the Etruscan: a historic tale of ancient Rome. Courtesy of the Bibliothèque Nationale, Paris.

*Figure 3* Bronze coin of Antoninus Pius, showing Mars finding Rhea Silvia. The type stresses the divine origins of Rome. Courtesy of the British Museum.

*Figure 4* Faustina the elder (died AD 141), the wife of Antoninus Pius. Courtesy of T. Howard-Sneyd.

*Figure 5* Relief showing Hadrian (AD 117–138), Antoninus Pius and the infant
Marcus Aurelius. Courtesy of the Kunsthistorisches Museum, Vienna.

*Figure 6* Heroic depiction of the young Marcus Aurelius.
Courtesy of the San Antonio Museum, Texas.

*Figure* 7 Bronze equestrian statue of Marcus Aurelius, formerly standing on Rome's Capitoline Hill. Courtesy of the Capitoline Museum, Rome.

*Figure 8* Marcus Aurelius as priest. Courtesy of the British Museum.

*Figure 9* Faustina the younger (died AD 175), the wife of Marcus Aurelius.
Courtesy of the Capitoline Museum, Rome.

*Figure 10* Faustina the younger. The goddess Venus is shown
on the reverse. Courtesy of the British Museum.

*Figure 11* Lucius Verus. The war galley is accompanied by a
reference to FELICITAS AVGVSTI. Courtesy of the British
Museum.

*Figure 12* The Rain Miracle which reputedly saved the army of Marcus Aurelius: a scene from his column at Rome.

*Figure 13* The column of Marcus Aurelius, completed after his death (AD 180), shows a new appreciation of the horrors of war, including the distress of German prisoners.

*Figure 14* Bronze medallion, portraying Commodus as a boy, with his brother Annius Verus, who died young. Courtesy of the Bibliothèque Nationale.

*Figure 15* Commodus as the refounder of Rome, to be known henceforward as 'Colonia Commodiana'. Courtesy of the British Museum.

*Figure 16* Commodus in his last year (AD 192), described as 'Hercules Romanus Augustus', and wearing the lion-skin head-dress of the god Hercules. Courtesy of the British Museum.

*Figure 17* Commodus as Hercules. Courtesy of the Conservatori Museum, Rome.

*Figure 18* Dupondius of Pertinax, a general of Commodus
who briefly succeeded him (AD 193). He calls upon 'the
Providence of the Gods'. Courtesy of the British Museum.

Figure 19 Didius Julianus, one of Commodus' commanders, who reigned for a
short time after Pertinax (AD 193). He is 'Ruler of the World' (Rector Orbis).
Courtesy of British Museum.

Figure 20 The north African Septimius Severus, who
emerged from the chaos of AD 193 to rule until 211.
Courtesy of W. A. Seaby.

*Figure 21* Clodius Albinus, a claimant to the throne whom Septimius Severus diplomatically recognized as Caesar before suppressing him. Courtesy of the British Museum.

*Figure 22* Pescennius Niger, an eastern usurper whom Septimius Severus put down. Courtesy of the British Museum.

*Figure 23* Temple of Serapis at Ostia, showing brickwork. From a private collection.

*Figure 24* Reconstruction of the sanctuary in the so-called 'Temple of Bacchus' (Baalbek) in Syria, from Wiegand, Theodor (ed.), *Baalbek: Ergebnisse der Ausgrabungen und Untersuchungen in dem Jahren 1898–1905*, Vols I, II and III, Berlin and Leipzig, 1921–25.

*Figure 25* The Odeon of Herodes Atticus at Athens. Courtesy of The Ancient
Art & Architecture Collection.

*Figure 26* The Library of Celsus at Ephesus. Courtesy of Richard Stoneman.

*Figure 27* Sculpture from Palmyra. Courtesy of the Louvre, Paris.

# 8

# THE ANTONINE AGE

Edward Gibbon included the first, and larger, part of this period among the epochs to which he allotted the highest possible praise.

> If a man were called to fix the period in the history of the world, during which the condition of the human race was most happy and prosperous, he would, without hesitation, name that which elapsed from the death of Domitian (AD 96) to the accession of Commodus (180).[1]

In this book I am concerned only with the last two reigns within this period, those of Antoninus Pius and Marcus Aurelius.

Is Gibbon's pronouncement justified in relation to that epoch? The question has, of course, been much discussed; and it has been pointed out that its basis is very largely the speech of Aelius Aristides, which was delivered in AD 143 or not very long afterwards (Chapter 3).

> As on holiday the whole civilized world lays down the arms which were its ancient burden, and has turned to adornment and all glad thoughts – with power to realize them. . . . The whole earth has been beautified like a garden. . . . Thus it is right to pity only those outside your hegemony – if indeed there are any – because they lose such blessings.
>
> It is you again who have best proved the general assertion that Earth is mother of all and common fatherland. Now indeed it is possible for Hellene or non-Hellene, with or without his property, to travel wherever he will, easily, just as if passing from fatherland to fatherland. Neither Cilician Gates nor sandy approaches to Egypt through Arab country, nor inaccessible mountains, nor immense stretches of river, nor inhospitable tribes of barbarians, cause terror, but for security it suffices to be a Roman citizen, or rather to be one of those united under your hegemony.
>
> Homer said, 'Earth common to all,' and you have made it come true. You have measured and recorded the land of the entire civili-

147

zed world. You have spanned the rivers with all kinds of bridges and hewn highways through the mountains and filled the barren stretches with posting stations. You have accustomed all areas to a settled and orderly way of life.[2]

The empire was made up of a huge number of provinces, of which thirty-four were governed, mostly, by proconsuls and *legati Augusti propraetore*. Fronto (Chapter 5) knew how difficult its <u>unity</u> was to achieve, and offered an insight into the sort of preparations a conscientious man would make before taking up one of these jobs. (He finally decided not to do so, p. 87.)

> I took active steps to enlist the help of my friends in all that concerned the ordering of the province. Relations and friends of mine, of whose loyalty and integrity I was assured, I called from home to assist me. I wrote to my intimates at Alexandria to repair with all speed to Athens and await me there, and I deputed the management of my Greek correspondence to some most learned men. From Cilicia, too, I called upon eminent citizens to join me, for owing to my continual advocacy of the public and private interests of Cilicians before you, I had hosts of friends in that province. From Mauretania also I summoned to my side Julius Senex . . . in order to make use not only of his loyalty and diligence, but also of his military activity in the hunting down and suppressing of bandits.[3]

The eulogies of the empire by Aristides and Gibbon have often been criticized. It was not nearly such a safe area as Aristides said. Fronto referred to banditry: there was quite a lot of it, at various dates, if we use the word, as the Romans did, to include every revolt against authority. To deal with such revolts, indeed, was the day-to-day responsibility of the imperial administration in the provinces.

Sometimes this 'banditry' or 'brigandage' became quite conspicuous. In 175–6 it was rampant on the border between Macedonia and Thrace. In 184 the Danube region was 'full of brigands', as inscriptions from Lower Pannonia (Pannonia Inferior) reveal. In a time of national crisis Marcus Aurelius enrolled 'bandits of Dalmatia and Dardania' in the army. Commodus built forts to repel bandits (*latrunculi*), some of whom came from across the river frontier. On the Roman side of the sector between Viminacium (Kostolac) and Naissus (Niş) it was particularly unsafe. In Numidia (eastern Algeria), two highways were constructed for the safety of travellers, which was otherwise uncertain.

The rising of <u>Maternus</u> in 185(?) (Chapter 4) was especially significant.[4] It seems to have symbolized a massive popular reaction against the imperial regime, which was unprecedented both in its purpose and in its

magnitude. Maternus was a soldier in the Roman army, who had a cour-
ageous record but who deserted at about this time and induced certain
of his fellow-soldiers to do the same. Herodian writes that he soon

> collected a huge mob of desperadoes. At first they attacked and
> plundered villages and farms. But when Maternus had amassed a
> sizeable sum of money, he gathered an even larger band of cut-
> throats by offering the prospect of generous booty and a fair share
> of the loot.
>
> As a result, his men no longer appeared to be brigands but rather
> enemy troops. They now attacked the largest cities and released all
> the prisoners, no matter what the reasons for their imprisonment.
> By promising these men their freedom, he persuaded them to join
> his band in gratitude for favours received.
>
> The bandits roamed over all Gaul and Spain, attacking the largest
> cities. A few of these they burned; but the rest they abandoned after
> sacking them.[5]

Maternus only had to stage his rebellion to have what the Romans saw
as 'a numerous band of rascals' flock to his ranks. These were clearly
destitute individuals who were ready to take to violence in provincial
lands, and their numbers swelled: once Maternus had created the impetus
he found himself joined by a large number of runaway slaves, expropri-
ated peasants, bankrupt farmers, and deserters from the Roman forces.
As for the deserters, it was probably they who provided the leadership in
Maternus's force, although they were very far from the only element
in that force. The large scale of the movement shows that it was nothing
short of a perilous rebellion of the oppressed, submerged classes in a
number of provinces. Indeed, as Herodian points out, the men under
Maternus's command were strong enough to assault 'the largest cities'.
Many estates must have fallen to them. In the process, famines and
shortages must have occurred (see p. 152).

There are other grounds on which Aristides and Gibbon have been
taken to task. Gibbon speaks of 'the human race', but knows little about
its remoter areas. The Roman empire of which he was speaking, although
it was of enormous dimensions, comprised only a small part of the world
as a whole. What was going on in the rest of the world we cannot tell,
so that Gibbon's general statement is not based on any adequate knowledge or facts about those regions (p. 2).

Gibbon's pronouncement has also been criticized on the grounds that
it refers entirely to the richer groups who were the principal beneficiaries
of Roman society, which maintained 'a massive system of exploitation of
the great majority by the upper classes'.[6] The latter were favoured even
by the philosophical Marcus Aurelius (Chapter 3), and were the only

beneficiaries whom Aristides, in his praise of the Antonine empire, took into consideration when he stressed the cities that they controlled.

> Now all the Greek cities rise up under your leadership, and the monuments which are dedicated in them and all their embellishments and comforts are beautiful suburbs which redound to your honour. The coasts and interiors have been filled with cities, some newly founded, others increased under and by you. . . .
>
> Taking care of the Hellenes as of your foster-parents, you constantly hold your hand over them, and when they are prostrate, you raise them up. You release, free and make autonomous, those of them who were the noblest and the leaders of bygone days, and you guide the others moderately with much consideration and forethought. . . .
>
> All the other rivalries have left the cities, and this one contention holds them all, how each city may appear more beautiful and attractive. . . . Gifts never cease from you to the cities, and it is not possible to determine who the major beneficiaries are, because your kindness is the same to all. Cities gleam with radiance and charm.[7]

It was these local leading men who created and ran – and, Aristides adds, guarded – the cities throughout the empire. They, as well as the emperors to whom he pays tribute, were lavish benefactors of the cities. This had always been the situation, but it reached its climax in the second century, thanks to the wealth that had been accumulated during the Imperial Peace. True, the Antonines, even more than their predecessors, were eager to help small landowners, but 'Rich citizens', wrote Michael Rostovtzeff, 'were ready to help and gave money freely for everything that was needed for a city; we may say that most of the beautiful public buildings in the cities of east and west were their gifts.'[8]

The emphasis is on cities, because, as Aristides proudly records, it was a network of such cities that constituted the Roman world: that world had become thoroughly urbanized. In the second century AD the transformation of the empire reached its highest and most fully developed level. City life grew by a natural kind of process; and the emperors assisted it by awarding the status of a Roman colony or *municipium* to native centres, when it seemed that these now possessed a sufficiency of Roman or Greek habits or culture to make this kind of administration possible. Thus in Numidia, for example, whereas there had been only twelve municipalities in the first century, there were now nearly forty. It has sometimes been said that the Roman empire became 'a federation of municipalities'. That, indeed, is what it very nearly was in the second century AD. In the time of Marcus Aurelius, municipal dedications abounded.

Nevertheless, there was sometimes friction *within* the cities; we hear of it at Naucratis (Kom Gieif) and Rhodes, and Polemo had to deal with it (p. 96). Despite legislation humanizing their lot, the lower class of 'free' men, the depressed, illiterate workers, failed to derive any benefits from this process of urbanization, and clearly did not have a very good time under Antoninus Pius and Marcus Aurelius, any more than they had had before. Many of the people in the rural areas lived a miserable life of continual or sporadic destitution and starvation, in contrast to many of the 'city-dwellers' (who included, of course, tax collectors). The contrast is noted on an inscription from Prusias on the Hypius (Üsküb).[9]

It is strange that so little is heard about this.[10] What scholars of ancient history choose to write about, and choose not to write about, is equally surprising. No large percentage of the people in the Roman empire can have passed their lives without at least once wondering from where the next meal was to come. The circumstances in which such uncertainty could exist were of desperate interest to the people of the time.

Food shortages, under Marcus Aurelius alone, happen to be recorded at Concordia (Sagittaria), Ariminum (Rimini) and neighbouring towns, at Carnuntum (Petronell), and, further afield, at Ephesus (Selçuk) and in Phrygia. No doubt similar shortages occurred elsewhere.

Galen writes about the sort of lives these starving rural populations experienced.

> Immediately summer was over, those who live in the cities, in accordance with their universal practice of collecting a sufficient supply of corn to last a whole year, took from the fields all the wheat, with the barley, beans and lentils, and left to the rustics (*agroikoi*) only those annual products which are called pulses and leguminous fruits – they even took away a good part of these to the city.
>
> So the people in the countryside, after consuming during the winter what had been left, were compelled to use unhealthy forms of nourishment. Throughout the spring they ate twigs and shoots of trees, bulbs and roots of unwholesome plants. And they made unsparing use of what are called wild vegetables, whatever they could get hold of, until they were surfeited. They ate them after boiling them whole like green grasses, which they had not tasted before even as an experiment.
>
> I myself in person saw some of them at the end of spring, and almost all the beginning of summer, afflicted with numerous ulcers covering their skin, not of the same kind in every case, for some suffered from erysipelas, others from inflamed tumours, others from spreading boils, others had an eruption resembling lichen, and scabs and leprosy.[11]

The lower classes also suffered under what the ancient Athenians had called 'liturgies' (public service obligations which included the provision of food, lodging and transport to the imperial troops); their flights from such oppressions are confirmation of this.[12]

The criticisms levelled against Aristides and Gibbon, with regard to people and places, are justified, but that is not the end of the matter. Given that the lowest and poorest classes fared badly under the Antonines, have they fared any better in later ages? A study of history suggests that they have not. Let us look at our present century (and examples may be taken from the rest of 'the human race', outside what was once the Roman empire). Communist Russia professed to sponsor the cause of the 'working classes', but conspicuously failed, in practice, to do so. Indeed, it has shown a striking, and perhaps unparalleled, disregard for the securities and decencies of ordinary human life. Consider Africa. Have the 'working classes' there benefited from the comforts and ameni-ties of the western way of life? For the most part they have not. Those classes are no better off, to say the least, than were many inhabitants of the Roman empire under Antoninus Pius and Marcus Aurelius. We should be careful, therefore, not to conclude too rapidly that Gibbon was wrong when he asserted that the human race has never been happier than it was in their reigns.

That is not to say that all was well. It must be repeated that, as far as the Roman empire was concerned, this was an age of transition. As the religious developments of the era made abundantly clear, the classical world was virtually over, and the medieval age had not begun. Everything was being changed and transformed, though this may not have been apparent to everyone at the time.

The most significant instruments of change were the wars. In the time of Marcus Aurelius, the sinister outbreak of strife along the entire northern frontier, following so soon after the disruption of the eastern borderline, was a major sign that things were changing, and that the equilibrium of harmonious stability was at an end. The wars were so costly that life could never be the same again.

Partly because of the necessities imposed by these wars, the emperors, whatever their intentions, were becoming more autocratic. Thus Eudae-mon of Nicomedia (Izmit) addresses Antoninus Pius as 'Lord King' (*kyrie basileu*), and Commodus is called 'saviour of the world' at Attaleia (Antalya; 177–80).

'Democracy' in the Greek or other cities of the empire was just a farce. The speech by Aelius Aristides lavishing superlative praise upon Rome asserted that the Roman empire was the finest, ideal kind of democracy, because its population had voluntarily given up its right to rule into the hands of the man best fitted to do so: the emperor. This was merely the ultimate conclusion and degradation of political thinking, the out-come of a prolonged process in the course of which the ancient demo-cratic institutions of the Greek cities, and such democratic elements as existed in the Roman constitution and tradition, had been obliterated by the endeavours of the men who ruled the Roman world and the ruling elements in the Roman and Greek cities.

During the second century AD, this trend towards autocracy was propped up by the writers of a number of essays and pamphlets defining and explaining the regal, all-powerful position of the emperor. Aristides was one of them. Ecphantes was another.

> The king is like the rest [of mankind] in his earthly tabernacle, inasmuch as he is formed out of the same material. But he is fashioned by the supreme artificer, who in making the king used himself as archetype.
>
> Accordingly the king, as a copy of the higher king, is a single and unique creation, for he is on the one hand always intimate with the one who made him, while to his subjects he appears in the light of royalty. . . .
>
> So then I suppose that the earthly king can in no particular fall short of the virtue of the heavenly king.[13]

Another writer of the time, Diotogenes, presented a somewhat more human and less divine, but equally autocratic, picture of the emperor.

The same movement towards autocracy expressed itself legally not only in the recognition that an imperial ruling now had the force of law, but also in ever-growing paternalism, which meant an increasing bureaucracy (in which the ranks were stratified), and an imperial willingness to interfere in the lives of individuals and in the conduct of affairs on a local level. This tendency is illustrated by the presence of an imperial freedman, Marcus Ulpius Eutyches, at Albocolensis in Gallaecia (Galicia) to look after the mines,[14] which were under central control, and by the action of Marcus Aurelius in relation to the dispute between the authorities (landowners) and population of Saepinum (see p. 39). These phenomena were also elements of a much more general trend, which resulted, to some extent, from irresponsible attitudes on the part of the rich local people who so largely financed their cities. The requirement that they do so was inexorable, but how they did it was left (much too freely) to themselves. Since they wanted to be popular, they spent lavishly on things that produced an immediate dividend rather than on what would be permanently useful. Far too often they squandered their money on free meals or entertainments or gladiatorial games.

At times, it is true, a public-spirited rich man paid to build a school or market-hall or aqueduct, or to construct new drains or to effect much-needed repairs. But this did not happen often enough. The result was that the cities themselves had to meet these inevitable bills. Since they could not afford to do so, they had to satisfy the requirements by borrowing, and consequently fell into a condition of grave indebtedness. This meant that the imperial government had to become involved.

As long as the local authorities discharged their duties without going too far into the red, the Roman government was willing enough to give them a free hand. By the second century, however, it became evident that central intervention was necessary. First, under Trajan (98–117), it was resorted to only on exceptional occasions. But, once introduced, imperial supervision of local finances tended to become a regular practice. Under the Antonines, representatives of the emperor who arrived to set straight the affairs of provincial cities became more and more numerous. Thus Marcus Aurelius, for example, had to send the senator (formerly a knight) Gaius Vettius Sabinianus Julius Hospes to Gaul 'to examine the accounts' (*rationibus putandis*):[15] something had gone wrong, possibly because of exceptional demands during the northern wars.

Before the third century such direct interventions were still comparatively rare. Yet cities were already beginning to run into financial difficulties. This was not only because the munificence of local rich men was so badly directed but also because of inter-city rivalries, such as those which Polemo, for example, had to try to calm down (p. 96). Such occurrences became a matter of real and justified concern to the imperial government at Rome, which thus had to intervene, or interfere, more often.

In spite of the failures of the local rich, they continued everywhere (as at Rome itself) to become increasingly privileged at the expense of their poorer compatriots. This was particularly noticeable on local councils. Cities, which were only too aware of the consequences of their financial ineffectiveness, established hard and fast rules requiring every new member of their council (or candidate for one of their official posts) to pay a lump sum into the municipal treasury. Alternatively the person could undertake some expensive public work. This system of compulsory contribution once again favoured the rich. Poorer people were not able to afford such costly expenditure, and suffered from an excessive strain if they were obliged to serve as councillors. At Oxyrhynchus (Behnesa) in Egypt an inscription particularly praises a man who had *voluntarily* accepted such a post.[16] Antoninus Pius exempted town councillors from torture, which shows that they had previously been liable to such treatment.

In other words, the gulf between the *honestiores* and the *humiliores* became wider. This is noticeable from contemporary local sources, and was very evident at Rome itself. Of 'democracy' there is little trace, as has already been seen. But what did democracy mean? There had been *direct* democracy, once upon a time, in ancient Athens, where citizens flocked to the Assembly to vote. That was now out of the question, because the empire was much too large for direct democracy to be possible. *Representative* democracy, such as we have today in the election of members of parliament, or deputies, or congressmen to speak for us, had not been considered (and, even if it had, the Romans would have failed to comprehend or appreciate its advantages).

One example, already mentioned, of the social gulf which existed at Rome, and which was reflected by the law, was the fact that the *honestiores* were exempted from torture, and the *humiliores* were not.

> 'Torture traditionally was reserved for slaves, but free men of low rank were not immune in the second and third centuries,' and 'Torture of *honestiores* was not permitted in the Antonine and Severan periods.'
>
> These perfectly correct statements by P. D. A. Garnsey are characteristic of what is to be found in most writings on the subject. They conceal the fact that a striking *change* took place in the second century, very probably in the Antonine period. A curiously limited *constitutio* of Marcus Aurelius which excused certain descendants of the two highest grades of the equestrian order (*eminentissimi* and *perfectissimi*) 'from the punishments of plebeians or from tortures' has more than once been discussed, without the really remarkable thing about it being stressed: that it shows that most Roman citizens had now come to be regarded as legally liable to torture! . . .
>
> In various other ways, too, members of the lower classes who were charged with crimes were at a disadvantage compared with the propertied classes. . . . Evidence given in court by members of the lower classes, whether in criminal or civil cases, was accorded less weight than that of their social superiors.[17]

This growing gulf between the Antonine rich and poor, although partially concealed by a system of relief (*alimenta*) of earlier origin (and renewed by Antoninus Pius and Marcus Aurelius), owed much to the effects of a grim economic recession, involving rises in prices and increasing inflation, which, as always, hit the poor more severely than the rich. Most of the town councillors who suffered such ruin from the 160s onwards were naturally in the former category.

Owing to several bouts of legislation of a humane sort – and perhaps to the influence, or knowledge, of powerful empresses – women were faring rather better than they had before. Even concubines gained some legal status, and their sons went into the army. The discovery of heaps of women's and children's shoes at Bar Hill on the Antonine Wall in Scotland suggests that there was no lack of a feminine presence there. But the women were doing better in a world that was doing worse.

Gibbon did not believe that what he regarded as the extensive universal benefit continued in the reign of Commodus. Ernest Renan, too, considered that 180, the year of that emperor's accession, was the decisive moment, 'the end of the ancient world'. They were following Dio Cassius, who remarked of that change: 'our history now descends from a kingdom of gold to one of iron and rust, as affairs did for the Romans of that day.'[18] Certainly, the ominous signs began to multiply at the time in question, partly because of the new ruler's unsatisfactory personality.

An inscription has survived about how his father Marcus Aurelius dealt with an administrative problem, a complaint from Saepinum (Altilia) in Umbria about how the local authorities dealt unfairly with local cattle-farmers (c. 168).[19] The details of the dispute need not be repeated (see p. 39); what is important is the light that it throws on the increasingly bureaucratic machinery. The praetorian prefects, Marcus Bassaeus Rufus and Marcus Macrinius Avitus Catonius Vindex, were probably doing their best to be just, but we can detect the cog-wheels, procedures and phraseologies of the imperial administration, foreshadowing the apparatus and stereotypes of today. 'Facts such as these', observes Charles Parain,[20] 'help us to understand that the central power has always tended more and more to restrain local liberties, to impose its control and a uniformity of regulations upon the municipal officials.'

The provinces were now advancing at the expense of the capital in many different ways. In this process, of course, the ever-increasing urbanization (p. 150) played a leading part. The provincial areas became largely enfranchised; they contained more and more Roman citizens, and more and more holders of 'Latin rights' which were a halfway house to full Roman status. That the second-century emperors should have actively pursued this policy is hardly a matter for surprise, since most of them were, at least partly, of provincial origin themselves. Antoninus Pius was born in Italy, but his place of origin was Nemausus (Nîmes) in Narbonese Gaul. The family of Marcus Aurelius came from Corduba (Cordoba) in southern Spain (Baetica).

Rome, it is true, remained the universal, timeless centre; the emporium of the world – the city that had been singled out to receive the transported grain of Egypt, and later Africa (see pp. 157f.). It was also the headquarters of charitable imperial activities such as the *alimenta*. However, Italian senators, who had formed over 80 per cent of the senate under Vespasian, now comprised around 50 per cent or less – although Marcus Aurelius did his best to help them by reducing a senator's compulsory investment in Italy from one-third to one-quarter. Italian legionaries, to, had diminished from constituting 65 per cent of the legions under Augustus to something under one per cent: to satisfy the non-Italian majority, Commodus sanctioned the worship of native gods in military sanctuaries. Distinguished writers now much more often came from the provinces than from Rome (Chapter 6).

Indeed, there were countless signs that the provinces were becoming as important as the central city itself. The gap was sharply narrowing, partly because of the war crisis, which required the rapid promotion of capable provincials.

As regards the west, powerful men from Africa (and its capital Carthage) were on the increase. The highly developed Rhineland had become the workshop of Europe. Centres such as Colonia Agrippinensis (Köln) were gaining greatly in industrial and commercial significance. It was in that city (among others) that the glass-making industry established a principal centre. (In *c.* 170 it moved again, to Westendorf in Raetia [Bavaria].) After 150, although Gaul was in other respects at the peak of its trading activity, one of the main headquarters of *terra sigillata* (terracotta adorned with reliefs) was transferred from Ledosus (Lezoux in the Auvergne) to Tabernae (Rheinzabern near Speyer). Moesia (including Scythia Minor) was prosperous, in spite of its devastation by barbarians, and ironworks in Illyricum flourished at the time of Marcus Aurelius's German wars. Poetovio (Ptuj) in Pannonia became a major economic centre, and commercial enterprises based on Aquileia pervaded both Pannonia and Noricum.

The significance of the east was vastly increasing, as was shown not only by its encroachment on Roman religion but also by the host of eastern senators and writers, and by the mass of new architecture in eastern cities (Chapters 6, 7). Marcus Aurelius appointed professors for the great philosophical schools of Athens. But it was outside Europe that the most striking developments occurred: the early stages of the triumph of eastern over western ideas.

The eastern province in which events did not proceed smoothly was Egypt. At first, all was well. Alexandria was the second city of the empire. The first year of the reign of Antoninus Pius coincided, in Egypt, with the termination of the old and the beginning of the new 'Sothic period' of 1,460 years. This was believed to herald a renewal, a rebirth, the return of the Golden Age. Relations with Rome seemed especially close. There were references to 'concord' between the Tiber and the Nile. The Egyptian deities Serapis and Isis played more and more of a part on the Roman coinage (on which Mercury, under Aurelius, is the Egyptian Thoth [p. 43]). The Prefect of Egypt instituted special celebrations of Antoninus Pius's fourth consulship in AD 145.

However, during the same reign there was a serious riot at Alexandria, in which another Prefect was killed. Then, under Marcus Aurelius, there was a revolt in the Nile Delta, which caused severe damage to agriculture, and which was followed by the uprising of Avidius Cassius. In this Alexandria (like Antioch) took the side of the rebel, a decision which did not do the city any good in its relations with the imperial government. It is not surprising that, as we learn from Dio Cassius, the subsequent reign of Commodus witnessed Egypt, as Rome's supplier of grain, having to accept a share of this trade being given to Africa, where Carthage was so important and from where shipments were made.

Elsewhere in the east, the provinces were everywhere rising at the expense of Rome. Some easterners wrote about this with satisfaction. They gloated about the eclipse of the imperial city that they foresaw. That, for example, was the attitude of a Judaeo-Christian Sibylline soothsayer.

> On thee some day shall come, O haughty Rome,
> A fitting stroke from heaven, and thou the first
> Shall bend the neck, be levelled to the earth,
> And fire shall utterly consume thee, bent
> Upon thy pavements, thy wealth shall perish,
> And on thy site shall wolves and foxes dwell,
> And then shalt thou become all desolate
> As though thou hadst not been . . .
> Inexorable wrath shall fall on Rome,
> A time of blood and wretched life shall come . . .
> Woe, woe to thee, O land of Italy,
> Great barbarous nation . . .
> And no more under slavish yoke to thee
> Will either Greek or Syrian put his neck,
> Barbarian or any other nation.
> Thou shalt be plundered and shalt be destroyed
> For what thou didst, and wailing aloud in fear
> Thou shalt give until thou shalt all repay.[21]

The narrowing of the gap between the provinces and Rome was further stimulated by the large part which the provinces had to play in the ever-increasing trading contacts *outside* the empire. There were regular commercial routes linking the empire with Germany and Scandinavia. One such route passed overland to the Dutch coast, and either passed onwards to Denmark or veered into one of the German rivers. Another route proceeded along the amber merchants' road from Carnuntum (Petronell) and the middle Danube to the Vistula, and went on to cross the Baltic. Extensive finds of Roman coins, mostly of the second century, in the Poznan area and Silesia and the islands off Sweden, display evidence of quite a volume of trade.

Further east, too, during the time of Hadrian or Antoninus Pius, Greek merchants pushed out to Darantkurgan and Tashkurgan, on the edge of the Tarim plateau in Hsin-Chiang (Sinkiang). In 166 a group of Greek traders, who claimed to be 'ambassadors' from the emperor 'An Tun' (Antoninus, i.e. Marcus Aurelius), reached the court of the Chinese emperor Huan-Ti at Loyang on the Huang-ho (Yellow River), and initiated arrangements for regular trading operations between the Mediterranean countries and China. When the Romans were fighting against

Parthia (Chapter 3), these commercial contacts were never far from their minds. And they had to avoid Parthian territory in order to maintain them.

Within the city of Rome itself, towards the end of the period, sharp changes occurred, which presaged the difficulties of the future. The unworthy favourites of Commodus gained the upper hand, and so did the armies, foreshadowing the epoch of military monarchy that lay some way ahead. This was still an age of transition. Commodus is as much a product of transition as Marcus Aurelius. In that phenomenon of transition lies the fascination of the entire period. There was, it was said, already a touch of autumn in the air. And there were already those who foresaw the winter that was to come, when Rome would collapse and fall. 'One can already sense, as so often in times of outward peace, the underground rumblings of the earthquake which was swiftly to change everything.'[22]

Meanwhile, there was some popular anti-Romanism, as is evident from Lucian,[23] but it was not enormous. However, some of the Judaeo-Christian *Sibylline Oracles*, as we have seen, were exceedingly hostile to Rome.

Here we have seen the Roman Empire at its height. It was already beginning to suffer from some of the troubles that would eventually bring it down, but it was still enjoying a vast, imposing supremacy.

The relevance of the empire to modern times was briefly touched upon in the Introduction, and here the theme will be developed further. There is an obvious field for comparison between that towering Roman empire and the new Europe which so many are endeavouring to create today, and which undoubtedly, in some form or another, is taking shape. There are obvious differences, too. The first is geographical. The Roman empire was not limited to Europe, since it also took in huge areas of north Africa and the Near and Middle East. It did not include massive zones which form part of the Europe of today; notably Germany, although as we have seen the idea of inserting it into the Roman empire was actively considered and pursued. Nor did it include the great regions of eastern Europe in which, recently, Communist domination has collapsed (and for which plans exist to bring them into what is now the Europe of the European Union before long).

Nevertheless, despite all of these dissimilarities, the resemblance between the Roman empire and modern Europe remains, and the relevance of the former to the latter is valid. On no other occasion since Roman times has there been such extraordinary progress, on a huge scale, towards the unification that is now being sought. It has therefore seemed imperative to examine the Roman empire, at its height, in order to see what it has to tell us about ourselves. In particular, we have to face the somewhat depressing task of determining why that empire began to crumble away, so that we may, if possible, avoid undergoing the same fate ourselves. It is useless, and inaccurate, merely to conclude that great empires or groupings of nations just collapse in due course, like plants or trees, because they have grown old. Empires and groupings of nations collapse because they, or their leaders, have taken the wrong decisions, have made mistakes, or have failed to deal with difficult or impossible situations.

We need not, I think, be concerned today with one of the principal causes of the downfall of the western Roman empire: external invasions. External invasions, across the Danube (and, embryonically, across the Euphrates), have figured largely in the present book; they were unmistakably the forerunners of the even more perilous invasions which would contribute largely, during the times that lay ahead, to the downfall of the western Roman empire. From that particular danger, mercifully, we seem to be exempt today. The disappearance of Communism in the Soviet Union and the other regions dependent upon it means that we in western Europe no longer have any external invaders to fear. In that respect, at least, we are happier and better off than Marcus Aurelius and his successors.

That does not mean that we are exempt from all of the other problems that confronted them. Immigration was one such. The Roman empire, during the period that we have been considering, let in very many immigrants. So have we. Most of the immigrants into the Roman empire came from the north and north-east. Up to now, most of the immigrants into modern western Europe have come from Africa and Turkey. At present a flood of people from the north-west Balkans is joining them. It is a fairly safe guess that within the next few years an almost uncontrollable mass of immigrations from what was formerly the Soviet Union, and the countries adjoining it, will be taking the same paths. When that happens, the parallel with the Roman world, already close, will have become even closer: these migrants will hit the same borders of western Europe that were hit by migrants from the north and north-east during the age of the Roman empire.

What is to be done about this problem? How did the Roman emperors react? They did much too little about the problem, so that it became uncontrollable. It hopelessly debilitated the empire into which the migrants massed. As for our own, modern, immigration, we must control its dimensions. The task is not made easier by extremists in our countries who urge its total stoppage, on the grounds of what often sounds suspiciously like racism. Total stoppage would be both cruel and impossible. Yet, we ought to bear in mind what happened in Roman times, which is very relevant to our own situation.

The western Roman empire became subject to a sort of internal paralysis, which prevented the inhabitants from averting its downfall. In the end, they felt that their government did nothing for them, and so they did nothing to help it. This was partly as a result of economic recession and a rise in taxes. It also resulted from increasing autocracy; that could happen to us, too, but at present there is no clear indication that it will. Another consequence of the economic recession and rise in taxes in the Roman empire was a greatly increased bureaucracy; that, indeed, is a present danger.

An expanded bureaucracy brings with it increased centralization. This happened to Rome in the Antonine Age, and in the light of our current preoccupations it is well worth considering what M. Cary and H. H. Scullard say might have been done to counteract it.

> The difficulties attendant on any comprehensive social change could have been faced without the fear of general social dislocation.
>
> This problem of redistributing economic power and responsibility had its counterpart in the question of a better division of political functions, so as to counteract the tendency to excessive centralization of power in the hands of the emperors. While a return to the government of Republican times was neither practicable nor desirable, a devolution of administrative duties from the Caesars upon the provincial parliaments would at any rate have been deserving of experiment.
>
> The political utility of the *concilia* [provincial councils] had already been proved on a small scale ... and emperors had found in them a serviceable link for the transmission of messages to the municipalities. Though it was imperative that the control of the army and of foreign policy should remain in the hands of the emperors, the provincial Councils could fitly have been entrusted with other executive functions, such as the maintenance of internal order and the repartition of financial burdens among the constituent municipalities.
>
> A policy of decentralization carried out on these lines would have had the double advantage of easing the burden on the shoulders of the emperors, and of giving wider scope to the administrative talents of the municipal aristocracies. But ... the Roman world of that age demanded nothing more than good administration on established lines.[24]

Cary and Scullard are correct in saying that the emperors ought to have done more to delegate and to devolve power. However, not everything else that they say will bear close examination. Their main point is that the emperors ought to have decentralized more by handing over greater powers to the provincial Councils. At first sight that appears quite an attractive policy, and they are able to point to ways in which the Councils were useful. But whether they could, in practice, have taken on much wider authority is very doubtful. Their members, the rich men of the provincial cities, would not have cared to do so. They spent their time and money enjoying what they had, and passing on judicious gifts to their own municipalities in order to increase their popularity. Any idea that most of them might have assumed a more permanent share of the financial burdens which weighed upon those municipalities seems unlikely and purely hypothetical.

At that point, I think, the Roman empire parts company with the Europe of today. It might have been ideal if the government of the Roman empire could have been devolved to the provincial Councils, but it was not practical. Today, instead of provincial Councils we have independent countries. Instead of the central Roman imperial administration we have an embryonic, or foreseeable, government of Europe. How far ought this Europe to retain central powers, and how far ought these to be devolved to the member countries? In other words, do we want a Federal Europe, or a Europe of Nations? Opinions differ sharply on the matter (personally I want a Europe of Nations).

We ought to study the Roman empire, during its precarious height under the Antonines, before we even begin to address ourselves to that modern problem. That is why the present book has been written.

# CHRONOLOGICAL TABLE

### HADRIAN AD 117–38

| | |
|---|---|
| 138 | Antoninus Pius adopted as successor |
| 138 | Fronto made tutor to Marcus Aurelius and Lucius Verus |

### ANTONINUS PIUS AD 138–61

| | |
|---|---|
| 140–1 | Antonine Wall in Britain |
| 140/1 | Death of Faustina the elder, wife of Antoninus Pius |
| 143 (or a little later) | Speech of Aelius Aristides *To Rome* |
| 144 | Death of Polemo |
| *c.* 144 | Excommunication of Marcion |
| After 155 | New German frontier established |
| *c.* 159 | Dacia divided into three provinces |

### MARCUS AURELIUS AD 161–80

| | |
|---|---|
| 162–6, from 169 | Galen at Rome, Apuleius famous at Carthage |
| 163–6 | Lucius Verus, joint emperor, in the east |
| 165 | Execution of Justin Martyr |
| *c.* 166–8 | German tribes penetrated northern frontier |
| 169 | Death of Lucius Verus |
| 175 | Revolt of Avidius Cassius |
| 175 | Death of Faustina the younger, wife of Marcus Aurelius |
| 177 | Commodus, son of Marcus Aurelius, married Crispina and made joint Augustus (Caesar from 166) |
| 177 | Christians executed at Lugdunum (Lyon) |
| 177 and *c.* 178 | Deaths of Herodes Atticus and Ptolemy |
| 178–80 | Marcus Aurelius on northern frontier |

### COMMODUS AD 180–92

| | |
|---|---|
| After 180 | Deaths of Lucian and Appian |
| 182/3 | Conspiracy of Lucilla (widow of Lucius Verus) and Crispina |
| 182–9 | Government by praetorian prefects |

| | |
|---|---|
| *c.* 185 | Irenaeus *Against Heresies* |
| 186 | Revolt of Maternus |

## PERTINAX, DIDIUS JULIANUS AD 193, SEPTIMIUS SEVERUS AD 193–211

| | |
|---|---|
| *c.* 193 | Completion of Column of Aurelius |
| 193–4 | Revolt of Pescennius Niger |
| 194–7 | Revolt of Clodius Albinus |

# ABBREVIATIONS

| | |
|---|---|
| *BMC Imp.* | H. Mattingly, *Coins of the Roman Empire in the British Museum*, 1928–50. |
| *CIL* | *Corpus Inscriptionum Latinarum.* |
| Dio Epit. | Dio Cassius, *Roman History*, Epitome by Xiphilinus (ed. E. Cary, Loeb, Vol. IX, 1927). |
| Fronto | Marcus Cornelius Fronto, *Correspondence* (ed. C. R. Haines, Loeb, 1982). |
| *Med.* | Marcus Aurelius, *Meditations* (ed. M. Staniforth, Penguin, 1964). |
| *RIC* | H. Mattingly and E. A. Sydenham, *Roman Imperial Coinage*, Vol. III, 1930. |
| *SHA* | *Scriptores Historiae Augustae* (ed. D. Magie, Loeb, Vol. I, 1930). |

# REFERENCES

## 1 ANTONINUS PIUS

1  Dio Epit. LXIX, 20.2–5 (trans. E. Cary).
2  Eutropius VIII, 8.
3  *RIC* II, 294, 445ff, 483, 1078ff.
4  Ibid. 484, 1086, 1087.
5  *RIC* III, 28.18, 19.
6  Ibid. 21.
7  *CIL* VI.984.
8  *SHA: Antoninus* 2.3–7 (trans. A. Birley); cf. *Hadrian* 24.3–5.
9  *CIL* VI.1001.
10  *RIC* III, 28.24, 30.42, 31.52, etc.
11  Ibid. 35.79, 50.201.
12  Ibid. 165.1148, 169.1195.
13  Ibid. 30.69, 114.660.
14  Ibid. 155.1057A, etc.
15  Ibid. 35.77, 109.612f.
16  Ibid. 94.506, 192.1378.
17  Ibid. 49.190.
18  Pliny the younger, *Panegyricus,* 75.
19  *RIC* III, 25.3, 136.881, 139.907.
20  *SHA: Antoninus* 7.11; cf. M. Cary and H. H. Scullard, *A History of Rome,* 3rd edn, p. 433, and A. Piganiol, *Histoire de Rome,* p. 294, against Aelius Aristides and John Malalas (p. 280, Bonn).
21  *RIC* III, 112.642f, 116.691a; 34.73.
22  Ibid. 74f, 165.1149ff.
23  Ibid. 134.861ff.
24  *SHA: Antoninus* 7.11, 12.
25  *RIC* III, 37.94ff, etc.
26  Ibid. 110.624; cf. II, 425.623.
27  *RIC* III, 33.107.
28  Ibid. 104ff, 574ff.
29  *BMC Imp.* IV, p. xcv.
30  Ibid. 9.14.
31  *RIC* III, 37.100.
32  Ibid. 108.604, 12f.769; cf. II, 367.232.
33  *RIC* III, 111.634a, 119.721.

34 *SHA: Avidius Cassius* 10.1; cf. R. Syme, *Ammianus and the Historia Augusta*, p. 170.
35 *SHA: Antoninus Pius* 5.4–5.
36 Pausanias VIII.43.3.
37 C. Daniels, in J. Wacher (ed.), *The Roman World*, I, p. 227.
38 *RIC* III, 121.742.
39 Ibid. 110.620.
40 G. E. Bean, *Aegean Turkey*, pp. 132, 223.
41 A. Garzetti, *From Tiberius to the Antonines*, p. 465.
42 *SHA: Marcus Antoninus* 8.6; *CIL* IX, 2457; H. Dessau, *Inscriptiones Latinae Selectae*, 1076.
43 *SHA: Antoninus Pius* 12.7.
44 *Med.* I.16, VI.30.
45 *Regionary Catalogue*, IX.
46 *SHA: The Three Gordians* 3.3; Julian, *Caesars*, 312A.
47 *Med.* IV.33, VIII.25.
48 *SHA: Antoninus Pius* 13.4 (trans. A. Birley).
49 See W. Weber, *Cambridge Ancient History*, XI (1936), p. 328.
50 *RIC* III, 99.538.
51 *SHA: Antoninus Pius* 12.5; cf. *RIC* III, 43.139.
52 *BMC Imp.* IV, p. xcviii.
53 H. Marsh, *The Caesars* (1972), p. 92.
54 *Med.* I.16.
55 *RIC* III, 48.185, 134.859, 145.961; cf. E. Wistrand, 'Felicitas Imperatoria', *American Journal of Philology*, CVIII, 1986.

## 2 MARCUS AURELIUS AND LUCIUS VERUS

1 T. D. Barnes, *Journal of Roman Studies*, LVII, 1967, p. 78.
2 *RIC* III, 49.191; cf. 94.506, etc.
3 Ibid. 79.422ff, 171.1206ff.
4 Ibid. 79.424, 174.1234; 81.432, 175.1242; 79.423, 174.1238.
5 M. Grant, *Roman Imperial Money*, p. 225.
6 *RIC* III, 93f.494f, 191.1367ff.
7 Ibid. 95.50f, 192.1380ff; 94.503f, 191.1372ff; 95.509; 95.511; 94.505.
8 On these see *SHA: Marcus Antoninus* 1.5–9.
9 Ibid. 10.
10 Eutropius VIII, 11.
11 *SHA: Verus* 3.7 (trans. A. Birley; cf. note by D. Magie, Loeb edn, I, p. 212, n. 4).
12 Justin, *Apology*, 1.
13 *SHA: Verus* 3.4; cf. *Marcus Antoninus* 7.6.
14 Ammianus Marcellinus XXVII, 6.16.
15 *Med.* I.17 (trans. M. Staniforth).
16 *RIC* III, 250.444ff, 316.1276ff.
17 *SHA: Verus* 10.6–8 (trans. A. Birley).
18 R. Syme, *Ammianus and the Historia Augusta*, p. 90.
19 *BMC Imp.* IV, p. cxii n. 5.
20 *SHA: Verus* 1.4, 5.
21 Ibid. 2.9 (trans. A. Birley).
22 Dio Epit. 71.1.3.
23 *SHA: Verus* 6.8–7.1 (trans. A. Birley).
24 Ibid. 7.9.

25 J. M. C. Toynbee, *Roman Medallions*, pp. 84f.
26 *SHA: Marcus Antoninus* 20.2.
27 J. F. Gilliam, *American Journal of Philology*, LXXXII, 1961, pp. 215–26.
28 Caesar, *Gallic Wars*, IV, 1.3.
29 Tacitus, *Germania*, 42.
30 T. Sulimirski, *The Sarmatians*, pp. 17f, 31, 134, 171, 175, 177.
31 A. R. Birley, *Marcus Aurelius*, p. 169.
32 Ammianus Marcellinus XXIX, 6.1; cf. E. Scheidel, *Chiron* XX, 1990, pp. 1–8, who prefers 170 as the date.
33 Pausanias X, 34.5.
34 *SHA: Marcus Antoninus* 22.1: Ammianus Marcellinus XXXI, 5.13.
35 Eutropius VIII, 12.
36 M. Grant, *Roman Imperial Money*, pp. 248, 241ff.
37 Dio Epit. 71.3.1.
38 *SHA: Marcus Antoninus* 14.5.
39 *SHA: Lucius Verus* 10–11 (trans. A. Birley).
40 Pausanias VIII, 43.6.
41 J. M. C. Toynbee, *Roman Medallions*, p. 145.

## 3 MARCUS AURELIUS

1 *CIL* IX.2478.
2 *BMC Imp.* IV, p. cxlvii.
3 *Med.* I.11.
4 Ibid. XII.20.
5 Ibid. VI.13 (trans. M. Staniforth).
6 *RIC* III, 244.401; cf. *BMC Imp.* IV, pp. cxxx, cxlvi; *Med.* IX.1.
7 *SHA: Marcus Antoninus* 11.10.
8 *Med.* VI.44.
9 *SHA: Marcus Antoninus* 10.10.
10 Dio Epit. 72.6.2.
11 *RIC* III, 235.285, 248f.1070ff.
12 Dio Epit. 72.8.1–4, 10.1–3 (trans. E. Cary).
13 *SHA: Marcus Antoninus* 23.8, etc.
14 *Med.* I, 9.27.
15 Dio Epit. 72.3–6.
16 Tacitus, *Annals*, XV, 44.
17 *Med.* XI.3 (trans. M. Staniforth).
18 Eusebius, *Ecclesiastical History*, v.1.3–63.
19 *CIL* VIII.21567.
20 *RIC* III, 119.210, cf. 228.193.
21 *Inscriptiones Latinae Selectae*, 8977.
22 *SHA: Marcus Antoninus* 17.3.
23 *RIC* III, 294.1021ff, 297f.1058f; Dio Epit. 72.3.5.
24 Orosius 7.15.10.
25 Eusebius, *Chronological Tables*.
26 G. E. M. de Sainte Croix, in M. I. Finley, *Studies in Ancient Society*, p. 222. For the date, O. Salomies, *Arctos* XXIV, 1990, pp. 107–112.
27 *Med.* I.17.
28 *SHA: Marcus Antoninus* 24.3.
29 Ibid. 21.7f.
30 Dio Epit. 72.22.2.

31 Ibid. 72.3.1.
32 Ibid. 72.4.1–4.
33 Ibid. 72.22.3–23.2 (trans. E. Cary).
34 Ibid. 72.27.1; *L'Année Épigraphique*, 1956, 124.
35 *SHA: Avidius Cassius* 9.11, 10.5, 11.1.
36 *Med.* vi.13.
37 *SHA: Marcus Antoninus* 19.9.
38 *Med.* i.17; Fronto i, pp. 126ff.
39 *RIC* iii, 274.751ff, 346.1659ff, 350–1711ff.
40 Ibid. 115.678.
41 *SHA: Marcus Antoninus* 2.6.
42 Fronto i, p. 179, n. 1.
43 *Med.* ii.17, vii.16.
44 Ibid. xi.5, 7, i.17, viii.1, 8 (trans. N. Staniforth).
45 *SHA: Marcus Antoninus* 27.7; cf. Plato, *Republic*, v, 473D.
46 *Med.* vi.44 (trans. M. Staniforth).
47 Ibid. ii.5, iii.5.
48 Ibid. v.1 (trans. M. Staniforth).
49 Ibid. i.8, 17 (trans. M. Staniforth).
50 Dio Epit. 72.6.3–4, 34.2, 36.2–3.
51 Galen, *On Antidotes*, xiv, 3, 4.
52 Galen, *On Prognosis*, xi, 1–8.
53 Julian, *Caesars*, 317C.
54 *SHA: Marcus Antoninus* 29.6–7.
55 *Med.* i.17.
56 Ibid. n. 5.
57 *Med.* v.10.4.
58 Ibid. iv.12, vi.22, viii.5, xi.21, xii.20.
59 Dio Epit. 62.34.2f, 363 (trans. E. Cary).
60 C. Parain, *Marc-Aurèle*, p. 204.
61 Julian, *Caesars*, 312A–B, 328D, 333B, 334B, 335C.

# 4 MARCUS AURELIUS AND COMMODUS

1 Dio Epit. 72.10.33.1.
2 *RIC* iii, 343.1013 (AD 179).
3 M. Grant, *The Roman Emperors*, p. 95. See also M. Stahl, *Chiron*, xix, 1989, pp. 289–317.
4 *RIC* iii, 262ff.597ff, 334ff.1513ff; 264.623ff, 337.1550ff (dated a year earlier); 265ff.632ff, 338.1556, 339.1566ff.
5 W. Weber, *Cambridge Ancient History*, xi, pp. 376f.
6 Julian, *Caesars*, 312B.
7 *SHA: Marcus Antoninus* 19.1.
8 *BMC Imp.* iv, p. cxxvi, n. 4.
9 Herodian 1.5.6.; cf. *RIC* iii, 381.139 (NOBILITas AVGusti).
10 Dio Epit. 72.33.4.
11 E. Gibbon, *History of the Decline and Fall of the Roman Empire*, Ch. iii (Penguin edn, 1993, Vol. i, p. 90).
12 *RIC* iii, 337f, 264ff, 441, 654ff.

## 5 COMMODUS

1 *RIC* iii, 401.294–5.
2 Ibid. 366f, 3, 8; 401.292, 402.296.
3 Herodian 1.6.3.; cf. *RIC* iii, 370.38 (SECVRITAS PVBLICA).
4 *RIC* iii, 377f.110, 107.
5 Dio Epit. 73.7.4.
6 *CIL* viii.10570, 14464.
7 Trans. N. Lewis and M. Reinhold, *Roman Civilisation*, ii, p. 184.
8 *SHA: Commodus* 14.16.
9 Ibid. 1.7.
10 Dio Epit. 73.17.2., 21.1–2.
11 Ibid. 1.1–2.
12 *SHA: Commodus* 3.6, 4.5.
13 Dio Epit. 73.4.6; *SHA: Commodus* 5.9.
14 Herodian 1.8.4.–7.
15 Ammianus Marcellinus xxix, 1.17.
16 Herodian 1.10.3.
17 Ibid. 1.10.6–7 (trans. E. Echols).
18 *SHA: Commodus* 5.1, 6.6.
19 Herodian 1.9.1. (trans. E. Echols); Dio Epit. 73.9.
20 *RIC* iii, 420.468.
21 Herodian 1.9.10 (trans. E. Echols).
22 Dio Epit. 73.12.1–2, 3, 5 (trans. E. Cary).
23 Ammianus Marcellinus xxvi, 6.9.
24 *SHA: Commodus* 7.1 (trans. A. Birley).
25 *RIC* iii, 388.201.
26 *SHA: Commodus* 7.9.
27 *RIC* iii, 395.248, 438.631.
28 Ibid. 392ff.230ff, 433ff.595ff.
29 *BMC Imp.* iv, p. clxiii.
30 J. Aymard, *Revue des études latines*, xiv, 1936, p. 361.
31 *SHA: Commodus* 11.9.
32 *RIC* iii, 381.138.
33 Ibid. 396.255, 434.596; 396.256, 434.597.
34 *Inscriptiones Latinae Selectae* 400.
35 Cf. *CIL* iii.395f, 439; and see next note, and M. P. Speidel, 'Commodus the God-Emperor and the Army', *Journal of Roman Studies*, LXXXIII, 1993, pp. 109–114.
36 *RIC* iii, 390.221, 432.581, 433.591.
37 *CIL* iii.395.250ff, 394.249.
38 Dio Epit. 73.15.6, 16.1.
39 Ibid. 72.34.
40 *RIC* iii, 379.119.
41 Ibid. 457.628, 397.261.
42 *SHA: Commodus* 8.1.
43 *RIC* iii, 382.146.
44 Ibid. 430.561.
45 *BMC Imp.* iv, pp. xii, clxxxiv.
46 W. Weber, *Cambridge Ancient History*, xi, p. 392.
47 Dio Epit. 73.22.1–2, 4–5 (trans. E. Cary).
48 Julian, *Caesars*, 312C.
49 *SHA: Commodus* 16.19 (trans. A. Birley).

50  *CIL* vi.992.
51  *SHA: Commodus* 17.11, *Septimius Severus* 11.3f.

# 6 ANTONINE SPEAKING AND WRITING

## Latin

1  M. Hadas, *History of Latin Literature*, p. 336.
2  Florus 1.1.
3  Fronto i, pp. xxiii, 293, xi.
4  Eumenius, *Panegyric* v, 14.
5  Macrobius, *Satires* v.1; Jerome, *Epistles*, 12; Claudius Mamertus, *Epistula ad Sepandum*; Sidonius Apollinaris, *Epistulae* iv, 3.
6  See Fronto i, pp. xiiif, xxv, xxviii, xxiii, xxxv.
7  Fronto i, 18.
8  Fronto i, pp. 75, cf. 91, 77; pp. 109, 113; pp. 189, 113, 115.
9  Fronto i, 17.
10  Fronto ii, 74, 82.
11  *Med.* i.11; cf. vi.13, 20.
12  Fronto i, 241, 243; cf. pp. 39, 81, 173, 199, 201, 219, 223, 227, 231, 253.
13  Fronto i, 233.
14  Fronto i, 307, 309.
15  Gaius, *Institutes*, i.5.
16  M. Grant, in Apuleius, *The Golden Ass* (Penguin edn), pp. viiff.
17  Augustine, *Civitas Dei*, xviii, 18.
18  Apuleius, *Metamorphoses*, xi, 27.
19  Gellius, *Noctes Atticae*, praef. 4; cf. 23–4, 1, 2.

## Greek

1  M. Grant, *Readings in the Classical Historians*, pp. 522ff.
2  Fronto i, pp. 263ff.
3  For example, by E. Badian, *Aufstieg und Niedergang der römischen Welt*, i, i, p. 707.
4  E. L. Bowie, in K. J. Dover, *Ancient Greek Literature*, p. 160; A. Lesley, *History of Greek Literature*, p. 846.
5  M. Grant, op. cit. pp. 544ff.
6  P. E. Easterling and B. M. W. Knox (eds) *Greek Literature*, p. 887.
7  M. Grant, *Greek and Latin Authors*, pp. 368f.
8  Ibid. pp. 38f; cf. F. Gasco, 'The Meeting between Aelius Aristides and Marcus Aurelius in Smyrna', *American Journal of Philology*, cx, 1989, pp. 471–8.
9  C. P. Jones, *Classical Review*, lxii, 1979, pp. 134ff, against S. A. Stertz, *Classical Quarterly*, 1979, pp. 171ff.
10  M. Grant, op. cit., pp. 171ff; F. Kudlien and R. J. Durling (eds) *Galen's Methods of Healing: Proceedings of the 1982 Galen Symposium* (Kiel), 1991; J. J. Vallance, *Journal of Hellenic Studies*, cxiii, 1993, pp. 197f.
11  P. E. Easterling and B. M. W. Knox (eds) op. cit. pp. 674ff; J. Bompaire (ed.) *Lucien de Samosate*, Tome i, 1993 (Introduction générale).
12  Lucian, *Twice Prosecuted*, 33.
13  Lucian, *Alexander*, 48.
14  P. Levi, *History of Greek Literature*, p. 459.

15 Ibid.
16 M. Grant, *The Climax of Rome*, pp. 133ff; cf. P. A. Brunt, *Journal of Roman Studies*, LXIV, 1974, pp. 1ff.
17 Fronto I, p. 12, n. 1.
18 Ibid. p. 81.
19 *Med.* II.5, III.12.
20 *Med.* III.12.
21 *Med.* XII.26, II.17 (trans. M. Staniforth).
22 *Med.* XII.28.
23 Fronto I, p. cx.
24 *Med.* VII.69.
25 *Med.* x.5 (trans. M. Staniforth).
26 *Med.* VII.69 (trans. M. Staniforth); cf. IV.49.
27 *Med.* IV.33 and 48, v.10, VII.3, x.27.
28 *Med.* IX.20.
29 *Med.* VIII.59.
30 G. Anderson in D. A. Russell, *Antonine Literature*, pp. 10ff.
31 M. Grant, *Greek and Latin Authors*, pp. 314ff.
32 Photius, *Bibliotheca* 94.
33 M. Grant, *Greek and Latin Authors*, pp. 1f.
34 Pollux III.83; cf. G. E. M. de Sainte Croix, *The Class Struggles in the Ancient Greek World*, pp. 139f.

### Christian

1 M. Grant, *Greek and Latin Authors*, pp. 242f.
2 A. R. Birley, *Marcus Aurelius*, p. 173.
3 Lucian, *On The Death of Peregrinus*.

## 7 ANTONINE ARCHITECTURE AND ART

1 J. M. C. Toynbee, *Roman Medallions*, pp. 139, 146.
2 *SHA: Commodus* 17.5.
3 P. MacKendrick, *The Mute Stones Speak*, p. 321.
4 E. Strong, *Art in Ancient Rome*, II, pp. 129ff.
5 P. MacKendrick, *The Greek Stones Speak*, 2nd edn, pp. 476ff.
6 Ibid. pp. 468, 470.
7 A. Boethius and J. B. Ward-Perkins, *Etruscan and Roman Architecture*, pp. 417, 419, 421.
8 R. E. M. Wheeler, *Roman Art and Architecture*, p. 96.
9 A. Boethius and J. B. Ward-Perkins, op. cit. pp. 428, 434, 439, 441, 443.
10 S. J. Keay, *Roman Spain*, pp. 140, 113.
11 P. MacKendrick, *The Iberian Stones Speak*, pp. 186ff.
12 R. Brilliant, *Roman Art*, p. 180.
13 E. Strong, op. cit. p. 124; fig. 435.
14 R. E. M. Wheeler, op. cit. p. 170.
15 E. Strong, op. cit. p. 126.
16 *RIC* III, 111.629, 119.722, 120.733.
17 H. Kähler, *Rome and Her Empire*, pp. 164f.
18 R. Brilliant, op. cit. pp. 260f.
19 J. M. C. Toynbee, *The Art of the Romans*, p. 105; cf. p. 174.

20 R. Brilliant, op. cit. p. 257.
21 *CIL* vi.1585.
22 *RIC* iii, 233.264.
23 H. Kähler, op. cit. p. 167.
24 D. E. Strong, *Roman Imperial Sculpture*, p. 52.
25 *RIC* iii, 411.382.
26 J. M. C, Toynbee, *Roman Medallions*, pp. 112, 125, 132, 134.

## 8 THE ANTONINE AGE

1 E. Gibbon, *History of the Decline and Fall of the Roman Empire*, Ch. iii (Penguin edn, 1993, Vol. i, p. 90).
2 Aelius Aristides, *Roman Oration (To Rome)* 94, 96f. (trans. J. H. Oliver).
3 Fronto i, p. 73.
4 E. A. Thompson in M. I. Finley, *Studies in Ancient Society*, pp. 31f.
5 Herodian i.10.1f (trans. E. C. Echols).
6 G. E. M. de Sainte Croix, *The Class Struggle in the Ancient Greek World*, p. 445.
7 Aelius Aristides, op. cit.
8 M. Rostovtzeff, *Social and Economic History of the Roman Empire*, p. 148.
9 *Inscriptiones Graecae ad Res Romanas Pertinentes* 3.69.
10 R. MacMullen, *Enemies of the Roman Order*, p. 249.
11 Galen, *On Wholesome and Unwholesome Foods* (*De Probis Pravisque Alimentorum Succis*) i.1–7 (trans. G. E. M. de Sainte Croix).
12 Cf. Chapter 3 (p. 50).
13 Ecphantes, *On Kingship* (E. R. Goodenough, *Yale Classical Studies*, 1928, pp. 76–8); cf. *Digest*, xiv, ii, 9 (Eudaemon), *L'Année épigraphique*, 1960, p. 314 (Attaleia).
14 *CIL* ii.2548.
15 Merlin, *Comptes-Rendus de l'Académie des Inscriptions*, 1919, pp. 355ff.
16 *Oxyrhynchus Papyri* iii.473.
17 G. E. M. de Sainte Croix, *The Class Struggle in the Ancient Greek World*, pp. 459ff.
18 Dio Epit. 72.36.4.
19 *CIL* ix.2438.
20 C. Parain, *Marc-Aurèle*, pp. 119f.
21 *Sibylline Oracle*, viii (trans. M. S. Tercy); cf. M. Grant, *The World of Rome*, p. 60.
22 H. Kähler, *Rome and Her Empire*, p. 164.
23 Lucian, *On The Death of Peregrinus*, 19.
24 M. Cary and H. H. Scullard, *A History of Rome*, 3rd edn, pp. 449f.

# NOTES

## INTRODUCTION

**Antonines**   Sometimes the term 'Antonines' is loosely employed to cover the entire period from Nerva (AD 96–8) to Commodus. This is misleading.

**Coins**   Under Antoninus Pius alone there were more than a thousand separate issues, each conveying some propagandist message.

## 1 ANTONINUS PIUS

**Antoninus Pius**   For his biographies, see Bryant, Hüttl, Lacour-Gayet, De Regibus (pp. 194ff). With regard to his name, R. Syme (*Emperors and Biography*, p. 37) doubts whether Antoninus Pius was really called 'Boionius'; but he leaves the matter open. On most of his coins after he became emperor he is called 'Antoninus Aug. Pius P.P.', but from 150/1 he is described as 'T. Aelius Hadrianus Antoninus Pius' (*RIC* III, p. 50 nos 200ff, p. 52 nos 209ff, p. 135 nos 869ff, p. 137 nos 887ff, p. 138 nos 895ff, p. 144 no. 948, p. 149 no. 1005).

**Hadrian's speech**   Hadrian was probably intending to point out that a senator could become *princeps*.

**Deification and Cult of Hadrian**   This cult was sometimes assoicated with cults of Marciana (the sister of Trajan) and her daughter Matidia. In 119 Hadrian had apparently flanked a Temple of Matidia at Rome with halls commemorating both ladies.

**Pius**   A temple of Pietas (Eusebeia) was erected in Hadrian's house at Puteoli (Pozzuoli).

**Temples to Faustina the elder**   These were, for example, at Rome, with Antoninus Pius (S. Lorenzo in Miranda), and at Eleusis (Lefsina). Temples of Antoninus and Faustina the elder in Egypt were apparently the last independent temples to rulers that were erected in that country.

**Alleged stinginess of Antoninus Pius**   Certainly, expenditure on public works was carefully controlled – and restricted (Chapter 7). And Antoninus left 675 million *denarii* to the treasury at his death (Dio Epit. 74.8.3).

174

**Laws of Antoninus Pius** Hadrian had elaborated the Law to a remarkable degree. During the reign of Antoninus Pius a handbook of departmental rules was issued, the *Gnomon of the Idios Logos*, incorporating many instructions of earlier, and especially Augustan, date.

**IVSTITIA** It has been conjectured that this coin-type may have possessed some reference to the deportation of three persons, for an unknown reason (A. Garzetti, *From Tiberius to the Antonines*, p. 447). But Antoninus Pius was also keen on justice in general.

**Alimenta** For a discussion of the aims behind these schemes, see A. R. Hands, *Charities and Social Aid in Greece and Rome* (1968), p. 108, and C. Bossu, *Latomus* XCVIII, 1989, pp. 372–82; cf. M. Cary and H. H. Scullard, *A History of Rome,* 3rd edn, pp. 643f, n. 24. See also Chapter 2 and note, p. 177. Imperial *alimenta* were also supplemented from private sources, e.g. at Sicca Veneria (El Kef).

**Faustina the elder** Her coins, portraying Venus as 'Augusta' (*RIC*, III, p. 67 no. 333), recall that the goddess was the divine ancestress of the *Gens Julia*. These pieces, therefore, reflect Antoninus's special care for Italy (J. M. C. Toynbee, *Roman Medallions*, p. 141), as does her medallion-type SABINAE, illustrating a drive to revive ancient marriage customs (*ibid.* p. 144).

**Army of Antoninus Pius** In 140 there was a change in the formula of auxiliaries' diplomas (M. Hassall, in J. Wacher (ed.), *The Roman World*, II, p. 696).

**Britain** Not long after this period there were new confederacies of the Maeatae in the lowlands and of Caledonian tribesmen further north.

**Alani, Alans** Non-German nomadic pastoralists who at this epoch lived north of the Caucasus Mountains, which they often tried to cross.

**Trogodytes** These were a primitive people living between Suez and the Straits of Bab-el-Mandeb and further south to the Ethiopian escarpment.

**Antonine Wall** Possibly it was temporarily remanned under Commodus, but it may have been damaged in *c.* 184 and abandoned in 186/7. Was it briefly reoccupied in the time of Septimius Severus?

**Upper German Limes** Forts were built at Niederbieber and Holzhausen, and those at Kösching and Pförring were rebuilt. After the establishment of the new Outer Line the Inner line was soon abandoned. The last major change was the creation of the 'Pfahlgraben' (palisaded ditches), which is generally attributed to Caracalla (211–217), though some would ascribe this development as early as the middle of the second century.

**REX QVADIS DATVS** A *foederati* relationship (A. Lengyel and G. T. B. Radan (eds), *The Archaeology of Roman Pannonia*, 1080, p. 08).

**Antoninus Pius and the Greeks** Aristides perhaps overstresses his love of the Greeks and their education.

175

**Health**    Temples were built for Aesculapius (Asclepius) at Pergamum (Bergama), and elsewhere (Chapter 7).

**Antoninus Pius's reign static**    There was a certain lack of future promise; see H. Mattingly, *BMC Imp.* IV, pp. ci, xi.

# 2 MARCUS AURELIUS AND LUCIUS VERUS

**Antoninus Pius's chronology**    The dates of his tribunician power were retrospectively amended, apparently to stress the permanence of the dynasty (Mattingly, *BMC Imp.* IV, pp. xxxix, lxvi).

**Death of Galerius Antoninus**    This was probably before 138 (A. R. Birley, *Marcus Aurelius*, pp. 242f). There is a coin of his lifetime, of an uncertain Greek city, showing his head (H. Cohen, *Description historique des monnaies frappées sous l'empire romain*, II 2nd edn, p. 443).

**Marcus Aurelius**    The outstanding biography in our own language, to which I am happy to acknowledge a substantial debt, is that of A. R. Birley, op. cit. For others, see Carrata Thomes, Clayton-Dove, Cresson, Farquharson, Goerlitz, Hayward, Klein, Matheson, Parain, Piganiol, Renan, Sedgwick, Soleri, Stella, von Wilamowitz-Moellendorf (pp. 194ff), and studies of the *Meditations*.

**Powers and names of Marcus Aurelius under Antoninus Pius**    He became Marcus Aelius Aurelius Verus when the adoptive son of Antoninus Pius, and Marcus Aurelius Antoninus when he came to the throne. He was not at any stage given the title of *Princeps Juventutis*, because he moved up too quickly.

**Marcus Aurelius's engagement to Faustina the younger**    Perhaps his grandfather Marcus Annius Verus was behind this. At Hadrian's wish Faustina had previously been betrothed to the boy Lucius Verus. She became Augusta after the birth of her first child in 146 (whereas Aurelius did not become Augustus until 161). Her elder sister Aurelia Fadilla had died young.

**Honos and Virtus**    These were military virtues (Silius Italicus xv. 98f; Mattingly, *BMC Imp.* IV, p. xlviii n. 3).

**Hadrian and Marcus Aurelius**    Hadrian's interest has been criticized as the first attempt to name a successor's successor but, as stated in the text, this is doubtful.

**Lucius Verus**    According to one view, Hadrian kept him in the palace, because he feared that there might be efforts, after his own death, to claim the throne for him. Antoninus Pius, despite his liking for Lucius Verus, perhaps treated him somewhat as a child, and ignored him in the final gestures of his life. Some have concluded that Verus became co-emperor by the grace of Marcus Aurelius (although the 'corrrespondence' between them is a fake), and not of Antoninus Pius. But an inscribed relief of 160 does show Antoninus between the two of them (A. Garzetti, *From Tiberius to the Antonines*, p. 706). It is perhaps fair to call Aurelius and Verus complementary rather than harmonious. Verus's names were greatly mixed up by ancient authors (R. Syme, *Emperors and Biography*, p. 80). He and Fronto were fond of one another (and Verus was hurt when Fronto failed to visit him), though Fronto did urge him to improve himself.

**Marcus Aurelius and Lucilla**   Alarmed by Lucius Verus's infatuation for Panthea (mentioned in the *Meditations* VIII. 37), Aurelius said that he would accompany his daughter Annia Aurelia Galeria Lucilla (Verus's fiancée) to Syria, but eventually let her go alone. Born in *c.* 148, on arrival in the east in 164 Lucilla became Verus's wife at Ephesus (Selçuk); thereafter, Aurelius named the girl-orphans for whom he provided institutional assistance (*alimenta*; cf. Chapter 1 and note) after the two of them. (She must be distinguished from Domitia Lucilla, who was Marcus Aurelius's mother.)

**Britain**   Sextus Calpurnius Agricola was sent to crush the British troubles (162–6).

**Gaul**   There were disturbances among the Sequani.

**Parthia**   There seems to have been a decline in Parthian art from *c.* 150, probably due to the continual damaging tension with Rome.

**Babylonia**   This was for a short time Trajan's province of Assyria (AD 116).

**Seleucia-on-the-Tigris**   This city (beside Opis) had been the original capital of the Hellenistic monarch Seleucus I (d. 281 BC). It stood on a natural lake, with a port for river and even maritime shipping. The Parthian king Vologaeses I (AD 51/52–79/80) founded Vologaesia close to Seleucia in order to undermine its non-Parthian influence.

**Osrhoene**   Its capital was Edessa (see pp. 21, 31, 178). The kingdom was founded in 132 BC.

**Adiabene**   This was overrun by Trajan in AD 116, but the effect was only temporary.

**Armenia**   Its kings included the Arsacids Vologaeses (116–140/3), Sohaemus (of Emesa [Homs] C 140/3–160, 164–185 or *c.* 192), Pacorus (160–3).

**Rome and Parthia**   The Parthians endeavoured to prevent the Romans from communicating directly with China, which was why the Romans tried to develop a route that evaded them. A customs tariff of Palmyra (AD 137) has come to light (*Orientis Graeci Inscriptiones Selectae* 629: *Inscriptiones Graecae ad Res Romanas Pertinentes* III. 1056). Hadrian had favoured a peaceful settlement.

**Pressure from central Asia**   In 135/6 the nomad Alani, egged on by the border state of Iberia (roughly = Georgia), poured into the Parthian empire from the north and even broke into Roman Cappadocia.

**Vologaeses III of Parthia**   He called himself 'Philhellene', like his predecessors. But he was far from pro-Roman. He had invaded Armenia before, in 155, so as to overthrow the Roman protégé Sohaemus (of Emesa), but was warned off by Antoninus Pius and withdrew.

**Campaigns of 163–4**   Adiabene and Hatra (El Hadr) (which Trajan had failed to capture) may have accepted Roman overlordship. Part of a Roman legion (Legio I Minervia) seems to have crossed the Krestovy (Dariel) pass into Iberia.

**Lucius Verus and Parthia**   One view was that Verus offered Parthia terms, which Vologaeses III scornfully rejected (Nazarius, *Panegyric* XXIV, 6). Verus himself spent four winters at Laodicea (Lattakie), at the mouth of the River Orontes (Nahr el-Assi), and visited the pleasure resort Daphne, a suburb of Antioch (Antakya) (*SHA: Verus* 7.3). One of Verus's principal commanders was Marcus Claudius Fronto (*Inscriptiones Latinae Selectae* 1097, 1098).

**Edessa**   The city was located in a ring of hills open to the south and surrounded by a fertile plain. Although it had been more or less independent for a long time, its regal coinage begins under Vaël (AD 163–5), some of whose issues bear the head of his suzerain Vologaeses III of Parthia. In 166/7, however, the Romans placed Mannus VIII on the throne – but probably they had already attempted to do the same some three or four years earlier. Thereafter Edessa (like Carrhae [Haran]) became a Roman colony, Edessa coining in his name (he is described as *Philoromaios*) and with the heads of Marcus Aurelius and his family. Mannus was succeeded by Abgar VIII (AD 179–214).

**Seleucia destroyed**   This perhaps occurred because, after first opening its gates to the Romans, it subsequently broke an agreement.

**Ctesiphon destroyed**   Later it recovered to become the capital of the Sassanian Persians, who superseded the Parthians in 223–6.

**Marcus Aurelius and eastern wars**   One commander, Marcus Annius Sabinius Libo, was said to have sidetracked Lucius Verus and consulted his own cousin Aurelius. Lucian's *How to Write History,* was prompted, satirically, by the spate of histories of the Parthian War.

**Parthia: Aftermath of eastern wars**   In *c.* 175 Vologaeses III of Parthia threatened war in order to recover his losses, but took no action. The next king, Vologaeses IV (191–208/9), was clearly out to make trouble.

**Plague**   The Christians were blamed. Even Chinese records mention the epidemic, so that it presumably ravaged the Parthian empire.

**Gotones (Goths)**   They had left southern Scandinavia at the beginning of the first century AD, and between AD 100 and 200 migrated to lands north of the Black Sea. In 238 at the latest they began to conduct raids into the Roman empire. Their migration caused many hoards of coins to be buried.

**Quadi**   They traded, for example, with Quintus Atilius Primus in the second century (or early third?).

**Sarmatia**   In the first century AD the geographer Pomponius Mela called the land east of Germania by this name. The dividing line between the two moved somewhat to the east. When the Romans spoke of 'the Sarmatians', they often meant the western portion of that nation, the Jazyges, who had been moved from the Danube estuary by Tiberius (AD 14–37), or at least before the middle of the first century AD. Thenceforward the southern section of their people lived in what is now the Voivodina (ex-Yugoslavia), while the northern three-quarters dwelt in Hungary. The Jazyges had helped Trajan because the Dacians were their eternal enemies. The eastern portion of the Jazyges, the Roxolani, were sometimes described as 'western Alans' (see p. 175).

**Costoboci**  The suggestion that they came to Greece by sea has not been accepted. Julius Heraclides at Ephesus (Selçuk) preserved some of their cult objects.

**Marcus Aurelius**  According to one theory, he was 'caught in the middle' while planning an offensive on the Danube.

**Aurelius's excessive generosity**  Not only had he refused, or partially remitted, the 'voluntary' *aurum coronarium* but also (following Hadrian) he granted a huge remission of tax arrears (even later, in 178). His demand that the senate should vote funds was deferential yet exacting. But, in spite of his usual generosity with largesses, on one occasion he refused to award a donative to the troops, on the grounds that it would have come from the blood of fellow-citizens.

**Military pay**  This was 225 *denarii* under Augustus, 300 under Domitian, 375 under Commodus, 500 under Severus.

**Diminution of gold in aureus**  The suggestion that this was merely an adjustment to the market price of metals, and not therefore an economy, does not seem wholly acceptable. For debasements, see M. Grant, *Roman Imperial Money*, pp. 240, 242, 244.

**Emperors' expedition to north**  Chronology much disputed. The coins with PROFECTIO AVG. (the imperial departure) seem curiously late (*RIC* III, p. 290, no. 963 [Dec. 168–Dec. 169]). Had the plague caused a postponement of the emperors' departure (but see text)? It is not until Dec. 172–Dec. 173 that Marcus Aurelius is called RESTITVTOR ITALIAE (Restorer of Italy), (ibid. p. 299, no. 1077).

**Dacia reorganized**  Upper and Lower Dacia were divided (sometime after 158?) into three provinces (under procurators): Apulensis, Malvensis and Porolissensis. But in 169 or 170 Marcus Claudius Fronto took over all three. A former governor of Dacia had given up his post – perhaps he had died.

**End of German Wars**  The new Legio III Italica appeared in Raetia at some stage between 166 and 175. Coins honouring the sixth legion, on an anniversary occasion (M. Grant, *Roman Imperial Money* , p. 200), suggest that it had done well.

**Death of Verus**  The effects of debauchery, or of plague, were also surmised.

**Other troubles**  In *c.* 168 the Mauri crossed over into Baetica (southern Spain), of which the governor had to enlist the help of his colleague, the procurator of Mauretania Tingitana.

# 3 MARCUS AURELIUS

**Saepinum** The 'emperor's herdsmen' are presumably the *conductores*, holders of prime leases with tenants cultivating their lands (see p. 39). Marcus Aurelius exempted *conductores* from civic obligations.

**Marcus Aurelius and senate** He relieved the consuls by the appointment of an additional praetor (*SHA: Marcus Antoninus*, 10.11).

**Aurelius's help to honestiores** He reduced the demands on them by arranging that the senate should lay down maximum prices for gladiators (176–80) – who were becoming hard to find in sufficient numbers. There were complaints about landlords who sheltered strangers without enquiry.

**Aurelius and legislation** The praetorian prefects were consulted.

**Tellus** *Tellus, Terra Mater,* also appears on an Ephesus (Selçuk) relief, reclining below Marcus Aurelius in a sun-chariot.

**Christian social services** Christian banks and church property are heard of from the time of Commodus. Probably this sort of cohesion had earned admiration during the plague.

**Antoninus Pius and the Christians** His city prefect, Quintus Lollius Urbicus, was said to have condemned Ptolemaeus and Lucius.

**Marcus Aurelius and the Christians** His 'rescript' about persecutions (Eusebius, *Ecclesiastical History*, IV.13) is apocryphal. *Meditations* VIII.51 does not refer to the Christians. Did Aurelius feel some admiration for their stubbornness? It is questionable whether he added a direct impulse to the executions but he might have approved of them.

**Contemporary views of Christians** Celsus denounced them, Galen was against them, and Lucian did not think much of them, but handed them a back-handed, patronising tribute.

**Persecutions before 175** Eusebius's reports are of very doubtful veracity.

**Persecution at Lugdunum** The altar at Condate overlooked the confluence of the Rhodanus (Rhône) and Arar (Sâone). It was on the slopes of the Croix Rousse (once an island). The amphitheatre dated back to AD 29. The victims from Vienna (Vienne) must have been visitors from the Christian community there. The suggestion that the persecuted Christians were Syrians is unproved, although there were many Syrian businessmen in the neighbourhood.

**Persecution in 180** The *Acts of the Martyrs of Scillium* (or *Scilli*), relating to that year, is the earliest document of the church in Africa and the earliest specimen of Christian Latin.

**Rhine front** The Chatti returned to the attack (with a sea-borne invasion), and were defeated by Marcus Didius Julianus, the *legatus* of Belgica (and future emperor) in 170/2. It was also possibly he who dealt with a (partly sea-borne) attack from the Chauci, which could only be repelled after emergency provincial recruitment. Perhaps new army bases at Aardenburg (north-east of Bruges) and Oudenburg (south-east of Ostend) were the precursors of the subsequent coastal defence system.

**Danube front** Raetia was less affected by the wars than Pannonia. At some juncture Marcus Claudius Fronto was killed fighting *adversus Germanos et Jazyges* (H. Dessau, *Inscriptiones Latinae Selectae* 1098).

**Noricum** The provincial capital was moved to Ovilava (Wels), and the garrison from Virunum (Zollfeld) to the western Lauriacum (Lorch). There may also have been a detachment at Locica in the south east (west of Celeia [Celje]) until *c.* 187.

**Pannonia** Marcus Aurelius established a base at Ulcisia Castra (Szentendre), north of Aquincum (Budapest).

**Moesia Inferior (Lower Moesia)** The date of the walls of Callatis (Mangalia), erected at the town's expense, is uncertain.

**Quadi** They expelled their king and appointed Ariogaesus, not recognized by Rome; and in 174 they helped the Jazyges (Dio Epit. 72. 13. 1f).

**Legionary moves** For example, the Legio v Macedonica was moved from Troesmis (Igliţa) to Potaissa (Turda) in *c.* 175. Troops were located to meet possible further attacks from the Jazyges.

**Immigrations** Some Cotini were allowed to settle near Mursa (Osijek) and Cibalae (Vinkovci). But in 171 the Asdingi (who had turned towards Dacia: Dio Epit. 72. 12. 1f) and Victofali (or Victuali), both (like the Lacringi) described as 'Vandals', were refused admittance to the empire. So the Asdingi settled in northern Bohemia, as neighbours of the Quadi.

**Avidius Cassius** It is disputed whether he was related to the royal house of Commagene (R. Syme, *Emperors and Biography*, p. 124 n. 3). Lucius Verus was said to have suspected his intentions a long time before the revolt, but his alleged letter on the subject is a fake. It has been suggested, doubtfully, that Avidius Cassius may deliberately have spread the false rumour about Marcus Aurelius's imminent death in order to undermine the army's loyalty to him. Alternatively, he believed the rumour, which may have rushed him into precipitate action. Marcus Aurelius, on arriving in the east, avoided Antioch, which was still holding out against the loyal Publius Martius Verus. The titles 'Certa Constans' of Legio XII Fulminata suggest that it, too, adhered staunchly to Marcus Aurelius.

**Faustina the younger and Avidius Cassius** She may, conceivably, have felt that he was the only insurance against Pompeianus or Lucilla. In her letter to her husband (which is fictitious), she was said to have mentioned the earlier rebellion of Celsus against Marcus Aurelius, which may be an invention. Aurelius's reply (*SHA. Avidius Cassius* 0–8) is also a forgery.

**Character of Faustina the younger** Faustina was said to have been the mistress not only of a gladiator (or sailor) – the alleged father of Marcus Aurelius – but

181

also of Lucius Verus, and to have poisoned him. Marius Maximus must be blamed for some of these scandalous stories, and Julian and Ausonius (died *c.* AD 395) believed them. So did Madame Anne Lefebvre Dacier (1654–1720), who remarked: 'The husband will always be deceived if the wife condescends to dissemble.'

**Marcus Aurelius and sex**  Aurelius was against passion – which he regarded as a powerful disease – but not sex, despite his disparaging remarks on the subject. After the death of Faustina the younger (who had given him many children), he took the daughter of her chamberlain as his concubine.

**Deification of Faustina the younger**  On some of the coins commemorating this she is depicted, veiled and holding a sceptre, seated on Juno's peacock which is carrying her to heaven (*RIC* III, p. 349, no. 1702 etc.). Other coins in the same series are inscribed AETERNITAS (ibid. p. 273, nos 738f., pp. 348f., nos 1691ff.).

**Marcus Aurelius and duty**  His review of duties performed and neglected goes back to Pythagoras (6th century BC) and Horace (65–8 BC). Yet, despite his stress on the philosopher-king, he regarded philosophers as greater than secular leaders (*Meditations* VIII. 3).

**Health of Marcus Aurelius**  'I', said Marcus, 'had no needs, but my wretched body has perhaps' (quoted in Julian, *Caesars*, 334f.). Aesculapius is prominent on his coins and medallions, referring to the health (1) of himself, (2) of the empire (J. M. C. Toynbee, *Roman Medallions*, p. 138). When Aurelius refers to an illness at 'Chrysa', is he alluding to a town in the Troad?

**Galen and Marcus Aurelius**  Galen at least once reverted to giving him these doses of theriac (which some derive from the Sanskrit *taraca*, relief from danger). By the later 170s Galen was said to have effected a remarkable cure. Cf. A. Birley, *Marcus Aurelius*, pp. 179, 190, 216.

**Criticisms of Marcus Aurelius**  He was annoyed by the jests of Marullus, but schooled himself not to become cross about them (*SHA: Aurelius* 8).

**Imperial grandeur**  Fronto had advised him not to assume too much of this (*Meditations* I. 11). Marcus Aurelius was perhaps the least divinized of all emperors in his lifetime.

**Legend of Marcus Aurelius**  This was encouraged when Septimius Severus declared himself his son (Chapter 4), and arranged that his own ashes should be placed in the tomb of Aurelius. Gordian I (238) wrote epics on Antoninus Pius and Marcus Aurelius – of whom statues continued to abound.

## 4 MARCUS AURELIUS AND COMMODUS

**Danube campaigns**  In *c.* 176 Syrian cavalry came to Intercisa (Dunaujváros, Dunapentele), where a camp was established for them.

**Commodus**  For his biographies, see Andreotti, Grosso, Heer, Traupman (pp. 193ff.).

**Marcomannia and Sarmatia**  It has been disputed when Marcus Aurelius, convinced that the cordon system based on the Danube was unsatisfactory (as Napoleon also later believed), at first entertained the idea of creating these two new provinces (rather than one, which would not have been practical). According to one theory, he initiated the plan quite early but later abandoned it, only to resume the intention in his last years. A Roman detachment was already located as far north as Trencin, seventy-five miles north of the Danube, on the upper reaches of the River Váh (a northern tributary of the Danube, and the frontier between the Czech Republic and Slovakia). Marcus Aurelius's Column shows a conscious desire that his wars should be comparable with those of Trajan (Chapter 7). He was credited with a wish to exterminate the Sarmatians (A. R. Birley, *Marcus Aurelius*, p. 183, doubts this; and, as Aurelius's *Meditations* may perhaps suggest [x. 10], he sometimes felt sorry for them). The unanswerable question arises: would his expansions have led to more extensive northward advances? Julius Caesar was ascribed a plan to allow no independent power in the north: did Marcus Aurelius have the same idea? If so, the two new provinces were only an inadequate step on the way. Besides, his wars caused the nervous German tribes to coalesce into more powerful groupings. e.g. the Alamanni.

**Powers of Commodus**  He did not receive the *praenomen imperatoris* and the tribunician power at the same time. Marcus Aurelius's elevation of his son to be Augustus meant that he had become the only emperor to share the title twice (the first time had been with Lucius Verus).

**Crispina**  Her coins give prominence to the happiness of her married life (CONCORDIA, FECUNDITAS, DIS GENITALIBUS – though we know of no children) and to her semi-divine role as empress (Ceres, Diana, Juno, Venus). 'Hilaritas' suggests the cult of Cybele with its festival of the Hilaria (*RIC* III, pp. 398ff., 442ff.). 'Pudicitia' marks Crispina as the model of all chaste matrons, associated in the ceremonies of the Vestal Virgins. For her downfall and end, see note, p. 69.

**Marcus Aurelius and the hereditary succession**  Septimius Severus later blamed him for not quietly putting down Commodus. A small medallion of Marcus Aurelius shows busts of Commodus and his twin, who died at the age of four (J. M. C. Toynbee, *Roman Medallions*, p. 139). For details of Marcus Aurelius's numerous children, see A. Garzetti, *From Tiberius to the Antonines*, pp. 710ff. One of them was Lucilla, the wife first of Lucius Verus and then (reluctantly) of Claudius Pompeianus: see Chapter 5.

# 5 COMMODUS

**Commodus's agreements with the Germans**  As usual, the stick and the carrot were combined: restrictions plus subsidies. He was avoiding the 'slippery slope of imperialism'. Commodus also resettled certain areas within the empire (A. Lenguel and G. T. B. Raban [eds] *The Archaeology of Roman Pannonia*, 1980, p. 152).

**Conductores**  They had been exempted from civil obligations by Marcus Aurelius. See also Chapter 8.

**Provinces under Commodus: Gaul**  The three Gauls were under effective governors: Marcus Didius Julianus (Lower Germany [Germania Inferior]), Lucius Septimius Severus (Gallia Lugdunensis), Decimus Clodius Albinus (uncertain). (The first two were future emperors, and the third attempted to become one.)

**Danube development**  Napoca (Cluj) became a Roman colony, and rectangular watch-towers were erected in Lower Pannonia (Pannonia Inferior). There were inscriptions in honour of Commodus in Scythia Minor and other parts of Lower Moesia.

**Royal Huntsman**  A coin of 181–2 shows Commodus on horseback in combat with a lion (*RIC* III, p. 407, no. 332, cf. p. 357).

**Lucilla**  Her part in the plot is discussed by A. Bianchi, *Miscellanea greca e romana*, XIII, 1988, pp. 129–44.

**Quintianus**  It has been suggested that his plot failed owing to its dual purpose: discontent with the ruler, and exploitation of the feud within his family. As a result of the conspiracy, Commodus decided to hold as hostages in the capital the children of provincial governors.

**Commodus and the senate**  Any pretence that there was a 'dyarchy' of emperor and senate was finished, even though, in 186–7, Commodus's coinage declared him 'Father of the Senate' (PATER SENATVS; *RIC* III, p. 424 no. 502).

**Tarrutienus Paternus**  He had been the emperor's (equestrian) private secretary. Subsequently, when joint praetorian prefect, he was promoted to the senate with consular rank. A successful general, he had helped Perennis to get rid of Saoterus. But Dio Cassius is probably right to blame Perennis for Tarrutienus's subsequent downfall – especially as Dio otherwise favours Perennis, who had perhaps secured his political advancement. Other important men who fell at this time, or after a second conspiracy, were Publius Salvius Julianus, consul in 175 and an important military commander; Vitruvius Secundus, one of the secretaries of the emperor (*ab epistulis*) and a friend of Tarrutienus; and the old and rich brothers or cousins Sextus Quintilius Valerius Maximus and Sextus Quintilius Condianus, the former of whom had a son who was also killed (though the other, Sextus, escaped).

**Perennis**  Ancient writers recorded coins of himself and his sons, probably erroneously, since none has survived. The story that his denouncers came from Britain has been queried. It has been suggested that he was executed secretly during the night, and that one of his sons was induced to come to Italy and was put to death on the way.

**Marcia**  She was a freedwoman, subsequently killed by Didius Julianus. She was said to be friendly to the Christians.

**Jupiter**  He also appears as IVVENIS, the god of early victory over the Titans (AD 186–8; *RIC* III, p. 424 no. 499, p. 426 no. 525, p. 427 no. 532).

**Hercules**  He appears as Commodus on a statue from a villa at Ajka (A. Lengyel and G. T. B. Raban [eds] *The Archaeology of Roman Pannonia*, 1980, p. 185). Hercules had received a dedication under Antoninus Pius and Marcus Aurelius, and had been revered as *Pacator* on coins of Lucius Verus (*RIC* III, p. 255 no.

510). A sarcophagus from the Via Cassia showing a relief of the Labours of Hercules (J. M. C. Toynbee, *The Art of the Romans*, p. 105) is perhaps of the time of Commodus, as is a mosaic of Asinius Rufinus (consul *c.* 184) from Acholla (Boutria). Commodus's identification with Hercules was later repeated by Postumus (259–68). Hercules was also one of the patron deities of the mint (*BMC* IV, pp. clxvi, clxxvii).

**Denunciations of dead Commodus**   His name was chiselled out of inscriptions, e.g. in Lower Moesia (Moesia Inferior).

**Rehabilitation of Commodus**   There was no precedent for Septimius Severus's 'posthumous adoption' by Marcus Aurelius (*CIL* VIII, 9317 etc.), which not only involved the rehabilitation of Commodus but also brought about, as 'heirs' of himself and his father Aurelius, many later imperial Antoninuses (including the emperors Caracalla [211–17] and Elagabalus [218–22]). Commodus is celebrated by CONSECRATIO on coins (*RIC* IV, p. 99 no. 72A, p. 191 no. 736A). He also appears as DIVVS (A. Mócsy, *Die Bevölkerung von Pannonien*, p. 28).

# 6 ANTONINE SPEAKING AND WRITING

## Latin

**Florus**   It is uncertain if he was called Julius or Lucius Annaeus or Publius Annius. If the last, as is widely supposed, he was a friend of Hadrian, and a poet, and the author of an imperfectly preserved dialogue about Virgil, in which Florus, if it is he, is stated to have come from Africa and to have resided at Tarraco (Tarragona) before coming to Rome. His *History*, which draws on other works as well as Livy, was a favourite school book in the seventeenth century, and was extensively read until *c.* 1800.

**Fronto**   He said that Marcus Aurelius's task was more difficult than the charming of animals by Orpheus; and one wonders whether Marcus Aurelius's coin-type of Orpheus at Alexandria was an implied compliment to the eloquence of Fronto (and/or a tribute to the unity which the singing of Orpheus was supposed to have brought about, in his capacity as the leader of men living in concord). The dates of many of Fronto's letters are speculative, and it is sometimes uncertain whether Marcus Aurelius or Lucius Verus is being addressed. There are also a number of other recipients. Aurelius remained curiously reticent about him in the *Meditations* (I. 11, cf. VI. 13, 30). As for the Games, Fronto stressed the importance of shows to keep people quiet.

**Apuleius**   Philosophical and religious works include *On the God of Socrates* (*De Deo Socratis*), *On Plato and his Doctrine* (*De Platone et eius Dogmate*) and *On the Universe* (*De Mundo*). His treatise *On the State* (*De Republica*) is lost, as is his Latin translation of Plato's *Phaedo* (later used to instruct Latin readers in Plato) and his *Investigations of Nature* (*Quaestiones Naturales*) on scientific themes. His novel, the *Hermagoras* (if he ever wrote it), has likewise not survived. Hellenistic predecessors writing on Transformations included Parthenius and Nicander. *Golden Ass*: see now E. J. Kenney, *Psyche and her Mysterious Husband*, in D. A. Russell, *Antonine Literature*, pp. 176–98. 'Golden' was the epithet which story-tellers applied to their stories, and in this case it seems to suggest 'the best of all tales about an ass'. The *Onos*

(*Lucius,* or *The Ass*) about Lucius of Patrae (Patras), from which Apuleius's work seems to be derived, is regarded as one of Lucian's works by P. E. Easterling and B. M. W. Knox (eds) *Greek Literature,* pp. 679, 687. As is stated in the text, Apuleius is also conscious of the Milesian Tales, of which Aristides and Lucius Cornelius Sisenna were the best known exponents, in Greek and Latin respectively. Apuleius's treatment of the bandits is mocking pseudo-epic. The spicier Greek novels that he had probably read, of which fragments are now known, include the *Iolaus, Timouphis,* and Lollianus's *Phoenicica.* Their dates are not certain, but it is possible that some of them belong to the Antonine age and so should have been included in the next section.

## Greek

**Greek poets of the Antonine age**  They perhaps include the satirical epigrammatist Diogenianus, a doctor from Heraclea Salbace (Vakif) in Caria (*c.* 150 or rather later); the elegiac poet Julius Heraclides, who wrote about Eleusis (Lefsina); the poet of hexameters and hymns, Paeon of Side (Manavgat), early in the reign of Antoninus Pius; and Marcellus of the same city, who spanned the reigns of Hadrian and Antoninus.

**Greek literature of the Antonine period**  The following have been particularly useful: P. E. Easterling and B. M. W. Knox (eds) *The Cambridge History of Classical Literature,* I, *Greek Literature* (1985), A. Lesley, *A History of Greek Literature* (1966), P. Levi, *A History of Greek Literature* (1985).

**Arrian**  Dio Cassius's biography of him has not survived.

**Albinus**  Owing to a misreading, the *Didascalicus* was formerly attributed to an unknown 'Alcinous'.

**Aristides**  The *Serapis* was perhaps among his earliest works.

**Galen**  He regarded Hippocrates of Cos (fifth century BC) as the basis of his entire medical faith. A. Prantera's book *The Side of the Moon* (1991) is an imaginative but evocative novel about his relations with the imperial house. Galen himself offers some autobiographical information in his work *On the Diagnosis of Different Pulses.* He gave definitive form to the theory of the four humours, which remained fundamental until the eighteenth century.

**Marcus Aurelius**  The idea that Stoicism nerved and strengthened him has been questioned: on the contrary, it has been conjectured, it insulated him from grim realities. Diognetus was one of those who turned Marcus Aurelius to philosophy (and painting). It has also been suggested (but denied) that Aurelius was less influenced by the Stoics than by the eclectic Posidonius (*c.* 135–51/50 BC). Although he disliked Seneca, he agreed with his saying that life is a kind of military service (Seneca, *Letters,* 96.5). The first certain surviving reference to the *Meditations* is in *c.* 900 (F. H. Sandbach, *The Stoics,* p. 178). For the book as evidence for Marcus Aurelius's position as the perfect transitional figure, see E. K. Rand, *Cambridge Ancient History,* XII, p. 588.

**Iamblichus**  He was not a Babylonian, as was sometimes stated. He was an approximate contemporary of Chariton, who provides the most important evidence for the Greek mime in Egypt in the second century.

**The Greek novel: Iamblichus and Achilles Tatius**   Many would include Longus's *Daphnis and Chloe* here, in the belief that the work was probably written in the later second century AD (B. E. Perry, *The Ancient Romances*, p. 350 no. 17; T. Hägg, *The Novel in Antiquity*, p. 35; P. E. Easterling and B. M. W. Knox [eds] *Greek Literature*, p. 885). But he could well be later (Easterling and Knox, op. cit; G. Giangrande, *Oxford Classical Dictionary*, 2nd edn, p. 619), so that it seems better to omit him. For the plot of *Daphnis and Chloe* see G. Anderson, *Ancient Fiction*, pp. 136–44. Longus came from Lesbos, or stayed there.

### Christian

**Spread of Christian culture**   Reference should be made to H. Chadwick, *The Early Church* (1967) and W. H. C. Frend, *The Early Church: From the Beginnings to 461* (1965, 1982).

**Worship**   Much of the Old Testament was available in Latin by the middle of the second century AD, and there is clear evidence of New Testament texts in the 180s. Quite a proportion of church literature is democratic, or at least anti-establishment (although there are exceptions).

**Gnostics**   They believed that the power of evil could be overcome by magic. Pagan Gnosticism possibly originated in the early second century AD. The debts of the Gnostics to Platonism were related to the current Platonic Renaissance (see Albinus, p. 103), and the influence of Christianity was apparent in the Gnostics' central concept of Redemption.

**Abrasax**   His name was said to add up to the mystic 365. He gave the world an existence of 6,000–7,000 years.

**Pantaenus**   He led up to the more decisive Origen (*c.* 185/6–254/5).

**Lucian**   He was violently denounced by the Christians as their enemy. His *Introductions* (*Prolaliai*) have earned recent attention by H. G. Nesselrath, in D. A. Russell (ed.) *Antonine Literature*, pp. 111–40.

## 7 ANTONINE ARCHITECTURE AND ART

**Sources**   I owe a substantial acknowledgment to (among others) A. Boethius and J. B. Ward-Perkins, *Etruscan and Roman Architecture*, although it is very selective.

**Church of Sant'Urbano, Rome**   This church (off the Via Appia Pignatelli) is on the site of a pagan temple dedicated to Ceres (Demeter). It appears to have become a church in the ninth or tenth century AD. In the second century the temple of Ceres had been attached to a villa of Herodes Atticus, who was said to have buried his wife Annia Regilla (although this is disputed) in what has been called the 'Temple of the Deus Rediculus', but is in reality a lavish sepulchral monument. Herodes Atticus was put on trial for murdering his wife (see p. 103).

**Other tombs outside Rome**   Tombs that may be of Antonine date are to be seen just off the Via Nomentana, to its south (the 'Sedia del Diavolo') and north.

**Carthage: Antonine Baths**   In addition to the usual offices, they contained an ingeniously designed ring of interlocking hexagonal hot rooms (*caldaria*).

**Athens: Odeon**   The important Odeon of Marcus Vipsanius Agrippa (d. 12 BC) seems to have been remodelled in *c.* AD 150.

**Dacia and Pannonia**   Villas abounded in Pannonia, where local potentates became great landowners (and Marcus Aurelius had a residence). For the Antonines in Dacia, see P. MacKendrick, *The Dacian Stones Speak*, pp. 108, 113, 121, 127, 129f, 135f, 142, 152f, 182, 206.

**Portraiture**   Some portraits and statues show strong Hellenizing tendencies, e.g. the figures of Commodus and Crispina (or Marcus Aurelius and Faustina the younger) in the National (Terme) Museum at Rome: they are represented as Mars (Ares) and Venus (Aphrodite). Other portraits appear to echo Greek originals. But Celtic influences have been detected in a gold bust of Marcus Aurelius from Aventicum (Avenches; Museum of Archaeology and History, Lausanne). The coin-portraits of the Antonine period deserve careful study. The portraits of Septimius Severus deliberately stress a link with the Antonines.

**Panels**   Panels at Rome (showing Marcus Aurelius) symbolize his Clemency, Victory and Piety: details in P. MacKendrick, *The Mute Stones Speak*, p. 382. The panels have also been said to illustrate a further innovation, ' "the bridge": that small span of stone deliberately left in the channels of the hair, connecting two ribbons of hair but not representing hair itself . . . to catch light, interrupting the dark line of the separate groove, and thus contributing to the luminous agitation of the surface', R. Brilliant, *Roman Art*, p. 261. Panels outside Rome: e.g. sculptured slab at Tomis (Constanţa), put up by a local Dionysiac association in honour of Marcus Aurelius (E. Strong, *Art in Ancient Rome*, II, pp. 135, 136 fig. 461); and a relief in a temple at Ombi (Kom Ombos) in Egypt.

**Sarcophagi**   R. Brilliant, *Roman Art*, p. 110, illustrates the 'Clementia' sarcophagus in the Vatican (*c.* AD 170), showing the dead man as a clement conqueror, i.e. a person of exemplary spiritual qualities. Greek influences are perceptible. The Velitrae sarcophagus displays affinities with Asian 'column sarcophagi', on which see J. M. C. Toynbee, *The Art of the Romans*, p. 104.

**Column of Marcus Aurelius**   This has also been interpreted as depicting two campaigns, separated by a figure of Victory inscribing a shield. It is uncertain if Rome's enemies in the Rain Miracle were the Quadi or the Cotini (A. R. Birley, *Marcus Aurelius*, pp. 173f.). The pathos of the reliefs on the Column is also displayed in other forms of art, e.g. the Sacrifice of Bulls mosaic in the Caserma dei Vigili at Ostia (P. Fischer, *Mosaic: History and Technique*, fig. 27).

**Tomb of the Pancratii**   The painted scenes include Admetus and Alcestis, the yoking of the boar and the lion (the dual forces of the soul), the Judgment of Paris (symbolizing the Last Judgment), and the Ransoming of the Body of Hector (divine mercy).

**Other Antonine stuccos and paintings** 'The vaults in two of [the recently discovered tombs beneath the basilica of S. Sebastiano] are divided into hexagonal or circular panels, with stucco rosettes and other ornaments in the centre. In another tomb the decoration is painted; on the space above the arch two birds (symbols of the soul) are seen pecking at a naturalistically represented glass vase full of fruit – another symbol of the *refrigerium* [consolation]. . . . Over another tomb, a mangificent peacock stands frontally.' (E. Strong, *Art in Ancient Rome*, II, p. 129). A villa which is likewise under S. Sebastiano displays a wall painting depicting a sea port. There are also late Antonine figure paintings from a villa at Tor Marancio, and religious themes in mosaic, such as the dramatic Sacrifice of the Bulls in the Augusteum at Ostia (see above; and Strong, op. cit. p. 130).

**Second-century mosaics from Antioch** These depict Oceanus and Thetis, hunchback, black fisherman, infant Hercules. From Daphne: Narcissus, Dionysus (two), Four Seasons (incorporating Calydonian Boar Hunt, Paris and Helen, Hippolytus and Phaedra).

**Medallions** They first became strongly developed under Hadrian. Under Commodus gold multiples appeared, and there were particularly impressive bronze medallions.

# 8 THE ANTONINE AGE

**Cilician Gates** Pass through the mountains north of Tarsus (Cilicia Pedias: in the plain), containing the River Cydnus (Tarsus Çayi).

**Unity of the empire** Stressed by Fronto (I, p. 73), who sees it as a harder task than the achievement of Orpheus in charming the wild beasts (Orpheus appeared on coins of Alexandria; see Fronto, p. 185).

**Maternus** See especially E. A. Thompson, in M. I. Finley (ed.), *Studies in Ancient Society* (1974).

**Glassware** The taste for this superseded the popularity of *terra sigillata*. For the vast Pannonian production, see A. Lengyel and G. T. B. Raban (eds) *The Archaeology of Roman Pannonia* (1980), pp. 381ff.

**Contacts outside the empire** Cf. the customs tariff of AD 137 (*Orientis Graeci Inscriptiones Selectae* 644; Chapter 3). The Romans' attempt to develop a separate route for trade with China was in an endeavour to avoid Parthian obstruction.

# SOME BOOKS ABOUT THE
# ANTONINE PERIOD

## ANCIENT WRITERS

Writers of the Antonine period have been summarized in Chapter 6. Some of them, notably Marcus Aurelius, throw light upon what was going on but no single, first-class historian has left us a story of the epoch. We must, therefore, content ourselves with such inadequate sources as we have and extract what we can from: the 'Unknown' [lost], Marius Maximus [lost], the writer(s) of the *Historia Augusta* in Latin, and Dio Cassius (and his Epitomator Xiphilinus) and Herodian in Greek. Having only these sources shows how difficult it is to discover what really happened, because historians tended to concentrate on the ruling class, and to assess emperors by their relationship to the senate.

### Latin

#### The unknown ('Ignotus')

Sir Ronald Syme argued with convincing skill that the more reliable portions of the *Historia Augusta* (see p. 191) were based on a collection of biographies which was written by an unidentifiable person and which has disappeared. He suggested that this 'Ignotus' may have witnessed the events of AD 193 and may have written his *Lives*, starting with Nerva (or Hadrian?) and continuing to Caracalla, in the early years of the reign of Severus Alexander (222–35). This is how Syme (1971: 33, 44) saw the Unknown (though the loss of the man's work does not permit us to confirm what Syme says):

> Though marred by error, abbreviation, and the intrusion of scandal or ineptitudes, the information is proved excellent ... sober, factual and accurate ... precise on Roman topography. . . .
>
> A conscientious scholar, averse from style and rhetoric, with no doctrine or fantasies, but addicted to facts and dates. . . . *Ignotus* had some legal competence and an interest in learning.
>
> He wrote at Rome – and may well have witnessed the momentous trans-actions of 193 (his exposition becomes more lively: also valuable details). A knight rather than a senator, and not necessarily in one of the high equestrian posts. In short, a recognizable successor of Suetonius [born *c.* AD 69].
>
> *Ignotus*, however, did not follow the master-biographer in his appetite for

drink and sex, anecdote and scandal. Readers in any age of imperial Rome would rate him dull and pedestrian. Abridgement did not make the product more exhilarating. On the contrary.

It appears, for example, that the life of Antoninus Pius, which we have in the *Historia Augusta*, is very largely taken from *Ignotus*.

## Marius Maximus

Marius Maximus was a biographer of the Roman emperors from Nerva (AD 96–8) to Macrinus (217–18) or Elagabalus (218–22). Thus, he was a continuator (as well as, to some extent, an imitator) of Suetonius; perhaps he wanted to emulate or supplement Dio Cassius (see p. 192). His work, like that of the 'Unknown' who has just been discussed, is no longer extant.

He was probably Lucius Marius Maximus Perpetuus Aurelianus. That man came of an African or Spanish family. He was born in *c.* 160 to a father of equestrian rank who was procurator of Gallia Lugdunensis and Aquitania. He himself pursued a long career; he became one of the consuls in 198 or 199 and in 223, he governed Gallia Belgica, Lower Germany, Africa and Asia (214–15), and he was prefect of the city of Rome in 217–18.

He is liberally cited by the *Historia Augusta* as a source. Some have argued (against others) that he does not appear to have been one of its principal sources, although certain of its passages (notably in the *Life* of Commodus) are based on what Marius Maximus wrote. The *Historia* did, apparently, reproduce a good number of the frivolities and pornographic elements that were produced by Maximus's fertile imagination. (In this he outdid his model Suetonius in uncritical partiality and piquant gossip; he believed that the 'Unknown' was too long and not scandalous enough.)

Curiously, however, the *Historia* complains of the verbosity and unreliability of Marius Maximus (*homo omnium verbosissimus, qui et mythistoricis se voluminibus implicavit*). This was probably a joke, because the *Historia* was equally guilty of such defects. Yet Maximus did reproduce certain aspects of the Antonine epoch.

## Historia Augusta

The *Historia Augusta* (its original title is uncertain) is a collection of Latin biographies of Roman emperors, princes and usurpers. All of the biographies, extending from Hadrian to Carinus and Numerianus (283–4), have survived, with the exception of a gap from 244 to 259. The alleged authors are Aelius Spartianus, Julius Capitolinus, Vulcacius Gallicanus, Aelius Lampridius, Trebellius Pollio and Flavius Vopiscus. The *Lives* of Antoninus Pius, Marcus Aurelius and Lucius Verus are supposedly by Julius Capitolinus. The *Life* of Avidius Cassius is said to be by Vulcacius Gallicanus, and the supposed author of the *Life* of Commodus is Aelius Lampridius.

There is every reason to suppose that all of these names are invented and that the *Historia*, which displays considerable stylistic uniformity, is instead the work of a single, unidentified writer posing as a sort of collective symposium. The biographies are ostensibly dedicated to Diocletian (284–305) and Constantine the Great (306–37), but they may all have been written towards the end of the fourth century.

The *Historia Augusta* is often our only surviving source of information. Some of it seems to be derived from Marius Maximus (see above), as frequent references in the *Historia* suggest, but the extent to which this is so has been widely disputed. The *Life* of Antoninus Pius is clear, convincing and unaltered; the *Life* of Verus is competent. But other, large sections are altogether unreliable. The secondary *Lives* are particularly untrustworthy, since they relate to persons who never came to the throne and so information about them is scanty. Most of the numerous quotations from documents are palpable forgeries, many of the proper names included are equally spurious, and even the events described are often suspect to the highest degree.

The work stands in the tradition of imperial biography as this was envisaged by cultivated pagans at the time when it was written. Why was it written? There has been much controversy about this. Possibly all that the writer was trying to do was to entertain like-minded readers by means of spicy and unscrupulous sensationalism. The author takes a poor view of the more factual 'Unknown', whose work he tampers with roughly, by transposition, abbreviation and addition. He quotes Marius Maximus as a source, but criticizes him (perhaps with tongue in cheek, since the two men rank more or less equal as scandalmongers).

The author of the *Historia Augusta* is also an erudite fancier and collector of archaic, flowery and precious words, but his writing is slapdash and hasty and his style flat and monotonous. He is not without a certain sly, tongue-in-the-cheek humour, and the barefaced effrontery of his fraudulent fabrications may well have raised laughs among his readers.

Moses Hadas advises:

> Though historians properly scorn [the minutiae the work contains] as trivial and frivolous, a reader may still relish them for their own sake – and justify his discreditable appetite by imagining himself edified by sociological data and deterrent examples. . . . Very uneven and badly organized, the book is nevertheless far from being the dullest in Latin, and a reader who is warned against accepting everything in the *Historia Augusta* as literal truth – and is willing to confess low tastes otherwise – will find the book interesting not only for its picture of the strange habits of a marked group of men, but also for lights upon the history of the empire which a more judicious book would deny him.

'Season and society', comments Sir Ronald Syme, 'fosters fraud and imposture as well as erudition. Combining both, the author of the great hoax concords with his time. He is also a comic writer . . . a clever rogue.'

## Dio Cassius (Cassius Dio Cocceianus)

A Greek historian, he was born at Nicaea (Iznik) in Bithynia (north-western Asia Minor) in *c.* AD 163/4 and died some time after 229. He was the son of Manius Cassius Apronianus, governor of Lycia-Pamphylia, Cilicia and Dalmatia. Early in the reign of Commodus he came to Rome, where he pursued a successful official career. He became quaestor in 188 or 189, which brought him into the senate; praetor in 194 or 195; and consul in *c.* 205. His career terminated in 219, the year of his second consulship, when the unpopularity of his strict ideas on military discipline caused the emperor Severus Alexander to suggest that he should leave the city: whereupon Dio Cassius withdrew to his native Bithynia.

He was the author of a Roman history in eighty books, extending from the beginnings to AD 229. The later part of his work has not survived, but the lost portion was summarized by the eleventh-century Byzantine historian John Xiphilinus of Trapezus (Trabzon), whose epitome (lacking the reign of Antoninus Pius and the first years of Marcus Aurelius) is extant and provides a somewhat erratic and spasmodic selection of the original. Fortunately, it also preserves many passages in uncondensed form.

The importance of Dio's work lies in the significant part that he himself played in the events of his time. Indeed, Dio Cassius could be the one historical writer of any note who enables us to build up a continuous and connected narrative of Roman history for the period from AD 70 onwards. However, although he aimed at (and mainly succeeded in) producing an accurate and systematic reconstruction, he was not a great historian. He judged emperors too much by their treatment of the senate, and scientific criticism was often beyond his knowledge and powers. An anachronistic perception of the monarchical conditions of his own day prevents him from doing justice to the gradualness of imperial development. He is too fond of dramatizing anecdotes. He steers too clear of detailed description, which he regards as incompatible with the dignity of history. Dio's stylistic aim is Attic archaism, and he employs rhetorical devices as well. He seldom achieves a vivid narrative.

## Herodian

Herodian, another Greek historian, was a Syrian, probably originating from Antioch, who later became thoroughly pro-Roman and anti-Syrian. He held a post in the Roman imperial administration, and died after AD 238. The post that he held was minor, which means that he cannot compete with Dio Cassius as a first-hand observer and recorder of contemporary events.

Herodian was the author of a historical work in eight books entitled *Histories of the Empire After Marcus*. This covered events from the death of Marcus Aurelius in AD 180 (which he probably, like Dio Cassius, saw as the end of an era) to the accession of Gordian III in 238.

Herodian is superficial, monotonous and derivative. Yet he is useful, especially for periods when Dio Cassius is lost or is available only in an epitome.

Herodian was described above as a Greek historian. Sir Ronald Syme preferred to call him 'a Greek rhetorician passing himself off as a writer of history'.

## MODERN WRITERS

Akirgal, E. *Ancient Civilizations and Ruins of Turkey*, 1983.
Allison, F. G. *Lucian: Satirist and Artist* [1927] 1992.
Ameling, W. *Herodes Atticus*, 1983.
Anderson, G. *Ancient Fiction: The Novel in the Greco-Roman World*, 1984.
Anderson, G. *The Second Sophistic: A Cultural Phenomenon in the Roman Empire*, 1993.
Andreotti, R. *Commodo*, 1942.
Astarita, M. L. *Avidio Cassio*, 1983.
Baatz, D. *Der römische Limes*, 1974.
Barnard, L. W. *Justin Martyr*, 1967.
Barnes, T. D. *The Sources of the Historia Augusta*, 1978.
Barry, B. *Studies in Lucian*, 1973.
Bean, G. E. *Aegean Turkey*, 1966.
Beltran, S. (ed.) *Traduzione e commento delle Istituzioni di Gaio*, 1992.
*Bilinguismo degli Antichi*, II (Atti delle Giornate Filologiche Genovesi), 1991.
Birley, A. R. *Marcus Aurelius: A Biography* [1966] 1987.
Birley, E. *Roman Britain and the Roman Army*, 1953.

Boardman, J. (ed.) *The Oxford History of Classical Art*, 1993.

Bodson, A., *La morale sociale des derniers Stoiciens Sénèque, Epictéte et Marc-Aurèle*, 1967.

Boethius, A., and Ward-Perkins, J. B. *Etruscan and Roman Architecture*, 1970.

Bolin, S. *State and Currency in the Roman Empire to AD 300*, 1959.

Bompaire, J. *Lucien écrivain: imitation et création*, 1958.

Boulanger, A. *Aelius Aristide et la Sophistique dans la province d'Asie au 2ème siècle de notre ère*, 1923.

Bowersock, G. W. *Greek Sophists in the Roman Empire*, 1969.

Branham, R. B. *Unruly Eloquence*, 1989.

Breeze, D. J. *The Northern Frontiers of Roman Britain*, 1982.

Breeze, D. J. (ed.) *The Frontiers of the Roman Empire*, 1986.

Brock, M. D. *Studies in Fronto and His Age*, 1911.

Brunt, P. A. (ed.) *The Roman Economy*, 1984.

Bryant, E. E. *The Reign of Antoninus Pius*, 1895.

Burn, A. R. *The Government of the Roman Empire from Augustus to the Antonines*, 1952.

Bury, J. B., Cook, S. A., Adcock, F. E., Charlesworth, M. P., *Cambridge Ancient History*, XI, 1936.

Caprino, C., Colini, A. M., Gatti, G., Pallottino, M., Romanelli, P. *La colonna di Marco Aurelio*, 1955.

Carrata Thomes, F. *Il regno di Marco Aurelio*, 1953.

Cartwright, F. E., and Biddiss, M. D. *Disease and History*, 1972.

Cary, M. and Scullard, H. *A History of Rome*, 3rd edn, 1975.

Caster, M. *Lucien et la pensée réligieuse de son temps*, 1937.

Cerfaux, L., and Tondriau, J. *Le culte des souverains dans la civilisation gréco-romaine*, 1957.

Chadwick, H. *Early Christian Thought and the Classical Tradition*, 1966.

Chadwick, H. *The Early Church*, 1967.

Champlin, E. *Fronto and Antonine Rome*, 1980.

Chrysos, E. K., and Schwartz, A. (eds), *Das Reich und die Barbaren*, 1990.

Clayton-Dove, C. *Marcus Aurelius*, 1930.

Coarelli, F. *Guida archeologica di Roma*, 1974.

Cohn, J. *L'empire des Antonins et les martyrs gaulois de 177*, 1964.

Colledge, M. A. R. *The Parthians*, 1967.

Cresson, A. *Marc-Aurèle: sa vie, son oeuvre: avec un exposé de sa philosophie*, 1939.

Cunliffe, B. W. *Rome and the Barbarians*, 1975.

Cunliffe, B. W. *Greeks, Romans and Barbarians*, 1988.

Dalfen, J. *Formgeschichtliche Untersuchungen zu den Selbstbetrachtungen Marc Aurels*, 1967.

Degrassi, A. *Il confine nord-orientale dell'Italia romana*, 1954.

Delehaye, H. *Les origines du culte des martyrs*, 2nd edn, 1933.

Dill, S. *Roman Society from Nero to Marcus Aurelius*, 1904.

Dodds, E. R. *Pagan and Christian in an Age of Anxiety*, 1965.

Druge, A., and Tabor, J. *Noble Death: Suicide and Martyrdom among Christians and Jews in Antiquity*, 1992.

Duncan-Jones, R., *The Economy of the Roman Empire*, 1974.

Easterling, P. E., and Knox, B. M. W. (eds), *Cambridge History of Classical Literature*, 1985.

Edelstein, L., *The Meaning of Stoicism*, 1966.

Farquharson, A. S. L. *The Meditations of Marcus Aurelius*, I, II, 1944 (with supplementary material by R. B. Rutherford, 1990).

Farquharson, A. S. L. (ed. R. Rees) *Marcus Aurelius: His Life and his World*, [1951] 1952.

Faye, P. de *Gnostiques et gnosticisme*, 2nd edn, 1925.

Filoramo, G. *The History of Gnosticism*, 1992.

Finley, M. I. *The Ancient Economy*, 1973.

Finley, M. I. (ed) *Studies in Ancient Society*, 1974.

Frank, T. (ed.) *An Economic Survey of Ancient Rome*, i-v, 1933–40.

Frend, W. H. C. *Martyrdom and Persecution in the Early Church*, 1965.

Frend, W. H. C. *The Donatist Church*, rev. edn, 1985.

Frend, W. H. C. *The Early Church*, [1965] 1991.

Gagé, J. *Les classes sociales dans l'empire romain*, 1964.

Garnaud, J. (ed.) *Achilles Tatius: roman de Leucippé et Clitophon*, 1991.

Garnsey, P. D. A. and Saller, R. *The Roman Empire: Economy, Society and Culture*, 1987.

Garnsey, P. D. A. and Whittaker, C. R. (eds) *Imperialism in the Ancient World*, 1978.

Garnsey, P. D. A., Hopkins, K. and Whittaker, C. R. *Trade in the Ancient Economy*, 1953.

Garzetti, A. *From Tiberius to the Antonines*, 1974.

Gibbon, E. *History of the Decline and Fall of the Roman Empire*, 1776–88 (Penguin edn, 1993).

Goerlitz, W. *Marc Aurel: Kaiser und Philosoph*, 1954.

Goodenough, E. R. *The Theology of Justin Martyr*, 1923.

Goodspead, E. J., and Grant, R. M. *A History of Early Christian Literature*, 1966.

Graindor, P. *Un milliardaire antique: Hérode Atticus et sa famille*, 1930.

Grant, M. *The Climax of Rome*, 1968.

Grant, M. *Greek and Latin Authors 800 BC-AD 1000*, 1980.

Grant, M. *The Roman Emperors*, 1985.

Grant, M. *Guide to the Ancient World*, 1986.

Grant, M. *Greeks and Romans: A Social History* (*Social History of Greece and Rome*), 1992.

Grant, R. M. *Early Christianity and Society*, 1959.

Grant, R. M. *Gnosticism and Early Christianity*, 1959.

Greenslade, S. L. *Schism in the Early Church*, 2nd edn, 1964.

Griffe, E. *Les persécutions contre les chrétiens aux Ie et IIe siècles*, 1967.

Grimal, P. (ed. G. M. Woloch) *Roman Cities*, 1983.

Grosso, F. *La lotta politica al tempo di Commodo*, 1964.

Grünert, H. (ed.) *Römer und Germanen in Mitteleuropa*, 1976.

Hachmann, R. *The Germanic Peoples*, 1971.

Hägg, T. *The Novel in Antiquity*, 1983.

Haight, E. H. *Apuleius and his Influence*, 1927.

Hamberg, P. H. *Studies in Roman Imperial Art*, 1945.

Hammond, M. *The Antonine Monarchy*, 1959.

Harnack, A. von *Marcion*, 2nd edn, 1926.

Harnack, A. von *Early Christian Doctrine*, 1958.

Hartley, B. and Wacher, J. S. (eds) *Rome and her Northern Provinces* (Papers Presented to S.S. Frere), 1983.

Hayward, T. H. *Marcus Aurelius: A Saviour of Men*, 1935.

Heer, J. M. *Der historische Wert der Vita Commodi*, 1901.

Harmatta, J. *Studies in the History of the Sarmatians*, 1950.

Hijmans, B. L. and Van der Paardt, R. T. *Aspects of Apuleius's Golden Ass* , 1978.

Hobsbawm, E. J. *Bandits*, 1969.

Holford-Stevens, L. *Aulus Gellius*, 1988.

Honoré, A. M. *Gaius: A Biography*, 1962.
Hout, P. J. van den *The Meditations of Marcus Aurelius* [1954] 1988.
Howe, L. L. *The Praetorian Prefect from Commodus to Diocletian*, 1942.
Hüttl, W. *Antoninus Pius*, I, II, 1933–6.
James, P. *Unity in Diversity: A Study of Apuleius's Metamorphoses*, 1987.
Jolowicz, H. F. (with B. Nicholas), *Historical Introduction to the Study of Roman Law*, 3rd edn, 1972.
Jones, A. H. M. *The Greek City from Alexander to Justinian*, 1940.
Jones, A. H. M. *Cities of the Eastern Roman Provinces* [1937] 1971.
Jones, A. H. M. *The Roman Economy*, 1974.
Jones, C. P. *Culture and Society in Lucian*, 1986.
Káhler, H. *Rome and her Empire*, 1963.
Kahrstedt, U. *Die Kultur der Antoninenzeit* (Neue Wege zur Antike, III).
Kaimo, J. *The Romans the Greek Language*, 1949.
Kan, A. M. *Jupiter Dolichenus* [1943] 1979.
Kelly, J. N. D. *Early Christian Doctrines*, 5th edn, 1978.
Kent, J. P. C., and Hirmer, M. and A. *Roman Coins*, 1978.
Kerler, G. *Die Aussenpolitik in der Historia Augusta*, 1970.
Klein, R. (ed.) *Marc Aurel*, 1979.
Kluse, J. *Roms Klientelstaaten am Rhein und an der Donau*, 1934.
Krüger, B. (ed.) *Die Germanen*, 2 vols, 1976, 1983.
Labriolle, P. de *La crise montaniste*, 1913.
Lacour-Gayet, G. *Antonin le Pieux et son temps*, 1888.
Langmann, G. *Die Markomannenkriege 166/167 bis 180*, 1981.
Layton, B. *The Gnostic Scriptures*, 1987.
Lefkowitz, M. R., and Fant, M. B. *Women's Life in Greece and Rome*, [1982] 1992.
Lengyel, A., and Raban, G. T. B. (eds) *The Archaeology of Roman Pannonia*, 1980.
Lepelley, C. *Les cités de l'Afrique romaine*, I, 1979.
*Les Martyrs de Lyon*, 1977.
Long, A. A. *Problems in Stoicism*, 1971.
MacMullen, R. *Enemies of the Roman Order*, 1967.
MacMullen, R. *Paganism in the Roman Empire*, 1981.
MacMullen, R., and Lane, E. N. (eds) *Paganism and Christianity 100–425 CE* 1992.
Magie, D. *Roman Rule in Asia Minor*, I, II, 1950.
Markus, R. A. *Christianity in the Roman World*, 1974.
Marotti, V. *Multa de iure sanxit: aspetti della politica del diritto di Antoninus Pius*, 1388.
Matheson, P. E. *Marcus Aurelius*, 1922.
Mathieson, H. E. *Sculpture in the Parthian Empire*, 1992.
Mattingly, H. *Coins of the Roman Empire in the British Museum*, IV: *Antoninus Pius to Commodus*, 1940.
Mattingly, H. *Roman Coins* [1928] 1962.
Mattingly, H., and Sydenham, E. A. *Roman Imperial Coinage*, III: *Antoninus Pius to Commodus*, 1930.
Mauro, M. *Bellum iustum: die Idee des gerechten Krieger in der römischen Kaiserzeit*, 1990.
Meiggs, R. *Roman Ostia*, 2nd edn, 1973.
Merlat, P. *Jupiter Dolichenus*, 1960.
Millar, F. G. B. *A Study of Cassius Dio*, 1964.
Millar, F. G. B. *The Emperor in the Roman World 31 BC-AD 337*, 1977.
Millar, F. G. B. (etc.), *The Roman Empire and its Neighbours*, 1967.
Mócsy, A. *Die Bevölkerung von Pannonien bis zu den Markomannenkriegen*, 1958.

Mócsy, A. *Pannonia and Upper Moesia*, 1976.

Mócsy, A. *Zur Entstehung und Eigenart der Nordgrenzen Roms*, 1978.

*Mondo classico: mondo attuale* (Convegno, Rome, 1990), 1992.

Musurillo, H. *The Acts of the Christian Martyrs*, 1972.

Neumann, E. *The Great Mother*, 2nd edn, 1963.

Nordeblad, J. B. *Gaiusstudien*, 1932.

Ogilvie, R. M. *The Romans and their Gods*, 1969.

Oliver, J. H. *Marcus Aurelius: Aspects of Civic and Cultural Policy in the East*, 1970.

Owen, G. *The Germanic People: Their Origin, Expansion and Culture*, 1960.

Parain, C., *Marc-Aurèle*, 1957.

Pârvan, V., *Marcus Aurelius Verus Caesar si L. Aurelius Commodus*, 1909.

Pearson, B. A. (ed.) *The Future of Early Christianity*, 1991.

Pepe, L. *La novella dei Romani*, 1992.

Peretti, A. *Luciano: un intellettuale greco contro Roma*, 1946.

Perkin, S. P. *Gnosticism and the New Testament*, 1993.

Perry, B. E. *The Ancient Romances*, 1967.

Piganiol, A. *Marc-Aurèle*, 1939.

Portalupi, F. *M. Cornelio Frontone*, 1961.

Potter, D. S. *Prophecy and History in the Crisis of the Roman Empire: A Historical Commentary on the Thirteenth Sibylline Oracle*, 1991.

Prantera, A. *The Side of the Moon*, 1991.

Ragette, F. *Baalbek*, 1980.

Regibus, L. de *Antonino Pio*, 1946.

Rémondon, R., *La crise de l'empire romain: de Marc-Aurèle à Anastase*, 1964.

Renan, E. *Marc-Aurèle et la fin du monde antique*, 1882.

Richardson, L. *A New Topographical Dictionary of Ancient Rome*, 1992.

Rist, J. M. *Stoic Philosophy*, 1969.

Robertson, A. S. *The Antonine Wall*, 1960.

Robinson, C. *Lucian and his Influence in Europe*, 1979.

Rostovtzeff, M. *Social and Economic History of the Roman Empire*, [1926] 1957.

Rudolph, K. *Gnosis*, 1983.

Russell, D. A. (ed.) *Antonine Literature*, 1990.

Rutherford, R. B. *The Meditations of Marcus Aurelius: A Study*, [1989] 1991.

Ryberg, I. S. *Panel Reliefs of Marcus Aurelius*, 1987.

Sainte Croix, G. E. M. de *The Class Struggle in the Ancient Greek World*, 1981.

Salway, P. *The Frontier People of Roman Britain*, 1965.

Sandbach, F. H. *The Stoics*, 1975.

Sanders, J. T. *Schismatics, Sectarians, Dissidents, Deviants*, 1993.

Schlam, C. G. *The Metamorphoses of Apuleius: On Making an Ass of Oneself*, 1992.

Schulz, O. T. *Das Kaiserhaus der Antonine und der letzte Historiker Roms*, 1907.

Schwartz, J. *Biographie de Lucien de Samosate*, 1965.

Schwendemann, J. *Die historische Wert der Vita Marci bei den Scriptores Historiae Augustae*, 1923.

Scobie, A. *Apuleius and Folklore*, 1983.

Sedgwick, H. D. *Marcus Aurelius: A Biography*, 1921.

Seel, O., *Römertum und Latinitas*, 1964.

Schatzmann, I. *Senatorial Wealth and Roman Politics*, 1975.

Soleri, G. *Marc'Aurelio*, 1947.

Sommella, A. M. *Marco Aurelio in Campidoglio*, 1992.

Speake, G. (ed.) *A Dictionary of Ancient History*, 1993.

Speigl, J. *Der römische Staat und die Christen: Staat und Kirche von Domitian bis Commodus*, 1969.

Stella, L. A. *Marco Aurelio*, 1943.

Stemmer, K. (ed.) *Kaiser Mark Aurel und seine Zeit: das römische Reich im Umbruch* (exhibition, 1988).

Stern, H. *Date et destinataire de l'Histoire Auguste*, 1953.

Stillwell. R., MacDonald, W. L., and McAllister, M. H. *The Princeton Encyclopaedia of Classical Sites*, 1976.

Strack, P. L. *Untersuchungen zur römischen Reichsprägung des zweiten Jahrhunderts*, 3 vols, 1951–7.

Strong, D. E. *Roman Art*, 1976.

Strong, E. *Art in Ancient Rome*, 2 vols, 1929.

Sulimirksi, T. *The Sarmatians*, 1970.

Sutherland, C. H. V. *Roman Coins*, 1974.

Syme, R. *Ammianus and the Historia Augusta*, 1965.

Syme, R. *Emperors and Biography: Studies in the Historia Augusta*, 1971.

Tatum, J. *Apuleius and the Golden Ass*, 1979.

Taylor, L. R. *The Divinity of the Roman Emperor*, 1931.

Temporini, H., and Haase, W. (eds) *Aufstieg und Niedergang der römischen Welt*, II: *Principat, 34: Sprache und Literatur*, 1993.

Thompson, E. A. *The Early Germans*, 1965.

Tobin, J. *The Monuments of Herodes Atticus*, 1991.

Todd, M. *The Northern Barbarians 100 BC–AD 300*, [1975] 1987.

Todd, M. *The Early Germans*, 1992.

Toynbee, J. M. C. *Roman Medallions*, 1944.

Toynbee, J. M. C. *The Art of the Romans*, 1965.

Trannoy, A. I. *Marc-Aurèle: Pensées*. 1939.

Traupman, J. C. *The Life and Reign of Commodus*, 1956.

Vogel, L. (with W. H. Allen), *The Column of Antoninus Pius*, 1973.

Wacher, J. (ed.) *The Roman World*, 2 vols, 1987.

Wagner, W. H. *After the Apostles: Christianity in the Second Century*, 1993.

Walker, D. R. *The Metrology of Roman Silver Coinage*, II: *Nerva-Commodus*, 1977.

Wallinger, E. *Die Frauen in der Historia Augusta*, 1990.

Walsh, P. G. *The Roman Novel*, 1970.

Walzer, R. *Galen on Jews and Christians*, 1949.

Ward-Perkins, J. B. *Roman Imperial Architecture*, 1981.

Wegner, M. *Die Herrscherbildnisse in der Antoninischer Zeit*, 1939.

Wheeler, R. E. M. *Roman Art and Architecture*, 1964.

Wilamowitz-Moellendorf, U. von *Kaiser Marcus*, 1931.

Winkler, J. J. *Auctor and Actor: A Narratological Reading of Apuleius*, 1985.

Witt, R. E. *Isis in the Graeco-Roman World*, 1970.

Wittmann, W. *Das Isisbuch des Apuleius*, 1988.

Zahariade, M. *The Fortifications of Lower Moesia between AD 86 and 275*, 1993.

Zwikker, W. *Studien zur Markussäule I*, 1941.

# INDEX

199

210